DODGING THE BULLET

DODGING THE BULLET

FAILED ASSASSINATIONS THROUGHOUT HISTORY

M J TROW

Pen & Sword HISTORY

AN IMPRINT OF PEN & SWORD BOOKS LTD.
YORKSHIRE – PHILADELPHIA

First published in Great Britain in 2024 by
Pen & Sword History
An imprint of
Pen & Sword Books Ltd
Yorkshire – Philadelphia

Copyright © M.J. Trow, 2024

ISBN 978 1 39903 762 4

The right of M.J. Trow to be identified as the Author of this work has been asserted by him in accordance with the Copyright, Designs and Patents Act 1988.

A CIP catalogue record for this book is available from the British Library.

All rights reserved. No part of this book may be reproduced or transmitted in any form or by any means, electronic or mechanical, including photocopying, recording or by any information storage and retrieval system, without permission from the Publisher in writing.

Typeset in INDIA by IMPEC eSolutions
Printed and bound in England by CPI (UK) Ltd.

Pen & Sword Books Limited incorporates the imprints of Archaeology, Atlas, Aviation, Battleground, Digital, Discovery, Family History, Fiction, History, Local, Local History, Maritime, Military, Military Classics, Politics, Select, Transport, True Crime, After the Battle, Air World, Claymore Press, Frontline Publishing, Leo Cooper, Remember When, Seaforth Publishing, The Praetorian Press, Wharncliffe Books, Wharncliffe Local History, Wharncliffe Transport, Wharncliffe True Crime and White Owl.

For a complete list of Pen & Sword titles please contact

PEN & SWORD BOOKS LIMITED
47 Church Street, Barnsley, South Yorkshire, S70 2AS, England
E-mail: enquiries@pen-and-sword.co.uk
Website: www.pen-and-sword.co.uk

or

PEN AND SWORD BOOKS
1950 Lawrence Rd, Havertown, PA 19083, USA
E-mail: uspen-and-sword@casematepublishers.com
Website: www.penandswordbooks.com

Contents

Chapter 1	Gunpowder, Treason and Plot	1
Chapter 2	On the Trail of the Assassins	33
Chapter 3	To Kill a King …	53
Chapter 4	… Or Queen	67
Chapter 5	M'Naghten Rules, OK	89
Chapter 6	From King Richard to the Bull Moose	95
Chapter 7	Killing Hitler	104
Chapter 8	All the President's Men (and Five Women)	122
Chapter 9	The Man They Could Not Kill	156
Chapter 10	Wolves and Jackals	169
Chapter 11	'Dead at 4.30 pm'	190
P.S.		201
Appendix: The Guns		206
Bibliography		212
Index		214

Chapter 1

Gunpowder, Treason and Plot

Gunpowder ...

Nobody much liked the new king. Centuries later, the 'poet of empire', Rudyard Kipling, summed up James I admirably:

> The child of Mary Queen of Scots,
> A shifty mother's shiftless son,
> Bred up among intrigues and plots,
> Learned in all things, wise in none.
> Ungainly, babbling, wasteful, weak,
> Shrewd, clever, cowardly, pedantic,
> The sight of steel would blanch his cheek,
> The smell of baccy drive him frantic.
> He was the author of his line—
> He wrote that witches should be burnt;
> He wrote that monarchs were divine,
> And left a son who—proved they weren't!

His contemporary, Henri IV of France, who would become an assassin's victim in 1610, called him the 'wisest fool in Christendom'. Even his own doctor, Theodore de Mayerne, was dismissive:

> [His] legs were slender, scarcely strong enough to carry his body ... and when he vomited it was with so great an effort that his face would be sprinkled with red spots for a day or two ...

he was very clumsy in his riding and hunting and frequently met with accidents ... he was very often thirsty, drank frequently and mixed his liquors, being very promiscuous in his use of wines.

He was also bisexual, at a time when homosexuality was punishable by death. His tongue was too big for his mouth and growing up in the viciousness of Scottish politics, had learned to trust no one.

Elizabeth I's death, in March 1603, left England with a vacant throne. Despite umpteen attempts and a long line of suitors, no one could persuade the queen to marry. She would 'make no man my master'. The accession, therefore, slid sideways to the son of her cousin, Mary, Queen of Scots, a woman she had never met but nevertheless imprisoned for nineteen years and had executed in 1587. Almost from day one of his reign, James I alienated both his parliament and English Catholics, who had been hoping for more toleration than they ever received from Elizabeth.

On 19 November 1605, Sir Edward Hoby wrote to Sir Thomas Edmondes, ambassador to the Brussels court:

On the 5th of November we began our Parliament, when the king should have come in person, but he refrained though a practice [plot] but that morning discovered. The plot was to have blown up the king at such time as he should have been set in his royal throne, accompanied with his children, nobility and commoners and assisted with all the bishops, judges and doctors, at one instant – a blast to have ruined the whole state and kingdom of England.

It was arguably the most ambitious assassination plan in history. Had it worked, the entire structure of the government would have been destroyed, the key members of the royal family dead and the country would have been thrown into chaos. Unfortunately for us, the shadow of the conspiracy theory which runs throughout this book, looms large over any attempt to explain what actually happened.

In essence, a group of disgruntled Catholic gentlemen, unhappy with anti-Catholic measures brought in by the puritanical James, decided to kill him, cause the maximum chaos and then, presumably, revive a Catholic England loyal to Rome. The state opening of parliament was a perfect opportunity. The plotters, led by Robert Catesby from Warwickshire, hired a 'hitman', Yorkshireman Guido (Guy) Fawkes, who was an explosives expert with military experience with the Spanish Army in the Netherlands. Calling himself John Johnson, he placed thirty barrels of gunpowder, then the most devastating weapon available, in the vaults under the House of Lords. Unfortunately for the plotters, the ruse was rumbled and they were hunted down, some killed in the process. Other were tortured and stood trial. In January 1606, they were executed in public, much to the delight of the crowd. If only assassination history were that simple!

On the one hand, the story is taken by some to be straightforward. Inevitably, the Puritans saw themselves as victims and used their usual over-the-top language to deplore the event. In 1610, Dr Francis Herring wrote that the plot was 'the quintessence of Satan's policy, the furthest reach and stain of human malice and cruelty, not be paralleled among the savage turks, the barbarous Indians, nor, I am persuaded, among the more brutish cannibals'. By 1969, when conspiracy theories had already taken hold, it was, according to Jesuit Father Francis Edmunds, a carefully contrived 'sting' in which Catesby, Fawkes and a third conspirator, Thomas Percy, were double agents working for the government under Robert Cecil, James's principal secretary of state.

At the time and since, Guido Fawkes was seen as the mastermind, a double-dyed villain. William Hazlitt, writing in 1821, the year after the Cato Street Conspiracy (see below), described him as 'this pale miner in the infernal regions, skulking in his retreat with his cloak and dark lanthorn, moving cautiously about among his barrels of gunpowder, loaded with death'. It is his face, bland, goateed, that is used today to cover the faces of protestors too cowardly to show their own. Although he was one of several, it is Fawkes alone who stands accused; just as Lee Harvey Oswald could not possibly have been the only would-be assassin of John F. Kennedy, his is the face forever associated with Dealey Plaza, Dallas and the 'day the dream died'. As a consolation, in the case of Fawkes, the old joke goes that he was the only man to get into parliament with the right intentions!

The actual leader was Robert Catesby, a charismatic Warwickshire gentleman prepared to go to any lengths to re-establish Catholicism as the religion of the state. He had already been fined and imprisoned for recusancy (refusing to attend the Protestant church services) and as such was known to the authorities. This is a common feature of assassinations, especially religiously motivated ones; it does not mean that the zealot is always properly monitored or that his would-be victim is safe. In the early autumn of 1605, Catesby recruited twelve other conspirators, mostly gentlemen like himself, and one servant, Thomas Bates. It was vital that, apart from loyalty to the cause, and to Catesby, all the plotters had country houses to hole up in, good horses for a getaway and enough money to reach the Continent quickly should things go awry.

The plot, argued about over several months, was that with the king and the royal princes Henry and Charles dead, 9-year-old Princess Elizabeth would be hailed queen and married to a suitable Catholic prince who would rule England and restore the status quo. The plotters met at various London taverns, like the Mitre in Broad Street and the Irish Boy in the Strand. Others joined them, not as plotters, but broadly sympathetic people, such as the playwright Ben Jonson, who was probably a secret Catholic himself.

Then, on Saturday, 26 October, a leading Catholic nobleman, William Parker, 4th Baron Monteagle, received an anonymous letter after dark:

> My Lord, out of the love I bear to some of your friends, I have a care of your preservation. Therefore I would advise you, as you tender your life, to devise some excuse to shift of your attendance at this Parliament, for God and man hath concurred to punish the wickedness of this time ... retire yourself into your country [estate] where you may expect the events in safety. For though there be no appearance of any stir, yet I say they shall receive a terrible blow this Parliament and yet they shall not see who hurts them ...

The letter has, extraordinarily, survived, but who wrote it is a mystery. Everybody involved in the plot, as well as several others, has at one time or another been accused of authorship. Monteagle did not know what to do with it, assuming it might be a 'foolish devised pasquil' (nonsensical hoax) but he took it to Robert Cecil at Whitehall just in case. This was a shrewd move; not only did it scotch the plot and save lives, but got Monteagle a nice cash handout for the rest of his life. It also got him out of a jam; several of the plotters were his friends and relatives. It may be, of course, that Monteagle faked the letter himself, having been tipped off by the weakest of the plotters, his brother-in-law Thomas Tresham.

Cecil's reaction to the letter was extraordinarily calm. King James was away on a hunting trip at the time and he did not even bother to tell His Majesty of the threat. Why? Because he knew all about Catesby's reckless venture, at least the how, when and where, if not all the names of those involved. The deformed secretary, ridiculed by Queen Elizabeth as her 'elf' had inherited one of the best Intelligence services in the world from his predecessor, Francis Walsingham. Essentially, although Cecil did not create the Gunpowder Plot, he ran it by proxy, keeping a cool distance from the hysterics of others.

On 4 November, while Catesby rode to the Midlands to raise a rebellion reminiscent of the one in the North against Elizabeth I in 1569, Guy Fawkes was given a match with which he could set the fuses in the gunpowder he had placed in the cellar under the House of Lords; the cellar that had conveniently and mysteriously been available to rent by the conspirator Thomas Percy. There was a routine search of the premises in which the Lord Chamberlain, Lord Suffolk, noticed a considerable pile of firewood stashed in a corner. This was followed by a second, led by Thomas Knyvet, a member of the king's Privy Chamber and a JP for Westminster. Around midnight on 4/5 November, Knyvet's men found 'a very tall and desperate fellow' lurking near some barrels. His name, he said, was John Johnson and he was a servant of Thomas Percy.

By dawn, word had got round that the plot was blown. It was expected, given the overuse of torture by the government at the time, that Fawkes would talk and all but two of the plotters rode hell for leather out of London. During the chaos of the next day, Catesby's planned Midlands' rising raised fewer than fifty men and nine of these were the plotters themselves.

In London, the crowd, responding to rumours that became wilder as time went on, lit bonfires, an act of hysteria which survives nationally to this day. Most foreign ambassadors in London (most of them Catholic), wished to dissociate themselves from the plot and duly rained money down on the mob from their upstairs balconies.

Under interrogation, Fawkes admitted to planning to use gunpowder to kill the king, but he named no names and added that he had hoped the explosion would blow all Scotsmen back to Scotland. He came out with what became the usual response of the fanatic, that desperate situations (intolerance of Catholics) led to desperate measures (assassination). The information did not come from Fawkes, but by 6 November, the names of eight conspirators were known to the authorities. That was the day on which the king told his people to use torture on Fawkes 'ab ima' – to the greatest extreme. In his own account written later, James claimed that 'the gentler tortures' were to be used first. By the next day, under the joint-dislocating pressure of the rack, Fawkes cracked. His signature, a feeble attempt from crushed fingers, has survived.

Middle-of-the-road Catholics, like Father George Blackwell, urged national calm and were genuinely horrified by Catesby's gang of desperadoes. Several priests connected with the conspirators were arrested and interrogated. On Friday, 8 November, Catesby and a handful of his followers holed up at Holbeach House were surrounded by the authorities led by Sir Richard Walsh and decided to fight it out. Thomas Wintour, brothers Jack and Kit Wright and Ambrose Rookwood all went down in a fusillade of musket fire. John Grant was blinded and Henry Morgan suffered agonizing burns. The wounded Wintour, standing back-to-back with Catesby, was hit by a musket ball which killed his leader as well. The bodies of the dead – and of the wounded – were stripped and taken to London.

In the capital, the panic had subsided, especially when it was discovered that the gunpowder in Fawkes's barrels was 'decayed'. This meant that it would probably not have exploded anyway. Those who believe in conspiracy theories contend that Cecil had substituted the dangerous stuff for a harmless replacement, in case of accidents. This is to give Elizabeth's 'elf' superhuman qualities he did not possess. Some people fell over themselves giving the government information for the trial they knew would follow. Others distanced themselves loudly from any whiff of treason.

James made a speech to parliament on Saturday, 9 November 1605, which became the official version of events. In it, he was of course the hero of the hour, sensing instinctively what was afoot (all of which was nonsense, the man had no clue). He was unusually gentle with Catholics, however, separating the faithful from the fanatical delusionists already dead or in the Tower of London. The king's central point was the sheer indiscrimination of gunpowder – it killed anybody, not just the single target (him) at which it was aimed. This was to misunderstand the purpose. A musket or pistol ball or a sword thrust would have killed James, but he had sons. By destroying the males of the royal family *and* the most powerful politicians, total chaos would have resulted. It would be like the 9/11 terrorists hitting Capitol Hill as the president was inaugurated.

The plotters' trial in January 1606 was an opportunity for the government to damn them – and all would-be assassins and dissidents – to hell. The most appalling Roman emperors, like Caligula, Nero and Domitian 'were but each of them fly-killers to these wretches'. The king, at first so reasonable and generous to Catholics, now turned nasty, which was typical of him, promising damnation against all papists. The eight conspirators were brought by barge from the Tower and the Gatehouse prison to Westminster Hall which they had planned to blow up two months earlier, on Monday, 17 November 1605. This was, in effect, a show trial, without the modern annoyances of a defence counsel and the result was a given. The king and queen, and Henry, Prince of Wales, watched proceedings along with foreign ambassadors, from secret positions out of sight of the makeshift court. Perhaps as a deliberate joke against the king, some of the accused 'drank smoke', knowing full well how much James hated tobacco. They all pleaded 'not guilty', except Sir Everard Digby.

The charge, delivered by Sir Edward Phelips, Serjeant-at-Law, spoke of 'Such a King, Such a Queen, Such a Prince, Such a progeny, Such a State, Such a government', although historians since 1606 have viewed all of them rather differently. As for the conspirators, their crime was the worst ever heard of and the Jesuits were to blame for all of it. The Attorney General Sir Edward Coke, regarded today as one of the country's greatest jurists, spoke at length about the damage that would have been done had the gunpowder gone up, including, bizarrely, 'insensible creatures, churches and homes'. This should not surprise us too much; English law was always more concerned with property than people.

Everard Digby's trial was a farce and the conclusion the same. Coke quoted the Psalms, some of the cruellest words ever written when Digby asked for mercy for his children – 'Let his wife be a widow and his children vagabonds, let his posterity be destroyed and in the next generation let his name be quite put out.' It did not quite work out that way. Kenelm Digby, only 3 when his father was executed, went on to become a confidant of Charles I *and* of Oliver Cromwell, and founded the Royal Society in 1660.

On Thursday, 30 January, Digby, John Grant, Robert Wintour and Thomas Bates were dragged on hurdles through a braying crowd to face the gallows. Their bodies were cut down from their nooses while they were still alive and their hearts ripped out from their bodies. 'Here is the heart of a traitor,' the headsman bellowed after each one. Each man had crossed himself, the Papish symbol, and Digby prayed in Latin, refusing the support of the Protestant clergy present.

The next day, Fawkes, Thomas Wintour, Robert Keyes and Ambrose Rookwood followed suit in Old Palace Yard, Westminster. Keyes threw himself off the platform, presumably trying to break his neck rather than suffer partial strangulation and the horrors that were to follow. But the rope broke and he went through it all fully conscious. Fawkes was the last to die, 'the greatest devil of all', but he could not climb the ladder without help and, ironically, his neck *did* snap during the hanging.

For an assassination that never took place, the Gunpowder Plot earned a central place in history. It burned into folk memory and is still remembered today, vaguely, *almost* forgotten, on Bonfire Night.

All the more strange, then, that a very similar plot, to wipe out key members of the government, if not the king, and one that happened over two centuries later, should now be virtually unknown.

... Treason ...

'This is the head of Arthur Thistlewood, the traitor,' the hangman, James Foxen, shouted out to the crowd milling mutinously at the base of the makeshift gallows outside the Session House. It was 1 May 1820 and thousands had made their way to the Old Bailey that day to gawp, to protest, to cheer, to pray, but mostly to see dying men writhe at the end of the rope and the decapitated heads of the hopeless in all their gory horror.

Five years earlier, a British Army led by the Duke of Wellington and a Prussian under the command of Field Marshal Blucher had ended the tyranny of Napoleon Bonaparte and brought, in the case of Britain, an end to twenty-two years of warfare. And despite the lavish praise sung to the armed forces and peals of bells and services of thanksgiving, placards appeared in all of London's parks – 'No dogs – and no soldiers in uniform'.

It had not just been Napoleon who had been destroyed at Waterloo, it was the whole concept of revolution and unchecked popularism, exemplified in France in the 1790s by the ragged sans-culottes and their improvised anthem, the marching song of the soldiers of Marseille – 'To arms, citizens! Form your battalions!' And to make sure that ordinary people would not demand freedom and justice again, the powers of the *ancien régime*, in Britain as well as in France, were augmented as never before, from the Prince Regent at the top to the magistrate in his local court.

The years after Waterloo were years of discontent. The government brought in the Corn Laws in 1815, to protect British farmers from foreign competition, but they had the effect of forcing up the price of bread – and bread was the staple diet of the poor. Britain was already the leading industrial nation on earth, but the creation of wealth was certainly not general or fair and the teething troubles were horrendous. Machines replaced men in the workplace; steam was the way forward. And the men who could not adjust to this – and, more especially, their wives and children – went to the wall. There was no welfare state or anything like it. The Poor Law of 1601 was hopelessly inadequate in a country with a rapidly expanding population and the few scattered workhouses, which would proliferate in the 1830s, offered grim alternatives to outdoor parish relief. The people called them, after the ghastly Parisian prison, Bastilles.

Old ways were changing and fast. More and more people drifted to the towns and cities. They had to pay for firewood that had once been free. The tobacco in their pipes had a tax on it. The rabbit in their stewing pot was somebody else's and a man could be sent to Botany Bay, on the far side of the world, for poaching.

Let us take a look at a group of men for whom this way of life, of endless poverty and drudgery, became intolerable. James Ings was a butcher; so was James Wilson. Richard Bradham and John Shaw were carpenters. James Gilchrist and John Monument were shoemakers. Charles Cooper and Richard Tidd made boots, a subtle distinction from Gilchrist and Monument. William Davidson was a cabinetmaker; in the scheme of things in the occupational hierarchy of the day, above the others. He was different in another respect, too; he was a 'person of colour' at a time when slavery still existed in the British Empire and the slave trade had only recently ended. Five of these men died, along with their leader, Arthur Thistlewood, at the Old Bailey in May 1820, guilty under the law of treason, in the Cato Street Conspiracy.

The end of the war saw a sudden loss of jobs – not only were the army and navy reduced (as they always are in peacetime) – but there was now far less demand for the materiel they used: iron for swords, bayonets and guns; canvas for sail; timber for ships of the line; and cloth for uniforms. Taxation changed suddenly too. In 1799, the prime minister, William Pitt, had introduced income tax, which the poor did not pay. But this would be a temporary wartime measure. In 1816, the tax was removed and, to make up the deficit, duties were imposed on all sorts of goods that the poor had no choice but to buy. Overcrowded in foul-smelling, rat-infested tenements and 'back-to-back' houses built badly and cheaply by unscrupulous landlords, the people had few rights and no time or money to obtain redress for their grievances. The Trade Union Movement was in its toothless infancy and mill owners trampled all over it.

Given this economic hell, fanned by pamphlets like William Cobbett's *Political Register*, or *Twopenny Trash* as it was called, some men became extremists, plotted and went on the rampage. The people of France had overthrown a corrupt, greedy, self-obsessed government in 1789 and three years later had offered to take the theme of revolution – liberty, equality and brotherhood – to any other European people who wanted it. And there were men, intelligent, wealthy, privileged, who agreed with all that: Thomas Paine, who had backed the American colonists in the 1770s; Charles James Fox, the leader of the Whigs; Joseph Priestley, the dissenter and scientist. Change for the better *could* be achieved, but it would have to be done by force because there was no other way.

As we shall see, in May 1800 James Hadfield fired his pistol at King George III at a theatre in Drury Lane. Two years later, Colonel Edward Despard, one half of what may have been the only mixed-race marriage in England, launched a would-be revolution that was almost a blueprint for Cato Street. Allying himself with Wolfe Tone's United Irishmen and the London Corresponding Society (itself in regular touch with French revolutionaries) he dreamed up a plan that would include capturing the Tower of London, the Bank of England in Threadneedle Street and the huge arsenal at Woolwich. Troops were to be lured to the cause with the promise of cash and land once the revolution was over. If all this sounds far-fetched, the exact same strategies were used in Dublin in 1916 during the Troubles, and in St Petersburg and other Russian cities a year later as the Russian Revolution got underway.

In Despard's case, however, the whole thing collapsed when he and forty others were arrested by the Bow Street Runners after a tip-off in November 1802. Tried at the Session House before Lord Ellenborough, Despard and five of his inner circle were found guilty of treason and plotting insurrection. This was despite an eloquent character reference from Horatio Nelson, a national treasure and hero who lesser men crossed at their peril.

The sentence passed by Ellenborough is straight out of the James I playbook from 1606:

> Each of you [shall] be taken from the place whence you came and thence you are to be drawn on hurdles to the place of execution, where you are to be hanged by the neck, but not until you are dead; for while you are still living, your bodies are to be taken down, your bowels torn out and burned before your faces, your heads cut off and your bodies divided into four quarters ... to be then at the king's disposal.

Henry Addington, prime minister since William Pitt had resigned over the issue of Catholic emancipation, was worried about the reaction of the mob to all this. Nelson appealed too. In the end, the disembowelling was dropped and the traitors were hanged and beheaded on the roof of the gaol in Horsemonger Lane. As the nooses were hooked in place by the inept headsman, William Brunskill, John McNamara said to Despard, 'I'm afraid, Colonel, we've got ourselves into a bad situation.' Despard smiled. 'There are many better and some worse.' He declined the last rites (which appalled Nelson when he heard about it) and he was the first to die.

Astonishingly, the church agreed to Catherine Despard's request to have her husband buried in St Paul's and his head was the last to have a wax likeness made by Marie Tussaud, who had made death masks of most of the French Revolution's victims.

The Newgate Calendar said, 'It was certainly the most vain [futile] and impotent attempt ever engendered in the distracted brain of an enthusiast [fanatic]'. But eighteen years later, a very similar plot was under way again.

Rioting and discontent became worse with the end of the Napoleonic Wars and new leaders were thrown up, from northern locals like Samuel Bamford to the charismatic Henry Hunt with his trademark 'wideawake' hat. A year did not go by in British history without a rebellion, albeit usually localised and on a small scale. Somebody threw a stone at the Prince Regent's carriage in Westminster in the spring of 1817 – it could have been a bullet. There were agents provocateurs everywhere, shady characters working for the government, who sounded like particularly deranged men of the people. One of them, John Castle, proposed a toast at a dinner in London's Bouverie Hotel in 1816 – 'May the last of Kings be strangled with the guts of the last priest.'

In 1817, Jeremiah Brandreth, a stocking-frame knitter, led a would-be revolution in Nottingham. Workers were to turn on their masters (as the mill owners were called) – each village was 'to kill its own vermin'. Brandreth and his followers were found guilty in minutes and hanged.

The immediate background to Cato Street was Peterloo. On 19 August 1819, a crowd perhaps 30,000 strong flocked to St Peter's Fields on the edge of Manchester to listen to speeches from, among others, Henry Hunt. There were women and children there. No one was armed. No one, that is, except the Manchester and Salford Yeomanry, the 15th Hussars and the militia on standby. The local magistrate panicked and ordered the police, under the corrupt

Joseph Nadin, to arrest Hunt. When they could not get through the crowd to the wagons that served as hustings, the Yeomanry went in, hacking about them with their sabres. These men were middle-class shopkeepers and artisans with no love for the working class milling around their horses. They were also hopelessly untrained for crowd control and in retaliation for their violence, people began dragging the Yeomen from their saddles. At one point, a Yeoman came face to face with an old woman who had nursed him as a child – 'Nay, Tom Shelmerdine,' she said, 'tha'll not hurt me, I know.' He rode over her. The 15th had fought at Waterloo four years earlier and on that August day wore their medals on their jackets. At a walk, they rolled up the panicking crowd, leaving another battlefield behind. Eleven people had died and over 400 were injured. It was Samuel Bamford's paper that coined the name 'Peterloo'.

Arthur Thistlewood became the next Colonel Despard. An army officer, he had led riots in London before and had spent a year in prison for challenging the Home Secretary Lord Sidmouth, to a duel (illegal in Britain). Whether 'T' was deranged (the same accusation had been levelled at Despard) or was a genuine man of the people is in the eyes of the beholder. Almost everything Thistlewood advocated is the law today and we take it for granted. Only his means are questionable.

His original plan was to target every cabinet minister in their homes. Lord Liverpool, the prime minister, was of course at No. 10 Downing Street. The hated Lord Castlereagh, the foreign secretary, had a house in St James's Square. The Duke of Wellington, Master-General of the Ordnance, had a famous residence at Hyde Park Corner – 1, London. Lord Harrowby, President of the Council, owned 39 Grosvenor Square (today a five-star hotel). The death of George III, on 29 January 1820, provided an opportunity. The funeral was scheduled for 15 February and Thistlewood believed (wrongly) that virtually every soldier in London would be at Windsor as part of the ceremonies. Various conspirators were to seize artillery pieces, blow up barracks using hand grenades and the mayor's Mansion House would become the headquarters of the new 'People's Government of Britain' with Thistlewood himself as some sort of president. It was part Despard and part Spa Fields, a serious insurrection in 1816.

Then, the plan changed and we have no idea why. Everything focused on Harrowby's house, where the leading cabinet members would be dining on 23 February. The conspirators, who had been buying up old and obsolete weapons for weeks in advance, met in a hayloft in Cato Street, a narrow lane off the Edgeware Road near Hyde Park. Astonishingly, this house is still there and externally has changed little since 1820. Posing rather unconvincingly as decorators, at least twenty men entered the house between five and six o'clock that evening.

Unfortunately for them, but fortunately for Harrowby and his colleagues, the whole plot had been rumbled. One of the conspirators, George Edwards, was in fact a government spy. No one seems to have noticed that an unemployed journeyman was suddenly splashing cash in all directions, especially as most of it was spent on buying weapons. He had contacted the Bow Street Runners (London's police force) and Richard Birnie, the Bow Street magistrate, who had sworn out a warrant for the arrest of fourteen conspirators (including, cunningly, Edwards). They stormed the Cato Street house and in the ensuing struggle, Thistlewood ran his sword through the body of a Runner called Smithers, who died within minutes. Runner Ellis fired at Thistlewood but missed and a free-for-all ensued in what was a very confined space. As pre-arranged, Captain Fitzclarence and a detachment of his Coldstream Guards turned up. The fighting continued, but clearly the conspirators were outnumbered. 'Don't kill me,' one of them said to Fitzclarence, 'and I will tell you all.'

Of them all, William Davidson, fought most desperately, narrowly missing Fitzclarence with his sabre. Both conspirators and the whole arsenal of weapons were taken across the road to the Horse and Groom pub along with the body of Smithers. Charged by Birnie, the magistrate, who had got involved in the fisticuffs too, the conspirators remained defiant, Davidson unaccountably singing 'Scots wha ha'e wi' Wallace bled'. When Ellis clapped manacles on him, he snarled, 'Blast and damn the eyes of all those who would not die for liberty.' But Thistlewood, John Palin and Edwards had got away.

Thistlewood was hiding in one of the many criminal dens that dotted London in those days. Eleven Runners, led by George Ruthven, found him at 8 White Street, Little Moorfields. 'Mr Thistlewood, I am a Bow Street officer. You are my prisoner.' Ruthven pinned the rebel to the bed with his body weight and handcuffed him. He was still fully clothed and had flints and ball cartridges in his pockets.

The crowd was there already. 'Hang the villain! Hang the assassin!' Thistlewood said he knew that a man was dead and hoped that it was Chief Magistrate Stafford. By the afternoon, he was facing the Privy Council, many of them the men he had planned to kill at Harrowby's house. They put him, on a charge of murder and treason, in Coldbath Fields Prison.

Hundreds descended on Cato Street to stare at the hayloft, already infamous, where most of the miscreants had been arrested. An enterprising local was charging 1 shilling for admittance.

'Thank Providence and Heaven,' said a junior counsel at the trial that followed, 'which kindly watches over the acts and thoughts of men, mercifully interposed between the conception of this abominable act and its completion.' Providence and heaven had nothing to do with it. The conspirators' fate was sealed as soon as Edwards tipped off the authorities. None of the Council was at Harrowby's house that night, not even Harrowby. The warrant for the arrest of the plotters and the address of Cato Street were known before any steps had been taken. The *real* conspirators in 1820 were the Privy Council.

It was clear in the trial that followed that Thistlewood and several of his followers had been trailed for days by the Runners. The problem with any planned insurrection was that not everybody was 'on board'. In the deprived London of the post-war period, men's loyalties wavered easily, especially at the clink of a coin. People talked. The prisoners were separated between the Tower and Coldbath as various politicians came to gawp at them. The prisoners laughed at them. 'It is want of food which has brought us here,' James Ings, the Portsmouth butcher said. 'If I had fifty necks, I'd rather have them all broken ... than see my children starve.'

The authorities combed the city for anyone on the fringes of the planned revolution. There had been talk of thousands and memories of Paris were long. Thistlewood's home was turned over as his wife, Susan, stood by stoically, the picture of dignity.

There were four charges against the rebels. The first was high treason – 'to deprive and depose our said Lord the King of and from the style, honour and kingly name of the imperial crown of this realm'. It was the most appalling crime imaginable in 1820 and has all but disappeared from public consciousness today. The second charge was very similar – 'to move and excite insurrection, rebellion and war ... and to subvert and alter the legislature, rule and government and to bring and put the King to death'. In fact, in all the relevant literature and the oral testimony, there was only one tangential mention of an attack on George IV. The third count was that the accused threatened 'to levy war against the King, in order by force and constraint to compel him to change his measures and councils'. The fourth count said the same thing.

Today, a competent defence counsel would drive a coach and horses through these charges. There was only one – insurrection – everything else was built up and expanded, so that there was little chance of anybody getting off. The prosecution was composed of the legal heavyweights of the day. Four judges tried the case (one would have been ample), two of them chief justices. All the accused pleaded not guilty, Ings cutting to the chase – 'I will be tried by God and the laws of reason. The laws of reason are the laws of God.'

One hundred and sixty-two witnesses were called, almost all of them by the prosecution anxious to blacken reputations. Thistlewood was a known troublemaker; most of the others had 'previous' too. One man conspicuous by his absence was George Edwards, Lord Sidmouth's spy. He could not be found. In vain did defence counsel Curwood argue – 'barracks were to be taken, cannons carried away, Ministers assassinated, government subverted, the Mansion House occupied, all by fifteen or twenty men'.

It took the jury less than half an hour to find all of them guilty. Thistlewood was allowed to speak – 'A few hours hence and I shall be no more … I died when liberty and justice had been driven from [this country's] confines by a set of villains, whose thirst for blood is only to be equalled by their activity in plunder.' He cited the government-backed butchery at Peterloo, as did James Ings – 'These yeomen had their swords ground beforehand and I had a sword ground also …' Other conspirators were less defiant, blaming the others and pleading their innocence. Of course, it cut no ice. Chief Justice Abbott sentenced Thistlewood, Ings, John Brunt, Davidson and Tidd to death, intoning the same ghastly punishment of dismemberment that had been the norm for centuries. The condemned men showed no emotion; Thistlewood took a peck of snuff and looked around the court 'as if he were entering a theatre'. When told of the date for the execution – 1 May – he said to the governor of Newgate, 'The sooner we go, sir, the better.'

On the morning in question, Davidson and Brunt drank a toast to the king's health. There was no final service and everybody refused the last rites. The crowds gathered early, thronging along the Old Bailey and Fleet Street, creeping down Ludgate Hill. The Foot Guards, the Life Guards, the Royal Horse Artillery and the

City Light Horse were out in force, armed to the teeth and ready to prevent any trouble.

On the platform outside the Session House, the five were brought out, shackled, to meet their maker. 'Well, Mr Thistlewood,' Richard Tidd shook the man's hand. 'How do you do?' 'I was never better,' the leader told him. He was sucking an orange. Neither man wanted the hood over his face and Tidd ostentatiously bowed to the crowd in the three directions where they stood.

When the noose was put around Ings's neck, he shouted, 'Remember me to King George IV.'

'God bless you, Thistlewood,' somebody shouted from the crowd and the trapdoors crashed together, the five bodies twisting and writhing at the ends of the ropes. The hangmen, Foxen and Botting, had to grab the kicking legs of Brunt and Ings to finish them off. After half an hour, they hacked off the dead men's heads, not with an axe but a knife wielded by an anonymous civilian who may have been a surgeon, or, ironically, bearing in mind Ings's profession, a butcher. 'This is the head of Arthur Thistlewood, the traitor.'

Now the crowd grew restless. There had been no trouble so far, but heads in the morning air was a step too far and someone yelled, 'Shoot that bloody murderer,' aimed at either hangman on the roof. Blood dripped from Davidson's neck and groans and hisses filled the air.

The families of the men who died petitioned the home secretary for the return of their husbands' bodies. That was refused and the following night they were buried alongside an underground passage from Newgate, the coffins filled with quicklime and covered with earth and stones. The others were transported over the next few days to the far side of the world.

Could the Cato Street rebellion have worked? There was much talk at the time of the 'Committee of 200', a shadowy group of backers for Thistlewood who in turn were alleged to have other adherents in London and elsewhere. What is required for a successful revolution is large numbers and the support of the army, as well as intelligent, informed leadership. For all his nerve and sangfroid, it is unlikely that Arthur Thistlewood could have provided this. The army remained staunchly loyal, however many disgruntled *ex*-soldiers were in the mix.

So what we are left with is a failed assassination attempt, like all the others in this book. In the end, despite the terror of the *threat* of revolution, there was only one death, that of Runner Smithers, before the whole attempt came crashing down. And that, as the successful assassin John Wilkes Booth said (in Latin) when he shot Abraham Lincoln – 'So it always is with tyrants.' Despite the positive murmurings of the mob who went to see the men of Cato Street die, those who faced the drop or Botany Bay were regarded by the mass of the British people as wannabe tyrants. There was no guarantee that the 'Government of the People of Britain' would have been any different from the one they wanted to overthrow.

... And Plot

Irishmen and elephants, they say, never forget. And in some ways, the plot to assassinate the prime minister, Margaret Thatcher, and her cabinet at the Conservative Party conference in Brighton in October 1984 is a living example of that memory.

'English' occupation of Ireland goes back centuries, ever since the Normans established 'the Pale' in the 1070s, a narrow strip of castle-held territory run by the new masters who were doing exactly the same thing all over England. Henry II went so far as to claim that Ireland had been given to him by Pope Adrian IV and his son, King John, established Dublin as the English headquarters and administered English law from there. Successive kings bought the loyalty of Irish clan chiefs with titles, but the island, fiercely Catholic as most of it was after the Reformation, was always a potentially fertile ground for rebellion and war.

Under James I, Ulster in the north was settled by plantations owned and run by Scots and Englishmen and the mass of the peasantry, all over Ireland, stayed illiterate and half-starving because that was how the Scottish and English lords wanted them – a powerless and ignored workforce.

As there seemed to be a very real source of rebellion in Wolfe Tone's United Irishmen in the 1790s and the risk of Catholic Ireland throwing in its lot with revolutionary France, the prime minister, William Pitt, pushed through the Acts of Union in 1801. The agreement of Catholic Emancipation, to give Catholics the same rights as Protestants, would have to wait until 1829.

By the 1840s, an economic disaster highlighted the chronic poverty of the people. Unable to afford seed corn and growing crops in small, unprofitable land-holdings, the peasantry had gone over to the cheaper potatoes. In 1845, three successive harvests had failed – the 'praties' turned black in the ground and could not be dug up, still less eaten. A million people died and about the same number emigrated to the United States and Canada, taking with them a visceral hatred of the English and their 'absentee landlords' which has never gone away.

In his first ministry from 1868, Prime Minister William Gladstone promised to pacify Ireland and failed. His policy of disestablishing the Irish (Protestant) Church was neither here nor there and his far more important Land Act, which would have increased tenants' rights, was ignored by the great landowners.

By the early years of the twentieth century, a strong Home Rule movement had developed, the Irish bloc of MPs at Westminster led by John Redmond demanding radical change that amounted to a demand for independence. Among the people, the Fenians in the

1860s brought dynamite and terror to mainland Britain and the Irish Land League was only slightly less belligerent. The Irish Republican Brotherhood began as a cultural movement, extolling Irish poetry and music, but morphed into something far more sinister by 1916 in the form of the Irish Republican Army.

Like the wars against revolutionary France, the First World War was a potential catalyst for Irish unrest. The country now was divided into two distinct groups – the province of Ulster, with its Unionist majority that had no intention of leaving Britain, and the rest, keen after what they saw as centuries of alien military occupation, to form a breakaway state. The Easter Rising in 1916 was in some ways what might have happened had Cato Street become a reality. Sinn Fein – Gaelic for 'ourselves alone' – presided over an armed insurrection in the capital when key buildings were targeted and running gun battles ensued. The Irish Republic was declared and the names Pearse and McBride were added to a list of martyrs to the cause. The ringleaders were rounded up, à la Cato Street, and hanged.

Two years later, Sinn Fein swept the board in the elections and those who were not in gaol formed Dáil Éireann, a new government. Civil war raged in Ireland for the next three years, with murders of policemen, officials and anybody who did not follow the IRA's lead. It was modern, twentieth-century terrorism, copied by the Bolsheviks in Russia and for the same reason: to foment revolution. The official government, with David Lloyd George and Herbert Asquith at its head, launched the 'black and tans', auxiliary policemen wearing khaki uniforms and routinely carrying firearms, an unheard-of policy in British policing.

In 1922, Sinn Fein effectively got their way, which probably gave credence to the Grand Hotel bombers of sixty years later that terrorism works, however much governments deny that this is not the case. The Irish Free State had a similar status to that of Canada in the newly created Commonwealth. The irony was that Sinn Fein itself was not satisfied with this arrangement and a low-key civil war continued; one of the casualties was Kevin O'Higgins, shot dead one Sunday on his way to church. In the Irish parliament, Eamon De Valera's Fianna Fail party overthrew the existing government and stayed in power for seventeen years. Links with Britain and its monarchy were gradually whittled away. In 1937, the South coined the name Eire and was nominally neutral in the Second World War. An exception was made for Irish regiments in the British Army, such as the Irish Guards, the Royal Inniskilling Fusiliers and the Irish Rifles, because they were no longer considered 'Irish' in the modern sense.

Whatever decisions were made in London, Dublin and Belfast, there was always a rank-and-file element that recognized no such boundaries and agreements. The same had probably been true in 1605 and 1820, when unknown numbers of ordinary people were either unaware of events until they were over, or were standing on the sidelines to see which way the wind was blowing. The IRA was different. It was a splinter group of the Irish Volunteers formed in 1913 'to serve and maintain the rights and liberties common to all the people of Ireland'. From 1916, their metier was ambush and assassination which led to the organization being outlawed in 1922. Like other organizations, for instance the Ku Klux Klan in the United States, this simply drove the followers underground, quietly arming themselves and training for whatever violence the high command deemed necessary.

In 1939, the first bomb of the Second World War, which hit the shops in Broadgate, Coventry, was the work of the IRA. So were those partially dismantled by DI Robert Fabian of the Metropolitan Police in Piccadilly, London, months earlier. IRA leaders were rounded up and imprisoned, but the movement continued illicitly with an estimated membership of 5,000 led by the grandly named Supreme Army Council.

Then came the New Troubles, named to distinguish them from 1916–22. In 1968, when the world seemed convulsed with student protests, mostly against American involvement in Vietnam, rioting broke out in the Bogside area of Londonderry and a cameraman caught the heavy-handed response of the Royal Ulster Constabulary which ultimately led to the force being disbanded. Early in the new year, Catholic demonstrators were ambushed at Burntollet Bridge and the British Army was sent into Londonderry and Belfast to back up the exhausted police force. There were howls of protest – the 'black and tans' were back. The Republicans did not come out of the clash well – IRA, said the propaganda scrawled on walls all over Northern Ireland, stood for 'I Ran Away'. There was shooting in the Shankill Road and petrol bombs were thrown. Bernadette Devlin, at 22 the youngest MP for 200 years, was arrested for incitement in the 'Battle of Bogside'.

The whole fiasco blew up because Protestants in Ulster (the vast majority) resented privileges being given to Catholics in an attempt by the British government to keep the peace. From such small and relatively insignificant beginnings, revolutions grow. Devlin was hailed by her supporters as a reincarnation of Joan of Arc and Florence Nightingale (a very unlikely pairing) and condemned by her opponents as the devil incarnate.

In July 1970, virtual open warfare was going on in Belfast's streets, with bombed houses, burnt-out vehicles and armed men in combat gear and balaclavas patrolling the area. IRA suspects were interned without trial or even charges, contrary to the centuries'-old law of habeas corpus. Two years later, civil rights protestors were shot by members of 1st Battalion, Parachute Regiment in 'Bloody Sunday', a case that rolled on through the courts for years.

Then, the bombing came to mainland Britain. On 9 March 1973, explosions occurred outside Scotland Yard and the Old Bailey law courts, where the bodies of Arthur Thistlewood and his Cato Street conspirators lay under the tarmac. The papers carried horrific photographs of shell-shocked civilians, many of them injured by flying glass. It was the work of the Provisional IRA, one of many splinter terrorist groups bringing slaughter to London.

The following year, the 'Birmingham Six' made headlines when two pubs in the city were destroyed by bombs. The six men arrested for this were subsequently, after years of bitter litigation, released, but the actual killers have never been apprehended. In the middle of all this, only the faithful noticed the passing of Eamon de Valera, architect of the 1916 Easter Rising, in Dublin at the end of August 1975. The European Court of Human Rights, potentially past its sell-by date having been set up in the immediate post-war period, decided that Britain was guilty of 'inhumane treatment and torture' in the war against terrorism, but said nothing about the terrorists themselves, happy to kill innocent women and children.

In 1979, as the pope (John Paul II who would himself dodge an assassin's bullet) visited Dublin to promote peace, the IRA assassinated Lord Louis Mountbatten, the queen's cousin, as he was holidaying with his family on board his boat, the *Shadow V*. Months earlier, and much nearer to home, Airey Neave, the government's spokesman on Northern Ireland and a close friend of the prime minister, Margaret Thatcher, was killed when a bomb was placed under his car in the car park of the House of Commons. It went off on 30 March, yards from the spot where Guido Fawkes was caught with his barrels of gunpowder.

While IRA prisoners went on hunger strike in the Maze, the notorious Northern Ireland detention centre for suspected terrorists, Marcus Sarjeant fired blank shots at the queen during the Trooping of the Colour (see Chapter 4) which, it turned out, had nothing to do with the Troubles at all. There was a break-out at the Maze in September 1983, the largest in Britain, involving 134 escapees. Then, came the Grand Hotel.

Margaret Thatcher was a Marmite prime minister if ever there was one. Half the country loved her; the other half regarded her as a monster. The earlier leaders who were targeted in this section of the book, Robert Cecil and Lord Liverpool, were very different characters. It was the unparalleled growth of technology and the media by the 1980s that made Thatcher such a well-known figure. Ordinary people would have passed Robert Banks Jenkinson (Liverpool) in the street without knowing who he was. You could not miss Robert Cecil because his deformity made him appear dwarf-like, but he never went 'walkabout', as we might say today – he always travelled by coach. But everybody knew Maggie – her followers knew her by that epithet – because she was constantly in the headlines, in the press and on television. The bombing that nearly killed her was televised too, at least its aftermath, in marked contrast to the Cato Street attempt, which was snuffed out before it started and the Gunpowder Plot only remembered today by the setting off of fireworks.

On 15 September 1984, Roy Walsh signed the register at Brighton's Grand Hotel, an elegant nineteenth-century building along the resort's famous sea-front. He gave his address as London, SE4 and ticked the box that said British. In fact, none of this information was true. He was not British but Irish and he did not live in London. His real name was Patrick Magee, a Provisional IRA fixer known to authorities, because of the risks he took, as The Chancer. He was given room 629, overlooking the sea (he had asked specifically for such a view) because it was five floors above the apartments due to be occupied by the prime minister in October.

The IRA had form when it came to assassinations. Their Fenian forerunners had murdered Lord Frederick Cavendish, the chief secretary for Ireland, in Phoenix Park, Dublin, in 1882. In 1922, Field Marshal Sir Henry Wilson was gunned down outside his London home. The murders of Airey Neave, the groundbreaking oncologist Gordon Hamilton Fairley (killed in error as he walked past a car bomb) and the *Guinness Book of Records* compiler Ross McWhirter were more recent examples. Magee had already brought in a heavy suitcase and two women visited him later in the day bringing in more apparatus. The next day an 'engineer' called to set the bomb up. We still do not know who these people were. The time bomb had a long-delay countdown of twenty-four days, six hours and thirty-six minutes. That would make the explosion due just before three o'clock on 12 October, the last day of the Conservative Party conference. It was hidden behind panels in room 629's bathroom and Magee checked out the next morning, his suitcase presumably much lighter.

On the day in question, the Grand Hotel was temporary home to 220 guests, 32 visitors, 11 staff and 23 police officers, there because the party conferences were known to be the centres of demonstrations and unrest. Margaret Thatcher was notorious for her ability to cat-nap and her staff were run ragged trying to keep up with her. After a glitzy ball in the hotel, the prime minister worked on a speech she would give the next day.

The bomb went off at 2:54:01, a giant fireball rushing through the corridors on the sixth floor. Blast waves rocked outwards, shattering windows and crashing through bricks and masonry. As with the later bombing of New York's Twin Towers, the building itself would do most of the damage.

Donald and Muriel Maclean, asleep in room 629 were thrown through the air. The wall between them and 628 disintegrated and occupant Jeanne Shattock was killed as metal, ceramics and wood were driven into her body with the force of the blast. The blast struck up as well as sideways – in room 729, Harvey Thomas was blown into what he thought was space. Then the eighth floor went, then the roof.

The noise of the collapsing building was horrendous – Gordon Shattock felt himself falling, with no ceiling above him and no floor below him. The Taylors were caught up in the drop, in room 528. So were John and Roberta Wakeham in the floor below that. Room 328 ceased to exist, carrying with it Sir Anthony Berry and his wife,

Sarah. In 228, Norman Tebbitt yelled to his wife, 'It's a bomb,' and they both hurtled downwards.

The Thatchers, unbelievably, were unhurt. Had Maggie worked for three minutes longer on her speech, she would almost certainly have died. As it was, her husband Denis threw clothes over his pyjamas and dashed with her across the corridor to the secretaries' office. 'I think,' the Iron Lady said, 'that was an assassination attempt, don't you?' A giant chimney stack which sliced its way to the ground floor had missed her suite by literally inches.

The alarm system had gone off automatically and the fire brigade arrived to what looked like a war zone. We all saw those scenes the next morning on breakfast television – curtains flapping in the breeze, the pavement a chaos of bricks, window-frames and broken glass. People still in their evening dress were wandering dazed and uncomprehending. Masonry was still falling when the fire engines got there, screams coming from everywhere. 'They arrived absolutely silently,' said one eyewitness of the fire brigade, 'like angels from heaven.'

The fire brigade was supposed to stay two streets away in case of other bombs, but fire chief Fred Bishop ignored that and called for volunteers. All his men followed him into the Grand. The prime minister, stoical as ever and still in her ballgown, thanked the brigade for coming – 'I'm delighted to see you,' she said. She was rushed to the police station, but refused to leave Brighton, insisting that she must be back at the conference centre by nine o'clock.

Astonishingly, some of the guests at the Grand had slept through the whole thing. One of them, who was, according to a fireman, 'in bed with a lady who was not his wife' yelled at the man to get out. Then began the dangerous and urgent work of getting the wounded out from under tons of debris. Jennifer Taylor and Gordon Shattock had fallen five floors but were only slightly hurt. Eric Taylor was running out of oxygen under the roof above him. Muriel Maclean, who had been in room 629, had a crushed leg and head injuries.

Norman Tebbit lay half-conscious next to sparking live wires. His ribs were broken and his lung was punctured. Camera crews showed him being stretchered to safety, still in his pyjamas. His wife would never walk again. In the ambulance, an attendant asked Tebbit if he was allergic to anything. 'Yes,' he said. 'Bombs.'

When the dust cleared, Eric Taylor, Anthony Berry and Roberta Wakeham were dead. The cause was suffocation. Muriel Maclean died of injuries five months later. Jeanne Shattock's body was never recovered. Everyone who was there and the nation who watched the aftermath on television, were stunned by the reserve and sangfroid of the survivors, even those who had lost spouses and friends.

Inevitably later than advertised, Margaret Thatcher took the podium at two o'clock. 'The bomb attack,' she said, 'was, first and foremost, an inhuman and indiscriminating attempt to massacre innocent and unsuspecting people.'

One person watching this, on live television, was Patrick Magee, in a bar in Cork. 'I'd always be looking over my shoulder,' he said later. '[The British people] would never forget.' The IRA took responsibility for the bomb – 'Today,' they announced, 'we were unlucky, but, remember, we have only to be lucky once.'

Modern counter terrorism quite rightly keeps itself under the radar. We are only told in hindsight that a certain number of plots against the state have been thwarted and we are rarely given details. I would venture to suggest that we are *never* told the complete truth. There were no leads in the Brighton bombing case. It was not even known exactly where the bomb had been planted, so 3,798 black bins were commandeered and the debris of the Grand Hotel was stuffed into them, so that intensive laboratory work could begin.

When the bomb mechanism pieces were found, it did not help. It could not prove when the device had been planted. Over 1,000 people stayed at the Grand from 1 July and they came from all over the world. Clever detective work by the Met's Special Branch recovered the registration cards from the hotel. Roy Walsh of 27 Braxfield Road, Brockley, did not exist. Even those who had driven him to The Grand Hotel from the station and the receptionist who had checked him in had only vague memories of an ordinary Joe – in effect, a perfect hitman.

Red herrings were everywhere, taking the police down all sorts of blind alleys. It did not help that Brighton had long had a reputation for extra-marital flings. Only an hour by train from London, it was the perfect spot for 'Mr and Mrs Smith' to while away a weekend, even (and perhaps especially) when there was a party conference in town.

DCS Jack Reeve ran the investigation, pursuing every avenue, hiring in extra computers when Sussex CID's became overloaded. He appeared on BBC's *Crimewatch* programme, appealing for Roy Walsh to come forward. He did not.

On 17 January 1985, technology at last came to the police's rescue. High-resolution testing found a partial palm print on Walsh's registration card and it matched that of Patrick Magee, a teenager in 1967 when he had burgled a shop in Norwich. Special Branch moved in, checking on the movements of Magee's wife, Eileen, who lived in Belfast with their 7-year-old son. She led them to her husband's hideout in the slum Ballymun area of Dublin. The problem was that the British security forces had no jurisdiction in Eire, especially in view of the history between the two nations and the Irish government had repeatedly turned down extradition applications in cases involving 'politics' (a euphemism, of course, for terrorism).

Then Magee made the mistake of carrying on his work. He was arrested in Glasgow on 22 June 1985 along with four other terrorists planting more devices. At his trial in September of the following year, the judge described the Irishman as 'a man of exceptional cruelty and inhumanity' and sentenced him to eight terms of life imprisonment, meaning, in effect, thirty-five years.

But politics moves on. Just as the popularity of James I waned and his son leapt headlong into civil war; just as the powers that were after Cato Street had to concede to the growing pressure for democracy via successful reform bills; so the sentence against Magee was overturned by Tony Blair's Good Friday Agreement in 1999, by which a number of convicted killers were released. Magee had served only fourteen years, had remarried and had written two books. He admitted to *The Guardian* newspaper in 2000 that he was indeed guilty of the Brighton bombing, but has always refused to name his accomplices.

In the cases you have just read, the central target in the three assassination plans dodged the euphemistic bullet. James I did not die as planned as St Stephen's Hall crashed around him. Today, thousands of us every 5 November stand around bonfires watching Guy Fawkes burn, most of us wholly unaware that that effigy was once that of the king himself. The king was never a serious target for the Cato Street conspirators, but Lord Liverpool, the prime minister, was. Thanks to the insidious (and probably illegal) work of the spy George Edwards, he was never in any serious danger at Lord Harrowby's house in Grosvenor Square; in fact, he was not even there. Margaret Thatcher came closest at the Grand Hotel in 1984, death missing her by minutes or feet, depending on the comparative yardstick used. There is a certain irony that in the first two cases, the authorities acted with firmness and decision to ruin the plan. In the last one, despite the wizardry of technology and a wealth of information, the fortunes of those at the Grand Hotel were, in the end, down to pure luck.

Chapter 2

On the Trail of the Assassins

The title of this chapter comes from the book written by Jim Garrison (Penguin, 1992) about a specific group of killers – those involved in the murder of President John F. Kennedy in Dealey Plaza, Texas, in November 1963. Garrison was the district attorney for New Orleans and he uncovered a bizarre extension to the plot to kill Kennedy which many at the time and since have dismissed as conspiracy theory fantasy. The harsh fact is, however, that most assassinations, especially political ones, *are* conspiracies in that they involve more than one planner and plotter, even if the actual assassin appears to be operating on his/her own.

There are a number of subtly different definitions of assassination, but the one used by Richard Belfield in *The Secret History of Assassination* (2008) puts the subject succinctly. 'Assassination is political murder, where the motives, no matter how mixed, are all about power; those who do not have power assassinate to get it and those who have power assassinate to keep it.'

This book is not about assassination per se, but the *attempts* made by would-be assassins on their victims. In that sense, motivation and modus operandi is as valid as in instances where the 'hit' was successful. By referring to assassination as political murder, various writers have given a status to such killings they do not deserve. Assassins are murderers, pure and simple and if, as in the case of the Gunpowder Plotters, the Cato Street Conspirators and the IRA, their crimes are carried out for a cause, that makes no difference. In a less serious context today, in Britain we have police officers who check that protestors are comfortable when glued to roads; judges dole out soft sentences on eco-warriors; and one group of lawyers have stated they will not aid in the prosecution of environmentalists. The death penalty no longer exists in Britain and no environmentalists have planned murder as part of their campaigns.

Bestriding the Narrow World Like a Colossus

American law enforcement agencies have invented a new word – victimology. Sometimes, the victims of murder are entirely random – they were in the wrong place at the wrong time. This cannot be said of the victims of assassination, unless a mistake has been made by the assassin or innocent bystanders get in the way of the bullets.

Almost universally, and contrary to the examples we saw in Chapter 1, the victims of assassination are single individuals, usually men, who hold extraordinary power over their subjects. Mathematicians, anxious to prove that their subject is applicable in all walks of life, have even provided algorithms to create graphs of such things. The more power a man has, the more likely he is to abuse it – Stalin, Hitler, Pol Pot, Idi Amin, Mao Tse-Tung; the list is very long indeed. We have already seen examples of this in this book. James I, though bound to an extent by his parliament, rode roughshod over the principles and rights of Catholics who had been following their faith for centuries. Lord Liverpool was the prime minister in a country where the wealthy lorded it over the poor and kept them in that parlous state. Margaret Thatcher epitomized an uncaring government seen as a foreign power by the men who wanted her dead.

The murder of Julius Caesar on 15 March 44 BC is often used as a benchmark for assassination. As such, it is still studied by Intelligence networks around the world, even though it happened 2,000 years ago and achieved nothing but chaos. Historically, ancient Rome had thrown out its kings – the Tarquin family – 500 years earlier and the 'eternal city' was ruled by a series of committees of landowners (the patricians), the most famous of which was the Senate. Rome came to claim a God-given right of conquest, pushing out from its origins as a humble mud settlement on the banks of the Tiber to the most formidable state in the ancient world. Most of that state was achieved by force of arms – the Roman army was superior to anything the 'barbarians' could throw at it. And Gaius Julius Caesar was the most brilliant general the army produced.

Tyrants are made by armies and Caesar duly became one. He manufactured an unnecessary war against the Gauls, conquered what is today France and invaded (however temporarily) Britain. His soldiers loved him, as they did Napoleon Bonaparte 1,800 years later – another potential assassination victim. They smiled indulgently at his vanity, curling his hair to cover his baldness, singing dirty songs about his bisexuality. Others were not so sure. A group of politicians was convinced that Caesar intended to put the clock back to the days of kingship; that he wanted to reduce the power of the Senate, destroy the republic and declare himself – as the army already had – *imperator*, emperor. At a stroke, autocracy would be back, a despot backed by the military (which applies to all of them in the twentieth and twenty-first centuries) and everything that was good and virtuous about Rome would be gone forever.

So sixty of them decided to kill him, singling him out as he attended the Senate, wrapping him in his toga and stabbing him, according to various Roman writers, twenty-three times.

Julius Caesar proved that he was mortal, to the extent that, in the years ahead, when *actual* emperors ruled Rome (the murder of Caesar achieved the exact opposite of what the assassins intended), augurs rode in the imperial chariot, whispering 'Remember, you are mortal. Look behind. Look behind.'

'Let me have men about me who are fat,' William Shakespeare contends that Caesar said. 'Yon Cassius hath a lean and hungry look.' Cassius was one of the twenty-three who stabbed Caesar and the point that Shakespeare is making is that everybody in a position of power hedges themselves around with security forces, the most up-to-date technology, family members – *anything* that will keep them safe. It does not always work.

The attitudes of potential assassination victims vary enormously. Enemies of US Marshal James Butler 'Wild Bill' Hickok, who was murdered in Deadwood, Dakota Territory, in June 1876, contended that he always walked down the centre of the street rather than on the sidewalk because of his fear of lurking assassins. And that he covered the floors of his hotel rooms with crumpled newspaper to avoid late-night/early-morning attacks. Any number of emperors and kings had official food and drink tasters attached to their courts to prevent assassination by poison.

Kings and emperors in particular protected themselves with a cloak of religion and even the supernatural in order to deter would-be assassins. If a killer believed that he was killing not merely a man but a god, the moral implications were enormous. Deranged Roman emperors like Nero and Caligula took this power-obsession to extremes, although it did neither of them any good. Nero, it is true, committed suicide (but under considerable pressure from his many enemies) and Caligula was hacked to death by his own Praetorian bodyguard.

On the other hand, some victims were incredibly laid-back. A number of American presidents *after* the assassinations of Lincoln, Garfield and McKinley stood exposed on podiums making speeches, almost willing assassins to shoot them. Reinhard Heydrich, the *obergruppenfuhrer* who effectively ran Czechoslovakia, persisted in riding in an open-topped car without armour plating or outriders, despite earlier attempts on his life. On 27 May 1942, as the Mercedes slowed to take a bend, Czech and Slovak patriots, trained by the British, opened fire on him. Heydrich fought back, using his pistol, but he died from sepsis caused by pieces of the car's upholstery lodged in a stomach wound. Thirty-eight years earlier, the Archduke Franz Ferdinand and his wife Sophie were also riding in an open-topped car when they inspected troops in Sarajevo, Bosnia. A bomb was thrown at the motorcade, but it bounced off the archduke's car and hit the second vehicle. Franz Ferdinand checked on the wounded, then took the advice of his security adviser, General Oskar Potiorek (who seems to have been a complete idiot), and continued with the procession. Potiorek had assured the archduke that another attack was most unlikely, even though the motorcade's route was well-advertised in advance and obvious from the yards of bunting floating from rooftops and lampposts.

Another assassin, 19-year-old Gavrilo Princip, probably assumed that the bomb had done its work and was astonished to see the archduke's car moving at a crawling speed towards him. He shot Ferdinand in the neck, piercing his jugular, and Sophie in the abdomen. Both were dead in minutes.

In all the assassinations and attempts we have looked at so far, *nothing* was achieved from the assassin's point of view. After the Gunpowder Plot, England went on to become a fully Protestant country, its monarch even today unable to embrace Catholicism. The plotters themselves, as we have seen, met gruesome and mostly public ends. As far as the Cato Street conspirators go, it could be argued by the cynical that we have still not achieved the government of the people that they wanted. We have democracy, but we still have economic inequality and the self-interested quangos of the great and not-so-good still run the country. If the ultimate aim of the Grand Hotel bombers was to create a united independent Ireland, they have failed; Northern Ireland remains as committed to union with

Britain as ever. Julius Caesar was not an emperor – it could be argued that he never wanted to be – but his heir Octavian certainly was, becoming Rome's first emperor, twenty-four years after the Ides of March murder. Wild Bill Hickok was shot dead in a Deadwood saloon while playing poker. His death achieved nothing, except that today, Hickok's legend as 'the fastest gun alive' still stands and only a few Western buffs even know the name of his killer, Jack McCall. The assassination of Heydrich did not lead to a collapse of Nazism and the Third Reich, not even in Czechoslovakia. Instead, an entire village – Lidice – was wiped off the map, its menfolk dead, its women and children entrained to extermination camps.

It is an adage often forgotten by assassins – 'Be careful what you wish for'.

Such Men Are Dangerous

Just as there is no homogenous group who are the targets of assassination, so the killers themselves are a widely disparate group. First is the 'lone nut', stereotyped in folklore as a masked figure with a cloak and dagger hidden in his clothes and characterized by many people as Lee Harvey Oswald, who allegedly killed John F. Kennedy in Dallas in 1963.

A number of assassins fit this pattern and they are usually unbalanced, exhibiting a range of psychoses which explains their behaviour. The only British prime minister to have been assassinated was Spencer Perceval in 1812, but this was not the result of an Arthur Thistlewood-type conspiracy. Perceval's killer was a failed businessman, John Bellingham, who believed that the prime minister's foreign policy had prevented him from securing lucrative Russian contracts. He shot Perceval dead in the lobby of the House of Commons.

Bellingham's statement at his trial at the Old Bailey on 15 May tells us all we need to know about his state of mind. 'Gentlemen, when a minister sets himself above the laws, as Mr Perceval did, he does so at his own personal risk. If this were not so, the mere will of the minister would become the law and what would then become of your liberties?'

It all sounds rather grand, but in fact it was nonsense. Perceval had acted in accordance with his cabinet, his party and almost certainly, all of parliament. Russia had allied itself with Napoleon in 1808 and for Britain to cut off trading ties with her was entirely natural and sensible. Bellingham's defence team pleaded insanity but the court ignored this and he was hanged on 18 May 1812 to the delight of the crowd.

If the assassination of a British prime minister is unique, in the United States, the murder of presidents is almost a national sport (see Chapters 6 and 8). On 2 July 1881, Charles Guiteau killed President James A. Garfield at the Baltimore and Potomac Railroad Station in Washington DC. He looked at the prospect of murder as a 'removal' rather than an assassination and realized that the knife he had originally intended to use would not work – 'Garfield would have crushed the life out of me with a single blow of his fist.' He borrowed $15 from a relative and bought a British-made .442 calibre Bulldog revolver, one with an ivory grip that he believed would look better in a museum after the event. He was no marksman; the first time he fired the weapon, the recoil knocked him off his feet. Ironically, the exhibited gun was 'lost' by the Smithsonian Institute soon after Guiteau's trial.

Guiteau had postponed the shooting because Garfield's wife, Lucretia, was not well and he did not want to upset her. Accordingly, on the day in question, he paced the station's waiting room, had his shoes polished and, as Garfield passed, shot him twice in the back.

Guiteau was immediately arrested, claiming to be 'a stalwart of the Stalwarts', a loose political group of Garfield's opponents.

The president died of infection on 19 September and his killer stood trial in November. Guiteau consistently ignored his defence counsel, who pleaded insanity on his behalf (the first time that this had happened in an American court) and tried to defend himself. Using the British M'Naghten Rule (see Chapter 5) the judge explained to the jury what legally constituted insanity. The defence hired an alienist (we would call him a psychiatrist today), Edward Spitzka, who testified that Guiteau 'is not only now insane, but that he was never anything else'. He was 'a moral monstrosity', a 'morbid egoist' with 'a tendency to misinterpret the real affairs of life'.

The prosecution, of course, disagreed. George Corkhill, Washington DC's district attorney, said, 'There's nothing of the mad about Guiteau; he's a cool, calculating blackguard, a polished ruffian ... He was a deadbeat, pure and simple. Finally, he got tired of deadbeating. He wanted excitement ... and notoriety – and he got it.'

Throughout his trial, Guiteau consistently swore at the judge, counsel and jury, declaiming poems that he had written and passing notes to the court audience. He demanded that the new president, Chester Arthur, should set him free because he, Guiteau, had got him into power. He also demanded a consulship in either Vienna or Paris. He even tried to pass the buck in terms of medical malpractice – 'The doctors killed Garfield. I just shot him.' To this end, Guiteau expected to be released and planned a lecture tour of the United States, even intending to run for president himself. The jury found him guilty on 25 January 1882 and he was hanged five months later.

Guiteau had been a member of the Oneida religious sect founded in New York state in 1848, a group given to 'perfectionism', group marriage and a form of communism. Like many sects, it was based on free love, but it also featured a type of proto-eugenics to create 'perfect' children. Whether the bizarre ideas of the cult damaged

Guiteau or whether he was drawn to the Oneidas because he was already unbalanced will never be known. God, Guiteau contended, had ordered him to shoot Garfield. The dissection of the assassin's body revealed phimosis, a rare condition in which the foreskin cannot be retracted. Such was the confused state of medical diagnosis in the 1880s that this was thought by some to explain Guiteau's behaviour. Parts of his brain are still on display in the Mütter Museum in Philadelphia.

Leon Czolgosz does not *quite* fit the pattern of the 'lone nut' assassin. Although he claimed to have acted alone in the shooting of President William McKinley in the Temple of Music at Buffalo, New York, on 6 September 1901, he was clearly influenced by the anarchist group to which he belonged; that takes him into the much more common type of assassin, one who is the 'hit man' for a much wider conspiracy.

Conspiracy theories have a bad press today, largely because of an ever-growing intrusion into a legitimate historical study by half-baked delusionists. Princess Diana? Murdered by Special Services personnel posing as paparazzi working for the late Duke of Edinburgh. The American moon landing of 1969? Filmed in a Hollywood studio. Various forms of anti-COVID medicine? Part of an international plot by governments to control the minds of its citizens. QAnon? A widespread group of child molesters and rapists working with Washington DC and putting themselves above the law. All of this rubbish and much more besides has muddied the waters for those of us genuinely concerned with conspiracy in history – which is a shame, because most assassins and their attempts are up to their necks in it.

The anarchists to which Czolgosz belonged were a disparate group of nihilists devoted to the overthrow of existing order and the creation of a classless state. In that sense, monarchies, churches and capitalism all became legitimate targets, even if the aims of anarchists beyond destruction made little sense and were frequently at odds with each other. The period during which McKinley was murdered is regarded as the golden age of anarchism, in which similar ideas spread worldwide.

Czolgosz was a Polish American born in Detroit in 1873. He became caught up in anarchist philosophy in 1898, attending the lectures of Emma Goldman, a feminist and anti-capitalist who was herself implicated in the attempted assassination of financier Henry Clay Frick of the Carnegie Corporation. When Czolgosz read of the murder of King Umberto I of Italy in July 1900, he decided to kill the president 'for the sake of the common man'.

On 6 September 1901, Czolgosz stood in line in the Temple of Music to shake hands with McKinley. He was carrying, under a handkerchief, a .32 calibre Iver Johnson 'Safety Automatic' revolver. As the president extended his hand, the anarchist slapped it aside and pumped two bullets into McKinley at almost point-blank range. One bounced off a button and did no harm but the second ruptured his abdomen and, like Garfield, infection did the rest. The crowd jumped on Czolgosz while the president urged, 'Go easy on him, boys.'

Theodore 'Teddy' Roosevelt was McKinley's successor and he summed up governments' universal attitudes to anarchists. 'When compared with the suppression of anarchy, every other question sinks into insignificance.'

It was a sign of the times, perhaps, that the notion of insanity was uppermost at Czolgosz's trial, although he would have none of it and refused to co-operate in any way with his defence counsel. The jury ignored the insanity angle and Czolgosz went to the electric chair in Auburn prison on 29 October. The man who pulled the lever was Edwin Davis, known euphemistically as the state electrician, who held a patent on some of 'Old Sparky's' features.

Emma Goldman was arrested but released on the grounds of insufficient evidence. She wrote articles in Czolgosz's defence, comparing him with Marcus Junius Brutus, another of the assassins of Julius Caesar. The implications were obvious – Shakespeare had made it clear that Brutus was 'an honourable man'; so, by association, was Czolgosz. McKinley, on the other hand, was 'the president of the money kings and the trust magnates'. Many anarchists were quick to dissociate themselves from the killer, believing that he had damaged their cause. This defence of 'plausible deniability' became standard in the years ahead.

Anarchists were not pledged to assassination as the only means of effecting change, but it was a useful tool from time to time. The Jews of the first century AD had the Sicarii (the knifers) who targeted occupying Romans in Judea soon after the time of Christ and killed individuals in streets and marketplaces, hiding their weapons and pretending to be as grief-stricken as everybody else innocently walking past. Perhaps the only organization that had political murder at its heart was the Medieval Middle East sect the Hashashin, from which the word assassination is derived.

In the Muslim world, three of the four caliphs who ruled Islam after the prophet Mohammed died by assassination; it was a way of life – and death – in Saudi Arabia. The Hashashin emerged as a result of the Islamic split into Sunni and Shia camps. The dominant Seljuks who spread a huge empire in the eleventh century were Sunni; the Hashashin were Shia. It was the kind of vicious, daggers-drawn stand-off which characterized Catholics and Protestants in the western Europe of the sixteenth century. The sect's leader was Hasan-i Sabbah, perhaps the world's first terrorist philosopher, but he targeted other Muslims rather than the Jewish or Christian elements in the Middle East. One exception was Conrad of Montferrat, King of Tyre, who was stabbed to death in April 1192 by Hashashin disguised as Christian monks.

The sect had a rigid code of practice, which allowed working for anybody if the price was right. It had little to do with the Koran and relied on absolute obedience to the will of Sabbah. The killers themselves, young, impressionable men in their twenties and thirties who had been indoctrinated by him since childhood, were promised paradise and the bodies of virgins if they died for Sabbah's cause. Because of that, they made no attempt to hide after their murders and put up with torture and execution with stoicism. Horror stories of the 'Old Man of the Mountains' and the atrocities of his sect were no doubt embellished, especially by crusading Christians horrified by Islam anyway. The envoy of Frederick Barbarossa, the Holy Roman Emperor, reported back that the Hashashin took a mysterious drug that made them impervious to pain or fear, were equally addicted to eating pork and regularly committed incest with their sisters and mothers – everything a good Christian expected to hear. In fact, Sabbah was such a purist that he had one of his own sons executed for drinking wine!

Elements of the Hashashin could still be found among the followers of Al Qaeda and ISIS, the most infamous terror groups to come out of Islam in recent times. Those who hijacked the planes that hit the Twin Towers in New York on 9/11 and significantly damaged the west side of the Pentagon almost certainly saw themselves as the descendants of the Old Man of the Mountains.

From sects and minority groups like the Sicarii, the Hashashin, the anarchists and the IRA, the world of assassination has morphed into something altogether more insidious and terrifying. 'We now live,' writes Richard Belfield, 'in the age of assassinations', and in *The Secret History of Assassination*, he spends nearly 300 pages proving his point. According to him, virtually every government in the world uses assassination as a matter of policy, sometimes not even bothering to hide the fact.

Since 1945, the world has been split into east and west in terms of European politics. As Winston Churchill warned in a speech in Fulton, Missouri, in March 1946, 'From Stettin in the Baltic to Trieste in the Adriatic, an iron curtain has descended across the Continent.' Beyond that curtain was what was dubbed 'the evil empire' by President Reagan, a state brainwashed by Marxism in which individual freedom had ceased to exist. It surprised no one when it emerged that Josef Stalin, the Russian dictator, decided to assassinate President Tito of Yugoslavia because Tito did not toe the Moscow line. Only Stalin's death in 1953 took this threat away and his successor, Nikita Khrushchev, was far more cautious and put the plans on hold. Not that Khrushchev had any objections to political murder per se. When he was party secretary in Ukraine, he ordered the assassination of Archbishop Romzha of the Uniate Catholic Church. Another Ukrainian, Oleksander Shumskyi, was murdered on a train under Khrushchev's directive. Others followed. Late in 1953, Lavrentiy Beria, once Stalin's right-hand man, was accused by the Kremlin of trying to 'revive capitalism and restore the rule of the bourgeoisie', which was a ludicrous charge for a wholly committed Communist. Unlike most assassination victims, he went through a show trial and was executed in prison.

The hit list of the KGB (Russian secret intelligence) in the 1950s was not impressive. Despite intense training and the use of highly sophisticated weaponry of the sort mocked by Cubby Broccoli's James Bond franchise, the results were disappointing. By 1957, there had only been one successful assassination out of five and three of the survivors had defected to the West, taking with them an astonishing array of secrets.

The problem was the quality of the hitmen the KGB were using. These were not the 'old guard' of Bolshevik fanatics prepared to die for their beliefs, but thinking men who worked, essentially, for money. As the 1960s went on, the Kremlin used assassination less and less as an extension of policy, if only because of the poor success rate, but it has come back with a vengeance in recent years with the fall of the Berlin Wall and the collapse of communism. Vladimir Putin's state is now exposed as a pariah with its declaration of war against Ukraine, even though most of the planned assassinations had Ukrainians as their targets as early as the late 1940s. Putin's people can no longer hide behind 'the cause' of communism, which somehow makes the removal of Beria and Leon Trotsky acceptable. Russia is a gangster state, pure and simple, and it has put assassination back on the table. Poison is an increasingly common method. It was possibly warfarin (rat poison) that killed Stalin – only Lavrentiy Beria knew the truth of that. Potassium cyanide was used in hollow bullets in the 1950s plan to kill Georgi Okolivich, a prominent anti-Russian living in Frankfurt. In 1959, prussic acid was used to kill another Ukrainian separatist, Stepan Bandera.

The use of poison continued from the Communist era. The last known assassination under the old regime was that of the Bulgarian dissident Georgi Markov who had seriously affronted his government and their Soviet paymasters throughout a glittering career in journalism. In September 1978, Markov was waiting at a bus stop near Waterloo Bridge in London when he felt a sharp pain in his leg. He turned to see a man pick up an umbrella and then hurry across the road and hail a taxi. He died days later as a result of ricin poisoning, for which there was no antidote, and it was widely believed that the Bulgarian secret service had carried out the attack with the backing of the Soviet KGB.

Alexander Litvinenko was a former officer of Federal Security Service (FSB) and the KGB itself. In November 2006, he was poisoned in London with Polonium 210, which causes acute radiation syndrome. Like Markov, he had openly criticized his former bosses and, because of his former position, had inside knowledge of Putin's corrupt system. In a final statement from his bed in University College Hospital, he wrote to Putin personally:

> You have shown yourself to be as barbaric and ruthless as your most hostile critics have claimed ... You may succeed in silencing one man, but the howl of protest from around the world will reverberate ... in your ears for the rest of your life. May God forgive you for what you have done, not only to me but to beloved Russia and its people.

In September 2021, the European Court of Human Rights ruled that two hitmen were responsible, Andrey Lugovoy and Dmitry Kovtun, both former KGB agents. It also ruled that these men were working under direct orders from the Kremlin.

Sergei Skripal was a double agent who was providing intelligence to MI6. He was living in Salisbury in 2018 and his daughter Yulia was visiting him from Moscow. They were poisoned by a two-man team, caught casually strolling around the city on CCTV, using the nerve agent Novichok. Three others were affected, including Dawn Sturgess who died as a result. Both Skripals survived.

The fact that no actual action was taken against Putin or Russia for the murder of citizens on British soil probably tells you all you need to know about the casual attitude to assassination that pervades our society today. To reiterate, no one was surprised that Russia behaved like this – the 'evil empire' was beyond the pale, with a litany of vicious behaviour reaching back into the regimes of the tsars.

But when it emerged, as it did, that the West – the United States, Britain and France in particular – were using the same tactics, there was a jolt of disbelief. It goes without saying perhaps that 'no assassination instruction should ever be written or recorded', but that is an actual quotation from the CIA assassination training manual, a document that sounds as humdrum and unexceptional as the Highway Code until we consider its actual meaning. It means that the Central Intelligence Agency of the most powerful country in the world, descendant of the Second World War's Office of Strategic Services, orders assassinations as freely as it orders its stationery.

Murdering people who were opposed to American policy at a time when the United States was assuming its role as the world's policeman, was known as 'executive action'. The assassination programme itself was 'the opening of the hunting season'. A 'Health Alteration Committee' was the complex structure set up to make assassinations happen. The handbook, probably written by CIA agent 'Rip' Robertson in 1954 ran to eighteen pages and covered all aspects of a state-sponsored hit.

Weapons vary. Blunt objects are messy, heavy and bulky to carry and do not always do the job, despite their wide availability. The infamous ice pick used on Trotsky was rather niche, but the original weapon of choice in 1940 was a machine gun that jammed. Likewise, knives are not always efficient. Body armour and even thick clothing can deflect blades. Guns have problems too, but they are the best weapon available. Low velocity rifles (in the 1950s) are more likely to be fatal because of the damage done by a bullet after it enters the body. Silencers were frowned upon as achieving little and occasionally distorting the shot. Women could handle lighter rifles, but pistols and revolvers, even at close range, did not always get the job done. Bombs were largely a no-no. They had to be thrown, probably hitting innocent people or set (as in the Grand Hotel) with all sorts of technical deficiencies. Assassination by governments is not about widespread murder. Various fanatics believe that killing large numbers has a desired impact, but the United States' actions are all about taking out one individual. In the 1960s, the Kennedys were trying to kill Fidel Castro, not vast swathes of his people. Poison was regarded as highly by the West as it was by the East and as such toxins became more lethal and apparently innocuous (thallium and morphine, for instance) advocation of their use grew.

Allen Dulles was the first head of the CIA and his brother John Foster Dulles was secretary of state. Between them, these two were the epitome of the Cold War, loathing everything about communism in a way that left Joe McCarthy, the rabid anti-Red senator from Wisconsin, looking like a pinko-liberal. John Foster Dulles once said publicly, 'I confess to being one of those lawyers who do not regard international law as law at all.' How someone like him could have held the high office he did beggars belief.

In 1960, the CIA co-operated in the 'removal' of Patrice Lumumba, whose Congo was cosying up to the Soviet Union. African nations had always been prone to using assassination as part of their policy, quite prepared to order mass destruction as well as individual hits. And Africa was fertile ground for the East-West confrontation to be played out south of the Equator. Dwight D. Eisenhower, the American president, met Harold Macmillan, the British prime minister, to discuss tactics. 'Why aren't we getting rid of Lumumba now?' Lord Home, the foreign secretary, asked. They did in the following year. Michael Mulroney of the CIA was opposed to assassination on moral grounds but was prepared to prise Lumumba from the United Nations protection that he had been given. Two actual hitmen, known only by the codenames WI/WIN and WI/ROGUE enabled Lumumba to 'escape' from his security and fall conveniently into the hands of his rival, Joseph Mobutu. *Chambers Biographical Dictionary* calls Mobutu's regime 'harsh'; Richard Belfield calls him 'one of the most evil corrupt psychopaths ever to run an African state'. You decide! The promised trial of Lumumba, for alleged crimes, never happened. Instead, he was tortured for several days and shot by a Belgian firing squad. The entire history of Belgian involvement in the Congo was one of oppression and brutality. Those who look on the British Empire in this way would do well to compare the two.

The CIA made such a hash of the proposed invasion on Cuba in the Bay of Pigs in 1961 that the new president, John F. Kennedy, promised to smash them into a thousand pieces. Coming from a president who not only sanctioned the Bay of Pigs but ongoing attempts on Fidel Castro's life, this is hypocrisy at its most blatant.

The world seems to calm down a little in the 1970s because when Gerald Ford was in the White House he signed a ban on assassination of world leaders. His successor Jimmy Carter followed suit, as did Ronald Reagan, except that Reagan must have had his fingers crossed behind his back when he signed it. The CIA boss now was Bill Casey, a Cold War veteran who was cut from the same cloth as the Dulleses. He wanted to hit Muammar Gaddafi of Libya, not realizing that that removal would ultimately lead to the 'Arab Spring' and the rise of ever more deranged Islamic fundamentalism. A show of military strength from the Americans in 1986 and clashes between them and the Libyans masked the fact that the ultimate aim of the United States was to kill Gaddafi. When a bomb, planted by Libyans, blew up La Belle discotheque in Berlin, and a female police officer, Yvonne Fletcher, was shot outside the Libyan embassy in London, other nations were pulled into what might have become a full-on war. There is no doubt that Gaddafi was the West's worst nightmare, removing foreigners from Libyan soil and closing British and American bases. In the nineteenth century, the British had regarded the Gulf of Sirte off the Libyan coast as theirs. By the 1980s, the Americans claimed it (with even less justification than the British). Gaddafi calmly (and correctly) pointed out that it was Libyan.

Other than Castro, the colonel was the most elusive target the West had. American F111 bombers rained bombs on to his tents in 1986 and the British tried a similar operation ten years later. On both occasions, the dictator was not at home. Only three years after the last attempt, the British prime minister, Tony Blair, beamed in front of photographers as he hugged and shook hands with Gaddafi as both men co-operated against a mutual threat, Osama bin Laden's Al Qaeda.

It is by no means only the United States that has an assassination arm to its governmental structure. In 1956, Britain was faced with international humiliation when Colonel Gamel Nasser of Egypt sank ships in the international waters of the Suez Canal in a direct slap in the face to British involvement in the Middle East. Anthony Eden, the prime minister, was in no doubt how to end the crisis. Britain did not have the resources at the time to mount a full-scale invasion and the Americans, despite nonsense about a 'special relationship' saw no reason to intervene. 'I want him murdered,' Eden yelled at an underling, 'and if you and the Foreign Office don't agree then you'd better come to the Cabinet and explain why!' Sir Ivone Kirkpatrick, a hugely experienced civil servant, reminded him, 'I don't think we have a department for that sort of thing, Prime Minister, but if we do, it is certainly not under my control.'

The French routinely killed opponents in Algeria when it was under their control in the last gasp of imperialism, as one of its leading assassins, General Paul Aussaresses, admitted in May 2001. They also blew up Greenpeace's exploration ship *Rainbow Warrior*, trying to cover their tracks by claiming that the vessel was a front for the KGB. Then, falling back on centuries-old hostility, it was a frame-up by Britain's MI6. Or perhaps, because the Americans had not been grateful enough for the French gift of the Statue of Liberty, it was all the work of the CIA.

The Belgians, the Israelis and manufactured 'nations' like Islamic State, taking a leaf out of the Hashashin's notebook, have all used assassination from time to time. And of course, they routinely lie about it. Late in 2002, Secretary of Defense Donald Rumsfeld even refused to use the 'a' word in response to a reporter's question. He told the press that assassination 'is not what [our operators] are trained to do. They are trained to serve the country and to contribute to peace and stability in the world.'

And, as euphemisms go, that says it all.

Chapter 3

To Kill a King ...

'There's such divinity doth hedge a king,
That treason can but peep to what it would.'
William Shakespeare, *Hamlet, Act 4, Sc V.*

That was the dilemma for kings and for those who would kill them. The king was just a man, as mortal as anyone else, and centuries of rulers have hedged themselves around with a pseudo-holiness designed to deter the would-be assassin. Those assassins may well have bought into this elaborate PR exercise; if you kill a monarch, you are attacking the God who put the monarch on the throne in the first place.

It was a risk that many considered worth taking. In 1886, as the Egyptian Valley of the Kings gave up its secrets, archaeologists discovered the tombs of Rameses III and his son Pentaweret. Scans of the pharaoh's corpse, in 2011, have revealed that his throat was cut with a 7cm gash as far back as the vertebrae. It may have been an attempt at decapitation. The historical records in the papyrus trial transcripts found in Turin condemn thirty-two conspirators from the pharaoh's court, scribes, chamberlains and, crucially, the commander of Rameses' bodyguard. Pebekkamen was the chief cook, Panouk overseer of the harem and Pendua chief clerk. At the head of the plot, however, was the pharaoh's wife, Tiye, who intended that her husband's son by another wife should not succeed him. Replica assassinations have followed the same pattern, especially in Africa and the Middle East, ever since.

Pentaweret's body was not embalmed and wrapped in the pharaonic tradition, almost certainly because he was the instigator of the revolt against his father. He was wrapped in a rough goat skin and his internal organs had not been removed. A lung scan showed them swollen and distorted, possibly the result of strangulation, although the papyrus evidence contends that Pentaweret was one of a handful allowed to commit suicide. Such was the retribution of the pharaoh's court.

Philip II of Macedon, father of Alexander the Great, was assassinated in October 336 BC. In 1977, his tomb at Vergina (it was called Aigai when it was Philip's capital) revealed the body of a 45-year-old man. It had damage to the skull (Philip lost his right eye on campaign years earlier) and to the left knee, the result of another war wound. There was even a pair of greaves (shin armour) specially designed to fit such a disability. The cause of death was not obvious from the corpse, but the written evidence is that the king was stabbed in the back during a wedding ceremony by Pansanias, one of his bodyguard. The killer dashed for a waiting horse, but either he or his animal tripped in the confusion and Pansanias was stabbed to death by his own comrades. The assassin was crucified (an extreme and rare punishment in ancient Greece) despite being dead and even the relay of horses waiting to take him to safety were slaughtered. There was a purge of various suspicious noblemen and the king's soothsayer was also crucified for not predicting the murder!

Whether Philip's son Alexander and his wife Eurydice were involved is impossible to say; those theories, as bizarre as anything on today's internet, came years later.

Because of their unique position as heads of state, usually with divine associations, monarchs are natural targets. There were umpteen attempts on the life of Elizabeth I because of her anti-Catholic stance in creating the Church of England in 1559. The Presbyterian John Knox, even more deranged than his fellow Scot who became king of England in 1603, blasted her (as he did all women). She was 'repugnant to nature ... a thing most contrarious to [God's] revealed will and approved ordinance'. He fell short, however, of urging her murder. Not so the pope, Pius V, who effectively signed her death warrant in 1570:

> We do ... declare the foresaid Elizabeth to be a heretic and ... her adherents ... to have incurred the sentence of excommunication and to be cut off from the unity of the body of Christ. And moreover [we declare] her to be deprived of her pretended title to the aforesaid crown and of all lordship, dignity and privilege whatsoever.

In other words, it was open season for any Catholic madman to kill the queen and the pope would absolve him of his sin. The 'jezebel of England' deserved all she got.

The bull was nailed to the door of the Bishop of London's palace and the queen's government hanged him for that. The ink was still wet when the Ridolfi Plot broke out, involving a dodgy Florentine secretary, the Duke of Norfolk and, for all Elizabeth knew, half of her subjects, in an attempt to depose and kill her. Nothing came of it, largely because of the assiduous Intelligence work of Francis Walsingham and a small army of 'Projectors and Intelligencers' who lurked below stairs and listened at keyholes to keep the government informed. But the 'lone nuts' of assassin theories were everywhere. John Somerville from Warwickshire planned to use a pistol on the queen and to 'see her head upon a pole'.

The queen herself made light of all this, refusing an armed escort and ignoring the death threats she received. When she fell ill with food poisoning caused by infected barley 'sodden with nater and sugar', her fanatical favourite Christopher Hatton breathed a sigh of relief that it was not *actual* poison!

The first king to be killed with a firearm was William the Silent of the Netherlands in July 1584. William of Nassau was as talkative as any other member of his family, but the epithet came from his wisdom in keeping his mouth shut when it mattered. The Netherlands was Spanish territory as part of the huge Holy Roman Empire and the Dutch were engaged in a nationalist uprising to kick the Spaniards out. Switching from Catholicism to Calvinism, William protested against the harsh regime of the Duke of Alva, causing havoc in Holland and Zeeland. From 1572, he led the anti-Spanish revolt at the head of fifteen republics in the Dutch League. There was a price on his head and several attempts were made to kill him. On 10 July 1584, another 'lone nut', Balthasar Gerard, shot him twice at point-blank range, the balls passing through his body and biting into the wall behind him. With the naivety of the fanatic, Gerard assumed that removing the Prince of Orange would end the revolt of the Netherlands. In fact, it merely strengthened Dutch resolve and with (dubious) English help, removed Spain's army of occupation soon afterward.

The assassination had profound effects. In England, Francis Walsingham, always the queen's first line of defence, insisted on an act of obedience from all and sundry in an attempt to increase solidarity and to minimize the risk to Elizabeth. The knock-on effects may well have been the assassination of Henri IV of France and the attempted assassination of James I of England (see Chapter 1).

We have no clear idea of the type of pistol used to kill William the Silent, but it was probably a Dutch- or German-made wheel-lock, perhaps a petronel designed to be fired by holding the butt against the chest to prevent recoil. The fact that *two* bullets were fired indicates two guns, because the loading mechanism was slow and Gerard would have been grabbed by William's people before he could get off a second shot. Such weapons were notoriously unreliable. When an idiot who liked playing with these new contraptions shot a prostitute in the chin in Constance in 1515, the bullet came out of the back of her neck. Astonishingly, she survived and the miscreant had to pay her 40 florins and a further 20 florins a year for the rest of her life! Clearly, by 1584, the technology had improved.

The next king to die by an assassin's hand was Henri III of France, five years after William, but more infamous was the murder of Henri IV, who had so accurately ridiculed his contemporary, James I of England. France in Henri IV's time was convulsed by the Wars of Religion. He had been married only days when thousands of Protestants were butchered in Paris under the auspices of Catherine de' Medici. That year, he became king of Navarre and was allowed to live, on condition that he followed Catholicism. As a Protestant, he found this difficult, but four years later emerged as the leading Huguenot in France. He conducted two military campaigns against the Catholics, but the assassination of Henri III at his camp at St Cloud by Jacques Clermont, a deranged friar, in August 1589, meant that he, was next in line for the throne.

Unable to take Paris in 1593, he switched again to Catholicism – the capital, he joked, was worth a Mass – and he passed the Edict of Nantes, which gave freedom of religion to Huguenots. A popular and largely successful ruler, Henri was stabbed to death, nonetheless, on 14 May 1610 by a lone killer, Francois Ravaillac. The assassin was a former teacher who had done time for bankruptcy. His motivation, unsurprisingly in an age of religious intolerance, was that Henri of Navarre was too generous to Protestants (even though he supported the Jesuits too). Ravaillac was torn apart by horses harnessed to his wrists and ankles. Needless to say, Paris was delighted!

Religion faded as a cause célèbre as the eighteenth century dawned. It was the Age of Reason and the Enlightenment, when the old monsters of the Reformation had disappeared into folklore. Assassinations would continue in this new age, but it is noticeable that, in Britain at least, they became rarer and almost pitiful in both their motivation and execution.

George III was the first Hanoverian to be born in England and regarded himself fiercely as an Englishman. He was stubborn, bigoted, succeeded in losing the American colonies and descended into bouts of 'madness' which, from 1811, were permanent until his death nine years later. Today, the trend among historians is to attribute this to bipolar disorder and his most recent biographer, Andrew Roberts, follows this line. Bipolarism however does *not* produce the welter of physical symptoms from which George suffered, including his urine appearing purple and I much prefer the British Medical Association's earlier theory that he suffered from porphyria. This not only manifested itself among other members of his family, but explains *all* the king's symptoms.

In the early 1770s, George was being routinely lampooned by the country's lawless radical press, spearheaded by the troublemaker, John Wilkes, whose supporters turned a man who was a reprobate (albeit an intelligent one) into a folk hero. Someone threw rotten fruit at the king's carriage as he visited parliament in March. The mob carried effigies of Lord Bute, the ex-prime minister and the queen dowager, burning them in public in a reprisal of the claim that they were having an affair. The same mob let off fireworks on George's birthday in June which threatened serious damage to Somerset House in the Strand.

Two days later, Jonathan Britain was waiting in the foliage of St James's Park armed with a pistol. Guns had developed considerably since the days of William the Silent. They were flintlocks and were more accurate, and relatively easy to load and fire. Britain was a soldier and presumably knew how to use one. George was a stranger to security. He often wandered around Windsor on his own, browsing in the bookshops and on the night of 6 June, he was being carried in a sedan chair with two Yeomen of the Guard in attendance. All

London's parks were notorious hubs of vice – footpads and harlots lurked there unmolested by the authorities. To Britain's horror, he realized that he had not checked his weapon carefully enough. He lacked sufficient powder in the priming pan to make the gun fire and he ducked back into the shadows. None of this would have come to light were it not for the fact that in 1772, Britain was charged with forgery (at the time a hanging offence) and made a last confession before he faced the rope. This was written up later, as a spurious 'autobiography' in which Britain claimed that there was a plot by five Irish and French Catholics to burn down Portsmouth dockyard and to persuade British Catholics in the army and navy to desert and defect to the French.

There were large numbers of Irishmen serving in the armed forces, if only because even the hazardous life of a soldier or sailor offered more regular employment than anything in civilian life. But Frenchmen in England would have aroused interest and concern. That said, there was no actual conflict in the early 1770s. The American crisis was looming but actual fighting was three years away. There *is* a plan in existence for a French invasion of the Isle of Wight dated 1778 but that was part of genuine paperwork held by all countries in relation to potential enemies. Nobody was remotely prepared to put anything like it into practice until Napoleon's projected invasion of 1804. As for the Irish, Wolfe Tone's United Irishmen did not raise their heads over the parapet until 1798, when some kind of Franco-Irish alliance was very much on the cards. It is likely that the plot behind Britain's assassination attempt was either in his own mind or that of his 'biographer'.

It was in 1778, however that another assassination plot came to light. By this time, the American colonists had had enough of what they saw as George III's tyranny and were in serious discussions with the French to obtain cash, ships and troops to aid their cause. Two years earlier, the Americans had declared independence, citing highly dubious reasons for doing so and brazenly pinching highfalutin ideas from English and French philosophers of the past, because they had none of their own.

Parliament, even the cabinet, was divided over the American issue and the prime minister, Lord North, had no real idea what to do about it. Spain, too, was toying with helping the Americans. On 21 December, the king had planned to go to the theatre. North's agents had uncovered a plot and when told of it, George remarked that he always put his trust in God and in any case had had no intention of seeing the play. How many assassinations have been foiled by a simple change of heart it is impossible to say.

Female assassins are rare, but one who attacked George III on Wednesday, 2 August 1786 stands out uniquely in his reign. The king was stepping out of his carriage at the garden door of St James's Palace to attend a levée. Anybody who was anybody was there and public appearances like this were a rare opportunity for a petitioner to hand a paper, often for personal redress of grievance, to the man who, after all, effectively still ran the country. Margaret Nicholson was a maid, jilted by her lover and living in penury. As she handed a document to George with her right hand, she lunged with her left carrying an ivory-handled fruit knife (fruit knives were rounded at the tip and often did not even go through peaches). She was aiming for his heart, but George's waistcoat and shirt were embroidered, providing unintentional padding. He jerked backwards instinctively and she stabbed again, this time just grazing his waistcoat, before attendants grabbed her. Clearly, as in the cases of Henri III and Henri IV, a sharp-pointed dagger would have killed him and we have the unfortunate fact that attendants' reactions are all too often fatally slow in these situations.

George realized that using her left hand, rather than her right, would have slowed Nicholson down. A mob of courtiers and soldiers surrounded the king at once and were all for tearing the woman apart. 'The poor creature is mad!' the king shouted. 'Do not hurt her! She has not hurt me!' He smiled in front of the shocked crowd to show he was fine and ordered his would-be killer to be taken good care of. The levée went on as though nothing had happened.

The actress Fanny Burney was very impressed by George's cool courage:

> To feel no apprehension of private plot or latent conspiracy – to stay out, fearlessly, among his people, and so benevolently to see himself to the safety of one who had raised her arm against his life – those little traits, all impulsive, and therefore to be trusted, have given me an impression of respect and reverence that I can never forget.

When he got home to Windsor, George told his family, 'Here I am, safe and well, as you see. But I have very narrowly escaped being stabbed!' His daughters burst into tears and their father comforted them. Later in the day, he walked among crowds on the terrace of Windsor Castle with a single equerry in attendance. The children kept crying and Queen Charlotte held his hand and said, 'I have you yet.'

There were national celebrations for the king's narrow escape. Kew, whose royal gardens were much appreciated by George, turned out in force. The French queen, Marie Antoinette, blissfully unaware of course of the fate that would befall her seven years later, told English politician Willian Eden how shocked her husband had been to hear George's news. Oxford gave George a rapturous welcome, with speeches in the Sheldonian Theatre. Few of the university's dons had any idea how to behave in the royal presence. Some could not kneel to kiss his hand; some could not get up again. Several of them turned their backs on him, an unpardonable sin in the eighteenth century.

As for Margaret Nicholson, she claimed to be the rightful queen of England, and, simultaneously, a virgin *and* the mother of Chief Justice Mansfield, a man old enough to be her father. She ended her days in the lunatic asylum at Bedlam.

By 1795, the mood of both king and country had changed. The French people had rebelled against church and state in the summer of 1789, creating ever more bizarre experiments in democratic government until they were not only at war with most of Europe, but publicly executed Louis XVI and Marie Antoinette heralding a 'reign of terror' which few outside France (and many inside) could understand or tolerate. There *was* a pro-Jacobin group, the more extreme Whigs under Charles James Fox, but the vast majority stood behind the prime minister, William Pitt and, of course, the king.

When George opened parliament in October, there were loud protests and his coach was jostled by the mob. They threw stones at the king, who calmly picked them and the glass shards of the windows out of his clothes. A shot was fired, but whether this was actually aimed at the king or who fired it was never discovered. The king's bodyguard of the Household Cavalry rode the miscreants away. That night, the audience at the Covent Garden Theatre where George was in attendance, demanded that the orchestra play *God Save the King* three times.

The incident of 15 May 1800 unleased a rash of outrages bordering on the insane. With the French king guillotined and George III himself prone to bouts of inexplicable madness, the average Englishman could believe his world 'turned upside down' every bit as much as it had been in the days of the Civil War and Cromwell. The king was reviewing his Grenadier Guards during the day when a soldier standing near him was shot in the leg. The whole thing may have been an accident, but what happened later certainly was not.

George went to the Theatre Royal, Drury Lane, to watch a performance of Colley Cibber's comedy *She Would and She Would Not*. The star was Dora Jordan, mistress of the Duke of Clarence. News of the review incident had spread and the king arrived to a rapturous applause. In the middle of it a man stood up on a table in the orchestra pit and fired a pistol at the royal box. Some accounts talk of two shots, but, as in William the Silent's time, pistols in 1800 only carried one charge before they had to be reloaded. The ball hit the frame of the box and was found later, flattened on the floor.

George instinctively jerked backwards but refused to leave his box and stayed for the whole performance, even dozing during the interval. With astonishing presence of mind, the playwright Richard Brinsley Sheridan, also in the audience, rattled off new words to the national anthem which was sung at the end of the play:

From every latent foe,
From the assassin's blow,
God save the King!
O'er him Thine arm extend
For Britain's sake defend
Our father, prince and friend,
God save the King!

George was delighted by this, although he personally found Sheridan's politics too far to the left for his liking. He had watched the orchestra cowering as they expected a second shot from the assassin. The 'latent foe' was James Hadfield, an ex-15th Light Dragoon who had suffered head injuries on campaign. He had been grabbed and bundled into the rehearsal room under the stage. Four days later, the press issued images of him, his arms folded as though in a strait-jacket and a decidedly deranged look on his face. He had received eight sabre cuts to the head at the Battle of Tourcoing in 1794 where he was probably serving as a mercenary. On his return to England, he told Thomas Erskine, his defence counsel at his trial, he joined a millennialist movement in London, believing that his execution for the king's murder would lead to Christ's second coming. The Mint struck a medal to celebrate the king's survival, Hadfield's trial was called off by Chief Justice Kenyon on the grounds of insanity, and, like Margaret Nicholson, the would-be king killer was locked up in Bedlam where he died years later of 'gaol fever' (probably tuberculosis). In parliament, the results of this assassination attempt were the Treason Act and the Criminal Lunatics Act, both of 1800.

Over the next two years, no less than nine people were arrested trying to break into royal palaces or getting too close to the king. Catherine Kirby threw stones at him in June 1801 and Urban Metcalf, with a history of serious instability, threw a penknife at the king at Weymouth Theatre. Given the penchant for attacks in theatres, it might have been wise for George to give drama a miss, but he carried on regardless.

The next attempt on George III's life, in 1802, was altogether more serious, if only because it was an orchestrated conspiracy which would be echoed eighteen years later in the Cato Street incident.

We have met Edward Despard already. He was a wayward Irishman, born in Queen's County in 1751. He served with the navy and as an administrator in the West Indies, where he impressed Horatio Nelson with his competence. He married a Black girl, Catherine, and fell foul of the plantation owners in Honduras (today's Belize). In 1792 he was imprisoned for debt.

Two years later, Colonel Despard was a changed man. He joined the London Corresponding Society that was in frequent touch with French revolutionaries and spent time in the Irish ghetto of Gee's Court off Oxford Street mixing with disgruntled soldiers.

He hatched a plan, as we know, to bring about a coup against the government. And the king was to be targeted. Private Thomas Windsor of 3rd Battalion, Grenadier Guards had an insider's knowledge of royal routine. Before the royal coach picked up its cavalry escort, the two lead horses would be shot and the now stationary vehicle surrounded. Another variant was to hit the coach with cannon fire (a sort of early nineteenth-century version of Dealey Plaza) fired at point-blank range from a cannon behind the Admiralty building in Whitehall. Like Cato Street, the whole plan (even the king's murder) was hopelessly ambitious. Above all, it depended on the mutiny of the Grenadier Guards who were to grab both the Tower and the Bank of England. Clearly, they would do neither, if only because Thomas Windsor was a government spy who ratted on Despard and anybody else he could name.

Nearly forty men were arrested at the Oakley Arms pub in Lambeth on 16 November and were distributed to various London gaols, all of them grim and escape-proof. In the end, seven ringleaders faced the wrath of the court and the prosecutor, Attorney General Spencer Perceval, who would die by an assassin's bullet ten years later. Of the seven, three were soldiers, a pattern which would often develop in later assassinations and attempts around the world. In connection with the murder of the king, Despard said, 'I have weighed the matter well and my heart is callous.' It was the soldier John Wood who hit upon using the cannon on the royal coach.

'You have been separately indicted,' the judge, Lord Ellenborough, told the accused, 'for conspiracy against his majesty's person, his crown and government, for the purposes of subverting the same and changing the government of this realm.' All seven were found guilty, although the jury recommended mercy in the case of three of them. The others were to have the same punishment – hanging and quartering – as befell the Gunpowder plotters and would be passed on the men of Cato Street.

On the morning of Sunday, 21 February 1803, with police and the army on high alert in case of any nonsense from the mob, the condemned men took their places on the roof of Surrey County Gaol in Horsemonger Lane. Despard died first, 'launched into eternity' and all were decapitated.

Marie Tussaud made a death mask of the rebel and would-be king killer which was duly exhibited at her emporium at the Lyceum Theatre in the *Caverne des Grands Voleurs* (Cave of the Great Thieves) which would, in time become the Chamber of Horrors. It is possible that the wax head was burnt, ironically, in another insurrection, this time in Bristol in 1831 over agitation over the Reform Bill.

When George III heard that Despard had refused the last rites before he died, he said, 'It is melancholy that a man should appear so void of religion at so awful a moment.'

Chapter 4

... Or Queen

Despite the fact that both George's successors, his sons George and William, were deeply unpopular with sections of their people, nobody tried to kill them! Ironically, it was the breath of fresh air, the 18-year-old Victoria, who became queen in 1837 who became the next royal target. She was irritating, emotional, not very bright and reigned for too long, but she hardly deserved the threats she received. The only full book on the subject – *Shooting Victoria* by Paul Thomas Murphy (2012) – runs to a staggering 520 pages and paints a vivid picture of what it meant to be the target of an assassin.

On Wednesday, 10 June 1840, Victoria and her still-new husband, Albert of Saxe-Coburg and Gotha, 'took the air' in an open carriage around Hyde Park, as they did on most afternoons when the weather permitted. They were late today; it was six o'clock before the droshky emerged from Buckingham Palace. There were two riders on the pair of horses and two equerries riding behind. One of the little boys who doffed his cap to the royal entourage was 11-year-old John Everett Millais, not yet the doyen of portrait painters.

Albert caught a glimpse of a 'little mean-looking man' standing near the carriage no more than six paces away. He stood like a duellist, his pistol raised straight ahead and he fired. Victoria hadn't seen him, but felt her ears ring. When Albert looked at the shooter again, he had a pistol in his other hand. This time, he was resting the gun on his right forearm to steady the shot, having missed so spectacularly with the first. Albert's first reaction was to grab him, but the appearance of the second gun and the assassin's warning 'I have another here' made him think twice and he sat down again. The carriage had stopped by the time the second shot rang out and equerries, the crowd and scattered policemen surrounded the gunman. At Victoria's request, the carriage ride continued, to the applause and admiration of the crowd.

The courage of the royals could not have come at a better time. Albert was unpopular with most of the country – he was a foreigner and from a country that had no parliament at all, still less a reformed one. The 1832 Reform Act had doubled the electorate; Britain was still not remotely a democracy in the modern sense, but it was streets ahead of Medieval Saxony. It was feared that Albert would rule the roost, as Victorian men were supposed to do and, in his case, that roost was Britain.

News of the outrage spread like lightning. With nothing like social media available, word of mouth was enough and by the time the royals were completing their circuit of the park, the place was crowded with well-wishers and ghouls, from all walks of life, wanting to be part of the action.

The horror of the situation at the shooting site developed into farce. Albert Lowe, a spectacle maker, had been first to grab the assassin and wrestled him to the ground. No sooner had he done so than somebody else jumped on him, calling him a 'confounded rascal'. The gunman was incensed – 'I am the man who fired,' he shouted. 'It was me.' Everybody jumped on him instead. Three policemen from A Division rescued him from the crowd and dragged him to the station.

The would-be killer's name was Edward Oxford. He was found to be carrying two pistols, both discharged, wadding, extra ammunition and a knife. He was an unemployed servant. Under interrogation by the police and media, he had a field day, cracking jokes and claiming to be a member of the patriotic 'Young England' movement created by Benjamin Disraeli, then a young backbencher in the House of Commons. Clearly, from papers found in his lodgings at West Place, Young England meant something different to Oxford. He claimed to be a republican (which Disraeli et al. certainly were not) and thought it wrong that the country should be run by a woman. In theatres and churches throughout the land, there were prayers, cheers and rousing anthems in support of Victoria.

The crux of the assassination attempt was: were Oxford's guns loaded? Everybody at the scene had seen and heard the shots, but guns could fire a number of projectiles which did no harm (essentially, blanks) and there was a huge difference in law between frightening the queen and trying to kill her. A number of cabinet ministers interviewed Oxford the next day and, again, he lapped it up. John Cam Hobhouse found him little and insignificant, but when he spoke it was 'his insolent carelessness [which] gave him the air of a ruffian'. The gunman questioned various witnesses and interspersed this with cackling laughter. As usually happens in eyewitness accounts (the killing of John F. Kennedy in Dallas 123 years later is just the same) 'recollections vary' (to quote a different queen in a different context). A clever brief would have driven a droshky through this evidence, but Oxford had no brief; he wanted the limelight for himself.

Nobody really bought into Oxford's claim that he was part of a conspiracy and he was sent for trial on a charge of High Treason, waiting for that in Newgate Prison. Rumours abounded that the would-be killer was a Chartist, bent on creating a revolution of the people (although removal of the monarchy was not on the Chartist agenda); that he was obeying the orders of a secret Hanoverian society; that the police were in on it! It went on and on in the way that virtually all assassinations and attempts have throughout history.

In Newgate, Oxford 'entertained' a string of curious visitors, telling a different story of the assassination attempt and his part in it each time. In the meantime, Oxford's mother, Hannah, spread the news that her boy was unbalanced, and she gave childhood instances of this to the press. Her dead husband had been barking too. It was unfortunate for Oxford, to whom the limelight was everything, that while he was in gaol, the trial of the murderer François Courvoisier was taking place – the media and public talked of nothing else. The man had cut the throat of his master, Lord William Russell, succeeding in killing an aristocrat while Oxford had merely failed to kill the queen! Both men were held in Newgate.

Edward Oxford was probably the most starstruck would-be killer of all time. In the dock, he wanted to know all the famous people present in the audience, whether he was in the papers and what the French were saying about him. 'What a great character I shall be!' For a humble pot-boy in a pub, this was fame indeed.

Madame Tussaud, pre-empting the trial's verdict, had a plaster cast made of Oxford's head and mounted in a tableau in her emporium of the assassin in the act of shooting at Victoria. Her company had not only decided his guilt, but his motive too, as their handbills made clear – 'THE LUNATIC EDWARD OXFORD … in the act of attempting the life of Her Majesty …'

Various doctors (none of whom would be regarded as competent professionals today) were called in to examine the accused. Dr Chowne of Charing Cross Hospital was sure that Oxford was an imbecile. Dr Connolly, an expert in phrenology (the then-fashionable vogue for skull-shapes as an indicator of brain function) agreed. Oxford spent most of his trial at the Old Bailey sniffing the herbs scattered at his feet to prevent the spread of gaol fever in the courtroom.

Lurid details of the insanity of Oxford's father and grandfather were paraded by family doctors and friends from Birmingham. Young Edward showed the same tendencies. After two days, the jury gave a hopeless decision that made no sense. They had not been persuaded that Oxford's guns had been loaded, but if they were, he was insane. Prosecution and judge erupted, arguments raged and the jury were asked to reconsider. The upshot was that Edward Oxford was sent to Bedlam 'in strict custody during Her Majesty's pleasure'. The assassin's guns, 'Brummagem pistols', were for years believed to have been on show in Scotland Yard's Black Museum, but this never happened. From Bedlam, Oxford was transferred to Broadmoor in 1864, in the view of the hospital authorities, as sane as any of them. Before he left, he spent some time with an old man with visible head wounds: James Hadfield, who had tried to kill George III.

But a pattern had been established and six more people tried to kill Victoria. Charles Dickens wrote to a friend how much better it would have been to have executed Oxford (although he deeply disapproved of hanging) 'and dulled the sound of his glory very much. As it is,' he wrote with prescience, '[the queen] will have to run the gauntlet of many a fool and madmen, some of whom may perchance be better shots and use other than Brummagem firearms.'

John Francis was the first to attempt to murder the queen after Edward Oxford, but whether he was a fool or a madman is difficult to say. He took his first shot – or did he? – in St James's Park in May 1842. It is not clear whether his gun jammed or he lost his nerve at the last moment. Teenager George Pearson was standing nearby and heard him mutter, apparently to himself, 'They may take it if they like – I don't care – I was a fool not to shoot.' Once again, Victoria and Albert were riding in an open carriage; once again, they were sitting ducks. The attempt, however half-hearted, reached the authorities. The newly created detective branch of Scotland Yard swung into action, collecting seventeen witness statements.

Victoria was understandably worried at the thought of an assassin at large, so soon after the Oxford business, but she was determined to carry on her routine as usual. The only concession she made was that her ladies-in-waiting would not accompany her and her carriage should move faster than it normally did.

William Trounce of A Division was one of several plainclothesmen in the park on Sunday, 30 May. He had seen Francis skulking near some trees that fringed the royal route but when the carriage arrived, the policeman turned to salute the queen and Francis fired, the explosion in Trounce's ear nearly knocking him over. He was mortified that he had not acted sooner, but there was no reason to suppose that Francis was armed. He grabbed the man's gun and collar and the carriage hurtled forward, the equerries colonels Wylde and Arbuthnot covering the vehicle with their horses' bodies.

There was the same ludicrous argument in the weeks that followed. Was the gun loaded? If so, where did the ball go? Over the carriage or under it? No shot was ever found. Parliament's sitting was cancelled for the day as the news spread – *two* attempts in two days. Had the world gone mad? As with Oxford, a flurry of senior politicians interviewed Francis at the police station, including Prince Albert, now a privy councillor – 'He is not out of his mind,' the future consort wrote, 'but a thorough scamp [the word meant something stronger in 1842]. His answers are coarse and witty. He tries to make fun of his judges … a wretched creature!' He was charged with High Treason.

The theatres reacted as usual with rousing martial anthems in London, made all the more poignant because Francis's father was a stage scenery carpenter, and there was an unofficial holiday the next day, Victoria and Albert ostentatiously riding in the open as they always did.

Commissioner Charles Rowan of the Metropolitan Police was not concerned with cheering and adulation. He was painfully aware how close Francis had come to succeeding, from the ludicrously exposed queen to the bumbling incompetence of his own officers. The press, inevitably, picked up the dangers and castigated the police accordingly. Robert Peel's whole raison d'être behind the creation of the Metropolitan Police was that it was a *preventative* force. It was

Francis's assassination attempt more than anything else that led to the establishment, and expansion, of the detective department.

Francis's trial began on Friday, 17 June. Oxford was now regarded as a con artist whose insanity plea had been faked; Francis's defence team did not raise the same issue. Once again, the case revolved around the question: was the would-be assassin's gun loaded? Francis's stammer was miraculously cured by Thomas Hart, whose business blossomed as a result, and his performance in the dock was full of confidence. The prosecution produced damning evidence that, even if there was no ball in the gun, the wadding alone could cause injury to the skin and even set fire to the queen's dress.

Despite some muddle by the jury (as in the Oxford case) they found Francis guilty and the judge, Mr Justice Tindal, sentenced him to death, the traditional black cap placed on his head. In the event, the sentence was commuted to life imprisonment with hard labour. On 18 July, handcuffed and in shackles, he was taken aboard the convict ship the *Marquis of Hastings* for the long trip via Cape of Good Hope to Van Diemen's Land, Australia. And there, despite the obvious hardships, he lived happily ever after, marrying and fathering children before settling down as a moderately successful artisan as a 'ticket of leave' man. He died in 1885.

Francis had not even left Newgate on his way to what everyone hoped would be purgatory, when yet another attempt was made on the life of the queen, and in more or less the same spot. Among the crowd cheering Victoria and Albert on their way to the Chapel Royal on Sunday, 3 July 1842 stood 17-year-old down and out John Bean. Bean could not possibly have blended in with the crowd. He suffered from acute scoliosis, which curved his spine and gave him a height of only 3ft 6in. The press of the day, totally ignorant of most medical conditions, referred to him as both a dwarf and a hunchback. In common with society's views for centuries, such deformity went hand in hand with mental aberration. Victor Hugo's Quasimodo (*The Hunchback of Notre Dame*), Dickens' Daniel Quilp (in *The Old Curiosity Shop*) and Shakespeare's version of Richard III were all immensely popular characters that the contemporary reading public delighted to be frightened by. Freak shows all over the country drew crowds every summer, where dwarfs gambolled along with bearded ladies and other 'monstrosities'.

Bean's parents loved him, but he was ridiculed by everybody else, even his fit and able younger brothers who all towered over him. He sold his tiny book collection to buy a pistol and read avidly the news of the Francis trial. The gun was defective, an old flintlock, but Bean persevered in trying to fix it. He ran away from home and lived rough, carrying his meagre possessions on his back.

As the queen's carriage passed him, Bean had a problem. The vehicle was a closed Landau, not the open droshky of the Oxford and Francis attempts and, to cap it all, his gun still did not fire properly. Bean was grabbed by a boy younger than himself who stood alongside him. There were police everywhere, so soon after the Francis incident, but most of the crowd, looking at Bean's deformity, decided it was all a prank and laughed accordingly. Some told the other boy to give Bean his gun back and let him go. The policemen refused to do anything about it. Immediately, the crowd got the wrong end of the stick – it was the boy holding the gun who was the culprit – why was he strongarming that poor little hunchback? In the confusion, Bean got away and the boy, Charles Dassett, was taken into custody, followed by a huge crowd demanding his head.

When the dust settled, Dassett was a hero, with apologies all round and the hunchback would-be assassin was still on the run. In farcical scenes, which are totally impossible to imagine today, anybody with a deformity or undue shortness had his collar felt by a bobby in the London area. An unknown number spent the night in police cells;

one of them was John Bean. He ended up in Tothill Fields prison while the authorities decided what to do with him.

The press had a field day – 'Hunchbacked little miscreant', 'crooked piece of malignity', 'hump-backed boy of an idiotic appearance' were the usual headlines.

For all that many Britons could not understand the spate of assassination attempts – three in little more than two years – no one grasped the idea of the 'copycat' crime or the lure of notoriety that went with a queen killer. In the eighteen years of his reign, the 'citizen king' Louis Philippe of France faced no less than seven attempts to kill him. One French newspaper referred to a 'savage and impotent monomania' spreading from France to Britain, as if assassination was a psychological condition. Elizabeth Barrett noted (wrongly) that it was only 'liberal' monarchs who were targets. The reality was that in democratic countries, the authorities were less prepared to pull out all the stops to protect their rulers; among despots, it was de rigueur. In a despotic state, men like Oxford, Francis and Bean would all have been publicly hanged to discourage the others. Exaggerated stories of Oxford's 'life of Reilly' in Bedlam made king killing all the more glamourous.

The important difference between Louis Philippe's would-be assassins and the queen's is that all of them were politically motivated in a country notorious for its political extremes; it was only a generation before that the new republic's government had executed their king and queen. And French assassins were not content with ineffectual weapons of limited range. Giuseppe Fieschi fired an early machine gun at Louis Philippe in July 1835 which killed eighteen people, wounded twenty-two more and blew off half the assassin's face.

In an attempt to lessen the notoriety of assassination attempts, the government charged Bean not with High Treason, which sounded like some great cause, but with common assault. That, of course, carried no death penalty. As prime minister, Robert Peel rushed a bill through parliament, that of 'disturbing the queen's peace' by firing at her. That made the contents of a gun barrel irrelevant, a situation which was used as recently as 1985. Most of the House of Commons and House of Lords wanted public whipping to accompany the sentence.

Bean's trial in August was almost lost in the national events of the time. This was the 'hungry '40s' in which economic depression hit hard. Chartists and 'plug plotters' roamed the land demanding reform and the abolition of the hated Corn Laws. The usual crowds stayed away from the Old Bailey and Bean could only just see over the rail of the dock the three judges trying him. He was found guilty of 'harassing and alarming the queen and the public'. There was no talk of whipping. Bean was sentenced to eighteen months' hard labour at Millbank Penitentiary.

Because of his deformity, the wannabe-assassin's hard labour was actually tailoring, which is scarcely hard at all. On release, he married twice and became a newsagent before committing suicide with opium in the summer of 1882 as a result of 'temporary insanity'.

Victoria had just got back from a carriage ride on Saturday, 21 May 1849 and was rattling into the grounds of Buckingham Palace. Albert had left with her earlier but decided to ride back ahead for the return journey. At a little after six o'clock in the evening, William Hamilton pointed his pistol between the railings around the palace and fired. Astonishingly, footman Robert Resnick in the seat behind the queen, saw him aiming and actually ordered the carriage to stop, giving the killer a clearer shot.

'Resnick?' Victoria had heard the explosion. 'What was that?'

'Your Majesty has been shot at.'

The carriage moved on and equerry, Wemyss, wheeled his horse to confront Hamilton. Park-keepers, policemen and a soldier all leapt on the gunman. The crowd wanted him dead. Wemyss took possession of the gun and, yet again, the nonsense started – had it contained a bullet or not? Wemyss thought not.

At A Division station house, where the three other would-be assassins had been held, Hamilton told police that he was an Irishman from Adaire, County Limerick, a bricky's labourer and that he had acted alone. He had fired at the queen to get sent to prison, because life on the outside was so grim. The potato famine had hit Ireland three years earlier, with the loss of a million lives from hunger and disease. One million more emigrated, to the United States, Canada and Australia. The lucky ones found work on the railways in the days of the 'mania', an unprecedented period of track-laying. Hamilton had tried his luck in this job in France, but now he was in London and out of work.

The response had become almost laughably predictable by now – the great and good wishing the queen well in person; lesser fry cheering and singling loudly at theatres, drunks rolling around outside pubs even more tipsy than usual.

This time, however, nobody believed that the attempt had been real. The gun was empty; give the man a good whipping, sling him in gaol and move on. Nobody linked Hamilton's Irish pedigree with the attempt, which is odd given the mood in Ireland at the time. It may have been an example of the 'savage vindictiveness of the Celt', wrote the *The Daily News* pompously (such a phrase would be classed as a hate crime today) but it had much more to do with poverty. Irish newspapers distanced themselves from him as far as they could. Nor was it likely that Hamilton was a hitman for, for example, the Chartists. After their rally in the previous year, in which petition signatures were found to be bogus (the queen's 'signature' appeared four times!) and the police outnumbered the Chartists, the movement had gone spectacularly quiet and would disappear altogether by 1850. There were indeed revolutions across Europe, which were toppling ministries and regimes, but nothing like that, everyone contended, could possibly happen in Britain.

Hamilton was sullen and did not enjoy the limelight, which, in any case, was decidedly dimmed by the authorities who had had enough of the 'monomania' of 'king killing'. *The Illustrated London News'* hope that the man would receive 'weekly, semi-weekly or even daily infliction of the cat-o'-nine-tails for three months at least' was certainly in order.

Hamilton's trial opened on 14 July at the Old Bailey. He had no counsel and no family support, and was unsurprisingly found guilty and sentenced to seven years' transportation. He sailed to Freemantle, Western Australia, on board the *Ramillies*, having served several months imprisonment at Millbank and Pentonville, under the twin new regimes – the 'silent' and the 'separate' system, designed to break prisoners' spirits. Released in Australia on the 'ticket of leave' system, he vanishes from the historical record.

Robert Pate was an oddity. Immaculately dressed in bright clothing, he would parade around Green Park, Hyde Park and Kensington Gardens, goose-stepping along pavements and waving his arms in the air. He did this every day at exactly the same time. When the queen's carriage passed him, he would bow low; both Victoria and Albert found him amusing, one of life's 'characters'. His father was a wealthy corn dealer and unlike Victoria's earlier 'assassins', money, for him, was no object. He bought a commission for his son in 1841 in the prestigious 10th Hussars, the Prince of Wales's Own. Here, his behaviour began to deteriorate. His three horses and his dog were all bitten by a rabid dog and Pate went into a decline as a result, believing that people were trying to poison him. He sold his commission and settled in comfortable apartments above Fortnum and Mason's in Jermyn Street, London.

In the last week of June 1850, the dependably peculiar Robert Pate, waiting in the small crowd cheering the queen as she left the house of her ailing uncle, the Duke of Cambridge, stepped closer to the carriage and smacked the queen across the head with his cane. Footman Resnick had (nearly) been there before and he grabbed Pate. 'I am not hurt,' Victoria said, although her forehead was bruised. Somebody smacked Pate in the face and the crowd were screaming for him to be hanged. Sergeant James Silver of A Division hurried through the jostling mob and got Pate to safety.

As usual, Victoria behaved with dignity and stoicism, going to the opera at Covent Garden that night as planned. 'I never heard such shouting,' a *Punch* reporter recorded. 'It was a deafening tumult of love …'

The scar on the queen's head lasted for ten years, but it was the brutality of the attack that hurt most, especially when her children were in the coach with her. Victoria found this the worst of the attacks on her – missed gunshots were, after all, just that. This blow with a cane had actually hit her. The case was passed to the most famous detective of his day, Frederick Field of Scotland Yard, immortalized by Dickens later as Inspector Bucket in *Bleak House*.

Technically, the drawing of blood from the queen's head wound meant that High Treason should have been the charge. Instead, the lesser indictment of high misdemeanour was used. Pate could have asked for bail, but did not. Beautifully dressed as ever, he pleaded 'Not guilty' in the Old Bailey on 11 July. Doctors for the defence testified to Pate's insanity – loud (bad) singing, reciting nursery rhymes, bathing in Scotch and water. The prosecution pointed out that none of that met the *legal* definition of insanity; did Pate know what he was doing when he struck the queen and did he know it to be wrong? It took the jury four hours to find him guilty.

On that basis, Pate was sentenced to seven years in Van Diemen's Land, taken there aboard the *William Jardine*. He behaved himself in prison and on board ship and got his 'ticket of leave' in 1853 and a pardon two years later. Back home, Pate inherited his father's £70,000 fortune (around £7 million today) and married. He died in

Croydon in 1895. Four years later, Pate's cane, the weapon he used on Victoria, was offered for sale at auction. The queen, at Osborne, heard about it and effectively shut the sale down.

Unlike Francis, Bean and Pate, Arthur O'Connor was a man on a mission, a man with a cause. His family, he believed, were descended from the kings of Connaught and his great-uncle Feargus was the 'lion of liberty', the best known of the Chartist leaders and the man who ran its organ *The Northern Star.* But by the 1860s, the O'Connors were living in an Irish rookery in London and 17-year-old Arthur was a clerk working for a paint company in Southwark and was suffering from scrofula (cervical tuberculous lymphadenitis, a bacterial infection involving the lymph nodes of the throat and neck).

Victoria herself had become a recluse on the death of her beloved Albert. She was rarely, if ever, seen in public, even carrying out Privy Council meetings with her in one room and her councillors in another. By 1872, the politician Benjamin Disraeli and the Highland ghillie John Brown had conspired to lure the 'widow at Windsor' back into the limelight to quell a growing republicanism caused by her absence from public life. In doing so, they were unwittingly offering Arthur O'Connor a real-life target.

Ireland was in upheaval, as it had been for centuries, and Prime Minister William Gladstone's attempts to pacify the country, via Acts of Parliament involving church and state, had not worked. The Irish created the Land League and were inching their way towards Home Rule, independence. To that end, the Fenian Brotherhood brought terror to mainland Britain in the form of dynamite in the first wave of outrages that would continue intermittently up to the attack on the Grand Hotel, Brighton in 1984 (see Chapter 1). There were Fenian prisoners held in British gaols and O'Connor wanted them released. He wrote a declaration, to be signed by the queen as he held a gun to her head, which would have overridden parliament and upended the constitution. Expecting that death would result, O'Connor wanted execution by firing squad rather than at the end of a hangman's rope.

On Tuesday, 27 February 1872, he bought a tatty old flintlock pistol for 4 shillings, even though he had no idea how to use it. He tried to get into St Paul's Cathedral where a service was to be held the next day, but he was turned away by police. He left his gun at home when he went back and realized that the crowds were so immense, he could get nowhere near the queen. He failed again the next day, at Buckingham Palace, but at least he was armed this time. The next day he returned, determined to strike.

As the queen's entourage came back from the usual park visit, O'Connor scrambled over the 12ft fence, apparently unobserved by the large crowd who were all looking up Constitution Hill for the royal carriage. He dropped into the palace yard and hid behind a pillar. Here, an old gatekeeper saw him – 'What mischief do you want here?' – but O'Connor dashed past him and ran to the coach disgorging its passengers. Everybody took the killer to be a groundsman in the wrong place at the wrong time and John Brown, helping Her Majesty down from the carriage, pushed him away. Instead, O'Connor raised his gun and mumbled something about Fenian prisoners. Prince Arthur of Connaught heard him say, 'Take that from a Fenian,' and reached out to deflect O'Connor's pistol. John Brown, almost twice O'Connor's weight and a head taller, hauled him down and everybody, including the 20-year-old Connaught, pitched in. The police ran in from all directions, frisking the Irishman and finding a knife and the declaration. He was dragged away. When they found O'Connor's gun on the ground, Lady Jane Churchill started crying and Prince Leopold, Victoria's haemophiliac son, almost fainted. The gun, however, was not loaded.

Today, there is a perception that something was going on between Victoria and John Brown. Whatever the truth of that, she certainly 'bigged up' the part he played in the incident – 'It is entirely owing to good Brown's great presence of mind and quickness that he was seized' – ignoring the equally quick thinking of Connaught and an equerry, Lord Fitzroy. O'Connor's gun, useless as it was, was shown to MPs at Gladstone's insistence and had to be taken away by police as crucial evidence before it fell apart passing through so many hands.

Nosy MPs wanting to gawp at O'Connor in the A Division headquarters were turned away. Only Edward Henderson, the police commissioner, interviewed him. Overnight, republicanism disappeared in England – prayers, toasts, bunting, jubilation were once again the order of the day, even though it had been over twenty years since the last assassination attempt.

O'Connor appeared not in Whitehall, the venue for earlier assassins, but Bow Street Magistrates Court which was packed with the riffraff from the rookeries of Seven Dials and St Giles. They hissed as O'Connor appeared. When the Treasury Solicitor, Harry Poland, read out the Irishman's declaration, the place erupted with laughter. John Brown and Prince Leopold appeared as witnesses for the prosecution (Prince Arthur of Connaught had to rejoin his regiment that day). The prince told the adoring crowd that O'Connor's gun had been within 12 inches of the queen's face.

The press called the Irishman a 'crack-brained youth' and yet again, the Irish press expressed their loyalty to the queen. It probably did little to steady the queen's nerves as she travelled to Windsor the next day – 'Queen Victoria may rest assured that if she ever fell victim to an unhallowed hate it shall not be by the hand of an Irishman.' O'Connor's family were not even Irish – the original spelling of the name was Conner. Most politicians, including Gladstone and the Home Secretary Henry Bruce, thought that a flogging would be punishment enough. Victoria disagreed – Hamilton had been an Irishman too and she thought the use of Robert Peel's act (misdemeanour rather than treason) too lenient in this context.

Transportation had disappeared by 1872, so that a mere, relatively short, prison sentence, was all that remained.

Despite the boy's family and a slew of doctors insisting that O'Connor was deranged, he pleaded guilty. Bizarrely, the judge was persuaded by O'Connor's counsel that the plea itself was proof of insanity (which calls into question, not just the need to *prove* insanity, but the whole concept of justice). The question therefore became – was the Irishman sane when he pleaded guilty, or was he sane when he fired at the queen? This made a nonsense of the whole proceedings. The judge was Baron Cleasby, a typically over-promoted stickler for judicial protocol who had little experience of a criminal court. In the event, the medical evidence was split down the middle and O'Connor's mother made the situation worse by backing the guilty plea.

In the end, the jury interrupted to say they believed O'Connor was sane and Cleasby sentenced him to a year's imprisonment with hard labour and a whipping of twenty lashes, not with the cat but the far less vicious birch. The queen was furious at the lightness of the sentence and the prime minister and cabinet were as horrified as she was over Cleasby's softness, not the first nor the last time that a 'distinguished' judge got things appallingly wrong.

The government was anxious, on behalf of the queen, to send O'Connor into exile, without the whipping. This he was, but he returned within months, seeing himself as a future poet laureate. He wrote to the queen and when he received no reply, the letters became more threatening. He turned up on 5 May at the exact spot he had launched his attack before. The police were ready; O'Connor was not armed and he was whisked away without anybody much noticing. He now confessed to visions of angels and when two doctors pronounced him insane, he was sent to Hanwell Asylum with the diagnosis 'imbecile'.

O'Connor was released as cured eighteen months later and lived in penury in London. At the end of 1880, he suggested the government pay for his journey to Australia for a new life and they readily obliged. Down under, he called himself George Morton, went on a drunken rampage and was locked up in an asylum again. Umpteen asylum doctors put the cause of his intermittent mania down to 'onanism' (masturbation), which tells us all we need to know about the state of psychiatric diagnosis in Victorian England – or Australia, come to that! He died, a forgotten relic of another age, in December 1925.

The last man to try to kill Victoria was Roderick Maclean. He was waiting at Windsor railway station on 2 March 1882 as the queen's train arrived and he watched as the royal party – Victoria, her secretary, her equerries and her ladies-in-waiting – transferred to the familiar carriages. John Brown was there, handling the vehicle steps, but he was not the powerful giant of ten years earlier; his legs were weak and he drank. He would be dead within the year. Princess Beatrice and Lady Roxburghe joined the queen in her carriage.

The crowd cheered, as always, especially the boys from nearby Eton College in their frock coats and top hats. Behind them, Roderick Maclean raised his pistol, aimed at the queen and fired. Chief Superintendent Hayes of the Windsor Borough Police grabbed him by the neck while a local photographer, James Burnside, wrestled the gun out of Maclean's hand. Two Eton boys belted the gunman with their umbrellas and the entire school contingent wanted him hanged there and then. Despite the fact that this attack had been potentially more dangerous than earlier attempts, Victoria was less perturbed than she might have been. Beatrice, however, was in pieces. The royal family, scattered as they were and the prime minister (Gladstone again!) were informed by telegram that all was well.

At Windsor police station, Maclean was talkative, giving his correct name and address. Gone, by 1882, were the clumsy flintlocks used in earlier assassination attempts. Maclean had carried a Belgian pinfire revolver. Two of its chambers were empty; two held bullets; two recently discharged. There were no shell casings at the shooting site and no evidence of bullet marks on the queen's carriage. Had Maclean fired blanks, the press wanted to know next day.

The gunman was starving, he said, and was grateful for the meal and the bath the police gave him.

The usual aristocratic toadying took place of the great and good offering congratulations to the queen, but since she was not in London, noble carriages, flunkies in livery and telegrams flew about in all directions in the capital. Similar messages flashed to her from all over the world thanks to the speed of the telegraph system, even from Chester Arthur, now president of the United States as James Garfield had gone down to an assassin's bullet a little less than six months earlier. The queen went on an open-topped trip around Windsor Great Park later in the day – 'It is worth being shot at,' she wrote to her daughter Vicky, 'to see how much one is loved.'

Police found Maclean's bullet, which had passed between the queen and Brown. Now, there was no question; the bullets were live. The intention was clearly murder. The gunman made a statement to the effect that he wanted to scare the queen, not kill her. The authorities did not accept that and Maclean's cab was nearly overturned by a furious mob as he was hurried to Reading Gaol to await trial.

The press uncovered the fact that Roderick Maclean had been in and out of asylums for years. He had tried to kill his family, various reports ran, and to derail a train. Howard Vincent, head of the newly formed Criminal Investigation Department, checked links between Maclean and a German anarchist group in London headed by Johann Most, whose ambition was to kill a crowned head of state every month. He was currently in Clerkenwell Prison while many people contended he should have been in Broadmoor. Vincent found no links at all.

Gladstone pointed out, from his long experience of royal assassination attempts, that attacks on the queen were always by 'morbid minds, combined with the narrowest range of mental gifts' – in other words, the 'lone nuts' described by many Americans in our own time.

While awaiting trial, Maclean had the gall to write an autobiography – *The Story of my Life and Reminiscences*. In it, he outlined his special links with God and that he was mad. Victoria visited the French Riviera for the first time, accompanied everywhere by John Brown, who was convinced that Fenian terrorists were stalking the queen and would try to kill her in Paris.

Maclean's trial opened in Reading on 19 April. He cut a pathetic figure in the dock, shabby and fidgeting, clearly terrified at the panoply of the law all around him. For once, prosecution and defence were actually on the same side; they both wanted Maclean declared guilty but insane and to be detained at Her Majesty's pleasure. Nine doctors declared him insane, one commenting on a head injury he had sustained as a child. He was obsessed with the number four and the colour blue. Bombarded with evidence like this, the jury took less than ten minutes to find Maclean not guilty due to insanity.

Again, the queen was outraged and, predictably, because she hated him, it was all Gladstone's fault. Any lunatic, she contended, could now shoot at her and, effectively, get away with it. She insisted (which she had no right to do under the constitution) that Gladstone change the law. Henceforward, in the event of similar incidents, it would be 'guilty but insane'. The talentless poet William McGonagall penned twelve verses of his usual rubbish, one of which references the quotation which began Chapter 3 – 'There's a divinity that hedges a king/ And so it does seem/ And my opinion is, it has hedged/ Our most gracious Queen.'

Roderick Maclean spent the rest of his life in Broadmoor, writing endless petitions for his release on ever more spurious grounds and writing poetry even worse than McGonagall.

If Queen Victoria did not deserve to be a target for assassination, the same could be said in spades about Elizabeth II. 'The queen', as she was known to millions around the world, even to those whose queen she was not, had no political power whatever. Whereas Victoria used the royal veto to stop parliamentary bills in their tracks (most famously in Henry Labouchere's Criminal Law Amendment to punish lesbians in 1885), Elizabeth was meticulous in her careful avoidance of political issues. That did not stop four men from trying to kill her, although how serious the attempts were must be open to conjecture.

In 1970, the queen and Prince Philip were touring Australia as part of the bicentenary celebrations of Captain James Cook's discovery of the country. Near the town of Lithgow in New South Wales, a large log was discovered across the railway line along which the queen's train was travelling. It had not been there hours before and although no one was held accountable, the speculation was that this was the work of the IRA, then beginning their 'New Troubles' reign of terror in Britain. Since the log was placed close to a bend in the track which the train had to slow to negotiate, it may have been no more than a warning.

The year 1981 was a mammoth one for assassination attempts, the 'highlights' of which were attacks on President Ronald Reagan and Pope John Paul II. These apparently motivated a would-be queen killer, 17-year-old Marcus Sarjeant, who emptied all six shots of his blank-firing starter pistol at the queen as she rode side-saddle on her favourite horse, Burmese, during the Trooping of the Colour ceremony in June. Elizabeth was an accomplished horsewoman and steadied her mount while the police grabbed Sarjeant. It was noticeable that the queen's traditional bodyguard, the Household Cavalry, did *nothing* to save the life of Her Majesty. Sarjeant got five years. This was clearly not a genuine attempt; he merely wanted his fifteen minutes of fame.

Later that year, the queen was touring New Zealand and, on her way to a museum in Dunedin, 17-year-old Christopher Lewis fired a single shot with a .22 rifle from the fifth floor of a neighbouring building. For those who remembered Dealey Plaza, this was a chilling re-enactment, but in fact Lewis had no chance of finding his target. He was found to be deeply psychotic, with a history of arson and animal torture (two of the traits of the serial killer) and an obsession with the royals. Two years later, he tried to break out of prison to kill Prince Charles, on another royal progress.

In 2021, the assassination platform once again moved to Windsor where 19-year-old Jaswant Singh Chail was found lurking outside the castle with a crossbow. Among his possessions was a video in which he boasted of his intention to kill the queen because of Britain's guilt in the 1919 shooting of up to 1,000 Indian nationals at Jallinwallah Bay. Troops under General Dyer opened up on unarmed civilians carrying out a lawful protest and it remains one of the most shameful incidents in Anglo-Indian relations. Since Elizabeth II was not even born at the time, her role in the whole thing can only be in the deranged mind of Chail, who not only called himself Darth Jones, but claimed to be a Sith, a monastic order from the *Star Wars* movie franchise.

Unhappy young men, the easy availability of weapons and a woeful grasp by the medical community on how best to diagnose mental illness and keep the rest of us safe has combined over two centuries to keep the murder of monarchs on the front pages.

But there was one major attempt to solve the problem once and for all, when Daniel M'Naghten thought he had killed the British prime minister, Robert Peel.

Chapter 5

M'Naghten Rules, OK

The question had first arisen in the case of James Hadfield in 1800; could a man (or woman) who tried to kill a king (or queen) actually be sane? The question was (and is) often asked about the wider implications of crime; could a man or woman take someone's life and not be regarded as insane? The problem is that murder is as old as time, insanity is not a qualification to kill and anyway, society has continually changed its mind about what insanity actually is, to the extent that we have legal and medical definitions that do not necessarily match. Add to that the British and American legal systems, where adversaries clash over just about every aspect of a case and where prosecution and defence will wheel in their own 'experts' to bolster their particular argument.

Daniel M'Naghten brought the whole issue into sharp perspective. Today, thanks to the relentless ubiquity of the media, famous faces are instantly recognizable. The eleven assassination attempts on American presidents since 1974 (see Chapter 9) were all delivered against men whose faces were everywhere, in the press and on television. It was not like that in the 1840s; photography existed, but it was a clunky and expensive process. Images by Fox Talbot, Louis Daguerre and John McCosh were largely of inanimate objects, necessarily because a moving image hopelessly blurred the picture. Where the photograph was of a person, the subject had to remain still for up to seven minutes to perfect the shot. The first British prime minister to be photographed was John Henry Temple, Viscount Palmerston, in 1857.

There are no photographs of Robert Peel, prime minister between 1841 and 1846, merely drawings and etchings. And, however good these were (and some of them were not) it did not compensate for the realism and accuracy of a photograph. So, when Daniel M'Naghten looked squarely in the Peel family carriage, which he recognized from the heraldry on the door, the man he saw had to be Robert Peel he was looking for. In fact, M'Naghten was wrong about that; the man in the coach was Peel's secretary, Edward Drummond.

The occasion was Victoria and Albert's first visit to Scotland. She was the first reigning monarch to set foot on Scots soil since James I in 1603. The royal couple fell in love with the Highlands and when their estate at Osborne in the Isle of Wight became too public for them, they bolted to Balmoral instead.

The royal visit was a great success, but Edinburgh was a dangerous city, with its dark passageways and winding stairs. Only twenty years earlier it had achieved notoriety in its evil pairing of William Burke and William Hare, the 'resurrection men' who dug up bodies and murdered people to sell to the anatomists. What worried Peel, who was in the procession but riding in Lord Aberdeen's coach behind the royal couple, was that the place seemed full of Chartists demanding outrageous political reform at a time of serious economic discontent. These people were standing perilously close to the carriages and by no means all of them were smiling.

One who was not was Daniel M'Naghten. A native of Glasgow, infamous as the 'filthiest slum in Britain', M'Naghten had been educated by harsh Jesuit teachers and suffered from a persecution mania since childhood. Trained as a wood-turner, he got to know several Chartists in the workplace and it may be that his head was further turned by them. He came to regard the ruling Tory Party as his personal enemy and especially its leader, Robert Peel.

The Whigs had brought in the Reform Act in 1832 which doubled the electorate, but the franchise still rested on property and

Disgruntled Catholics led by Robert Catesby plotted to kill James I and most of his government. The enterprise would have used gunpowder to blow up the Houses of Parliament, but the government knew about it all along.

Deadly technology had moved on by the twentieth century and in 1984, the IRA were able to plant a bomb in the Grand Hotel, Brighton, three months before it went off. The target was prime minister Margaret Thatcher but by a miracle of timing, she escaped unhurt.

Above left: The medieval cult of the Assassins extended over the Middle East and this castle in today's Iran was one of their headquarters. Members of the group were purported to take the drug hashish (from which the word assassin comes) although this is unlikely as it impairs efficiency when it comes to killing. *Iran Tourism*

Above right: Catholics referred to Elizabeth I as 'the Jezebel of England'. The pope effectively put out a hit on the queen, encouraging Catholics in England and in Europe to kill her. A number of plots on her life were uncovered by her spymaster, Sir Francis Walsingham.

James Hadfield fires his flintlock at George III. Theatres were highly dangerous places for assassination targets. In this instance, Hadfield's ball hit the woodwork of the royal box before he was wrestled to the ground and taken into custody. The king continued to watch the play.

Above left: Female assassins are rare but are particularly dangerous because their targets do not take them seriously. Margaret Nicholson tried to kill George III with a fruit knife but only succeeded in scratching his waistcoat. She ended her days in an institution.

Above right: Daniel M'Naghten intended to kill the prime minister, Sir Robert Peel, but got his secretary instead. Arguments raged as to his sanity and continue to be argued about today. The M'Naghten Rules, which are a measure of criminal lunacy, were adopted both in Britain and the United States.

There were several attempts on the life of Queen Victoria. This one at Windsor in 1882 was foiled by John Brown (standing at the back of the carriage), a couple of policemen and two Eton schoolboys.

The problems of assassination in bad weather using damp gunpowder! A controversial president like Andrew Jackson had many enemies but one of his friends was the legendary frontiersman Davy Crockett, who wrestled his would-be killer to the ground.

The Colt .38 Police Special used by would-be assassin John Schrank to shoot President Teddy Roosevelt.

Two things saved the life of President Teddy Roosevelt when he was shot by John Schrank. Under his jacket, he carried a spectacle case and a folded up copy of a speech he was about to make. The bullet could not penetrate them both.

Adolf Hitler shows his fellow dictator Benito Mussolini the damage done to his headquarters at the Wolf's Lair by Claus von Stauffenberg's bomb in Operation Valkyrie. The Fuhrer was temporarily deaf and had a damaged arm. British and American intelligence had decided earlier in the war that it was better to keep Hitler alive because his strategy made less sense than that of most of his subordinates.

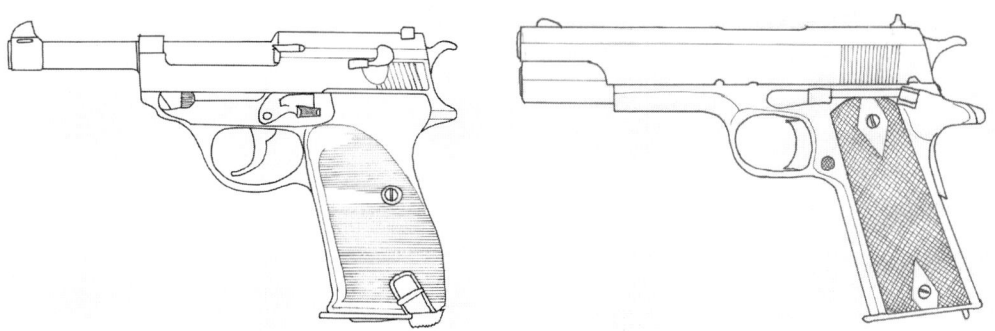

Above left: The Walther .38 used in an attempt to assassinate President Harry S. Truman. This was a two-man hit squad and Oscar Collazo was an amateur. His partner, Griselio Torresola, succeeded in killing a secret serviceman. Truman was unhurt.

Above right: Gerald Ford sat on the Warren Commission to investigate the most famous assassination in history – that of JFK – but was himself the target of assassins. Lynette 'Squeaky' Fromme had been one of the 'family' of serial killer satanist Charles Manson in the late 1960s and did not know how to fire the Browning 1911 shown here.

Moment of impact – President Ronald Reagan told his wife, Nancy, he 'forgot to duck' when he was fired at by John Hinkley, who was himself trying to impress the film actress Jodie Foster.

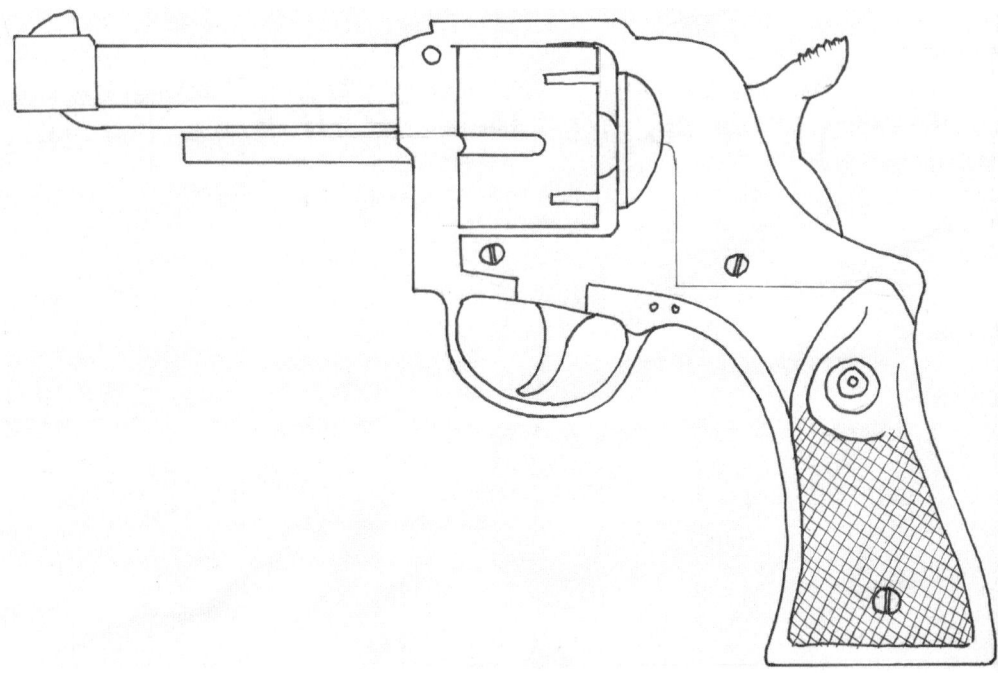

The Röhm RG-14 pistol used by John Hinkley in his assassination attempt on President Ronald Reagan. Despite the amateur looking weapon, it discharged all six shots in seconds and Reagan was lucky to survive.

Robert Pickett was charged with firing his Taurus .38 revolver 'in the general direction' of the White House while President George W. Bush was in residence. He was unlikely to have hit anybody at this distance and he used the Alford plea to avoid a lengthy jail sentence.

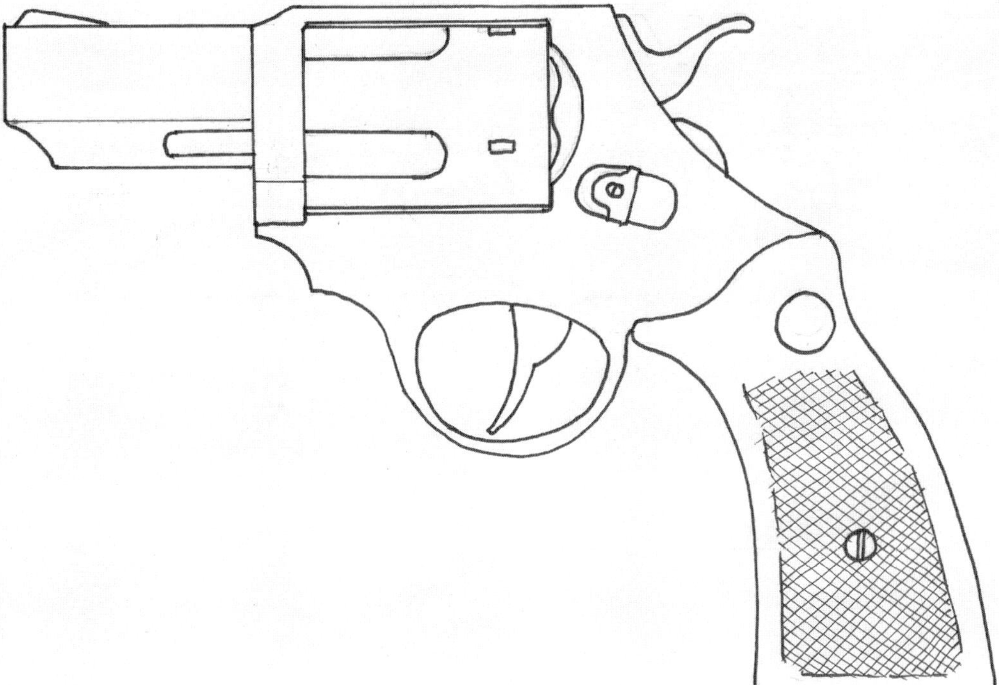

The snub-nosed Taurus .38 revolver used by Pickett to shoot at the White House! Some people do not include this as an assassination attempt at all.

Left: According to some sources, there were over 600 attempts on the life of Fidel Castro, the communist leader who took over Cuba in 1959. Most of these were the work of America's CIA and involved such bizarre techniques as exploding cigars. Castro evaded them all.

Below: There was more than one assassination attempt in 1981. In front of a horrified crowd outside the Vatican, Pope John Paul II was shot by Mehmet Ali Agca. The Pontiff survived and went on to meet his would-be killer in jail and to forgive him.

M'Naghten did not qualify. Ironically, from 1841, Peel's Tory Party was rapidly morphing into the Conservatives and Peel himself was already introducing budgets and promoting railways, both of which would alleviate the economic pressure on the poor. All this took too long for M'Naghten and anyway, Peel had made it clear that he was no friend of the Chartists. His father was a cotton spinner, on the other side of the political and economic divide.

For reasons he could not explain, Tory spies were following M'Naghten everywhere. They wrote libellous letters about him to *The Glasgow Herald* and *The Times* in London. They kept him awake at nights, tried to poison his food. One of them regularly threw straw at him. Needless to say, all this was in M'Naghten's imagination. In desperation, he asked for help – the Procurator Fiscal, the Lord Provost, the Sheriff, his MP – all the great and good of Glasgow. The Reverend Turner advised M'Naghten's father to have his son committed.

M'Naghten left Scotland and went to London, then to France, but his tormentors followed him and he realized the only solution was to kill their leader, Robert Peel. He was in London in 1843, eking out a living from his wood-turning, and took to hanging around the government's Privy Council offices. One man who saw him there was the same Constable James Partridge who had grabbed Edward Oxford after his attack on the queen and had arrested the innocent Charles Dassett in the John Bean attempt.

Like several prime ministers at the time, Peel did not live in 10, Downing Street, but conducted business there. Accordingly, he came and went several times a day, always with his secretary. M'Naghten even asked a patrolling policeman if that was the prime minister. The constable told him it was, but M'Naghten was looking at the wrong man.

On 20 January, M'Naghten was ready to strike. Drummond was alone as he left No. 10 and went into his brother's bank in Charing Cross. It was on his return journey that M'Naghten pulled a pistol from his coat and fired at point-blank range. The explosion briefly ignited the secretary's coat. Constable James Silver, who as a sergeant seven years later would arrest Robert Pate for his attempt on the queen, grabbed the man and kicked his legs from under him before M'Naghten could fire his second gun.

Drummond collapsed in the bank doorway, but the wound at first appeared superficial and the bullet was removed. He was bled and leeched, standard procedure which did no good and he died five days later.

Silver frog-marched the killer to Gardiner Lane police station and locked him in the same cell that Oxford, Francis and Bean had all occupied. It was not until that night that the police told M'Naghten that he had shot the wrong man. Victoria took the line that she maintained throughout on the various attempts on her – there was a crucial difference between someone not knowing right from wrong and someone deliberately buying a brace of pistols and stalking his target. Acquitting M'Naghten would merely encourage the others and commentators made the point that when John Bellingham was hanged for the murder of Spencer Perceval, there were no copycats. After Oxford was put in Bedlam, there had been two more attempts on the queen.

M'Naghten was given time to prepare his defence and had sufficient finds – £750, close to £80,000 today – to afford the best of lawyers. Just as officers of A Division featured in this case in other attempts, so legal counsel duplicated too – William Clarkson had defended Francis and William Bodkin was part of Oxford's team. M'Naghten also hired five doctors, all of whom declared him insane.

The trial began on 3 March before the usual panel of three judges. Unusually, M'Naghten was allowed to sit during the proceedings. The prosecution had a difficult job, trying to have their cake and eat it by claiming that M'Naghten was mad, yet at the same time 'morally aware and criminally responsible'. The solicitor general, William Follett, argued the law as it had stood since the late seventeenth century – 'To be acquitted on the grounds of insanity, that insanity must be total, negating any sense of moral awareness.' M'Naghten was rational – he answered questions, lived by himself, held down a job and had a sizeable income through careful saving. He had also bought two guns for a specific purpose. Who could claim that such a man was mad?

Various prosecution witnesses claimed that the man they knew was normal, both in Glasgow and London.

The next day, the defence, led by Alexander Cockburn QC made the extraordinary comment that Follett's definition, dating from the seventeenth century, was out of date superstition. This was extraordinary because the whole British system was – and is – based on precedent, what had gone before. To dismiss this as so much rubbish was a dangerous precedent. Especially as Cockburn contended that modern science had removed the 'darkness and solitude ... the dismal cell, the bed of straw, the iron chain ...' In this, Cockburn himself was delusional. Would this uplifting modern science be the same one that used leeches on Edward Drummond and opened his vein to ensure that he lost yet more blood? And clearly, the QC had not visited a London prison recently or he would have seen plenty of dismal cells, beds of straw and iron chains still in widespread use.

Be that as it may – and it is astonishing that Follett did not challenge it – Cockburn believed that there was a difference between 'understand[ing] the evil of what he did' and being controlled by impulses beyond his control. Nine doctors were wheeled out to testify to M'Naghten's obsessions and mania and again, this medical (as opposed to legal) defence went unchallenged. Two of the doctors had never met the defendant but were allowed to testify anyway in what was then, as now, a gross example of bad practice. Judge Tindal stopped the trial, having got out of Follett that he had nothing else to say and the jury had little choice but to find M'Naghten not guilty on the grounds of insanity.

The odd little miscreant, lost in his own world, died in Broadmoor in 1865 and was buried in an unmarked grave. But his name and the arguments about sanity and assassination lived on forever. Most of society was appalled – any lunatic was free to shoot anybody and a combination of law and medicine, arguably two of the most out of touch professions in the land, could get them off. Peel, who no doubt felt guilty about Drummond's death, wrote to the queen claiming that anyone who had planned a killing so carefully could not possibly be insane. Victoria agreed and slammed the judges as being utterly out of kilter with common sense and the opinion of the country.

The Judicate Supreme Court met the day after the trial to establish once and for all what the rules should be. Eleven of the twelve agreed and their judgement came to be known as the M'Naghten Rule, applicable in British and, as it turned out, American law. In a nutshell, the definition was 'to establish a defence on the ground of insanity, it must be clearly proved that, at the time of committing the act [the shooting of Drummond] the party accused [M'Naghten] was labouring under such a defect of reason [Peel was out to get him] from disease of the mind [undetermined in 1843] as not to know the nature and quality of the act he was doing [murder] or, if he did know it, that he did not know he was doing what was wrong.'

Yet Daniel M'Naghten had been brought up by God-fearing parents and the Catholic Church. Are we seriously to accept that he did not know murder was wrong? The M'Naghten rules were flawed as a result and have caused repeated problems over the decades, especially when genuine medical advances in psychiatry were made. We have already established in Chapter 3 that there have been hundreds of assassins and would-be assassins in history. Under the M'Naghten Rule as laid down by Judge Tindal, none of them would have been guilty of anything, just as Americans plead the Fifth Amendment in court which guarantees their right against self-incrimination, so assassins could merely plead M'Naghten!

Chapter 6

From King Richard to the Bull Moose

With hindsight, Andrew Jackson was one of the presidents of the United States most associated with violence. A tough, uncompromising soldier, he had defeated the British at the Battle of New Orleans in 1813 and did his best to wipe out the Creek Indian nation years later. One of his most famous quotations is 'I have only two regrets: that I did not shoot Henry Clay and did not hang John C. Calhoun.' That was because, at least in part, Calhoun was implicated in a plot to assassinate him.

Jackson's presidency began with riot and discord. 'Ladies fainted,' an eyewitness observed during his inauguration, 'men were seen with bloody noses and such a scene of confusion took place as is impossible to describe.' A great deal of drink was taken and the White House was trashed. Jackson himself retreated to a nearby pub!

Five years later, under fire from the Senate for misuse of power (contemporary cartoons show him with crown, orb and sceptre) Jackson attended the funeral of a senator at the Capitol Building in Washington DC. It was 30 January 1835, cold and raining, and as the president emerged from the service via the East Portico, 35-year-old Richard Laurence stepped out of the crowd and fired a pistol at him. The gun misfired. Laurence whipped out a second from his coat and the same thing happened again. Stunned, but nevertheless showing lightning reaction, Jackson beat his would-be killer with his hickory cane before the crowd leapt on the assassin. One of these was David Crockett of Tennessee, the legendary Indian fighter who was a congressman at the time.

Once in custody, bizarre details emerged about Richard Laurence. He was born in England, probably in 1800 and his family moved to Washington DC twelve years later – bad timing, because Britain and the United States were at war. Laurence's childhood was conventional and he became a house-painter, but in his thirties he began exhibiting symptoms of mania. He turned viciously on his siblings, beating up his sisters, and claimed that he was prevented from leaving the country by the government who did everything in their power to keep him in the United States. In a similar way to Daniel M'Naghten in England eight years later, Laurence believed that the newspapers carried libellous articles about him and that he was actually King Richard III of England (ignoring the fact that the real one had been killed at Bosworth in 1485). Specifically, it was Andrew Jackson who was preventing him claiming his rightful inheritance because of the president's attack on the Second Bank of America, which he saw as an example of unbridled financial corruption.

Laurence began to wear flamboyant clothes, changing them three or four times a day. He burst into fits of laughter, swearing and talking to himself. On 30 January, he closed the book he was reading and left his workshop, muttering, 'I'll be damned if I don't do it.' His trial began in Washington's City Hall on 11 April; Francis Scott Key prosecuted. Throughout the proceedings, Laurence laughed, cursed and utterly refused to recognize the authority of the court – 'It is for me, gentlemen, to pass judgement on you, and not you upon me.' It took the jury five minutes to find him not guilty by reason of insanity and he spent the rest of his life in various institutions, dying in June 1861.

At the time and since, the question of a conspiracy arose. Jackson was not a popular president, even if he was a populist one, and the list of his enemies would have stretched all the way along Pennsylvania Avenue. Foremost among these were George Poindexter, a senator from Mississippi, and John Calhoun of South Carolina, who had been a thorn in Jackson's side throughout both men's careers. Rumours became so entrenched that Calhoun had to deliver a speech to the Senate, denying involvement in any such conspiracy.

If Andrew Jackson was the first president in history to appear in an assassin's sights, Abraham Lincoln was the first where a gunman actually succeeded. But four years before John Wilkes Booth shot Lincoln in Ford's Theatre, Washington, in April 1865, there had been an earlier attempt on the life of the man who, today, always tops opinion polls of presidential popularity.

We have to forget the cult of sainthood that exists around Lincoln today; much of that is because of his actual assassination and the motives for it. In February 1861, he had yet to undergo his inauguration and not everybody was happy about it. The scrawny, scruffy senator from Illinois, with his log cabin to White House fairy story, was the first Republican to obtain the presidency; that alone alienated him from half the voting population. He was seen by many as an abolitionist, yearning to free the slaves, although he had not yet come to that decision. He was a Marmite president – people loved him or hated him and it would only be a matter of weeks before the Southern states deserted the Union and set up their own government – the Confederacy – with their own laws, armed forces, currency and president.

Lincoln and his family planned to carry out a whistle-stop train tour of seventy towns and cities, from Springfield, Illinois to Washington DC. There was no official security for presidents then (which would lead directly to Lincoln's death four years later) and Lincoln hired Allan Pinkerton's Detective Agency to protect him on this journey. Railway magnate Samuel Morse Felton got wind of a plot to seize the railways and the Capitol and tipped Pinkerton off.

Pinkerton and his lead detective, Harry W. Davis, discovered that the heart of the plot lay in Baltimore, Maryland, a city with pro-Secessionist (Southern) sympathies where slave-holding was the norm. Rather like Dallas, Texas just over 100 years later, Baltimore was not a place where presidents trod lightly.

Or, at all, in fact. Pinkerton persuaded Lincoln to disguise himself and swap trains, travelling with his family from Harrisburg by night, so that when the presidential train arrived in Baltimore, it was empty. The problem with the city was that its regulations prevented trains from passing through. Passengers, even presidents, had to travel by cab or on foot between stations. This was the perfect place for an assassination attempt. Pinkerton's undercover agents unmasked a number of shady characters who planned to mingle with the crowd as the train arrived on 23 February and stab Lincoln à la Julius Caesar. The leader of the group was believed to be Cipriano Ferrandini, a Sicilian who had recently arrived in Baltimore and was the barber at the prestigious Borman's Hotel in the city.

Pinkerton's problem was that Abraham Lincoln was 6ft 4in tall and highly recognizable from recent press coverage of political debates and electioneering. In the end, the president-elect went along with the ruse, wearing a Scottish bonnet (cap) and long cloak. The press got wind of the subterfuge and had a field day. Everywhere, cartoons of Lincoln appeared of him in full Highland fig, including kilt and tam o'shanter. *The New York Times* was vitriolic and *The Baltimore Sun* said, 'We do not believe the Presidency can ever be more degraded by any of his successors than it has by him, even before his inauguration.'

But by eliminating Baltimore as a stop, there was no assassination attempt. Pinkerton telegraphed, 'Plums delivered nuts safely' (the President is safe).

Was this conspiracy and concomitant assassination threat real? Certainly, Lincoln did receive death threats at the time, ranging from shooting and stabbing to poisoned ink and dumplings filled with poisonous spiders! Pinkerton clearly took it seriously, but the fact that the only named conspirator, Ferrandini, was never charged with any crime (he continued to cut Baltimore hair throughout the Civil War) is perhaps very telling. Ward Hill Lamon, Lincoln's bodyguard, doubted whether the president was ever in any danger. There was no conspiracy 'of a hundred, of fifty, of twenty, of three, no definite purpose in the heart of even one man to murder Mr Lincoln'.

But those who do not believe in conspiracies should take note of a remarkable photograph taken at Lincoln's second inauguration, in March 1865. It was one of several taken by Alexander Gardner, a fashionable Washington photographer and, when the crowd of the great and good are analysed face by face, standing outside the Capitol's columns is the actor John Wilkes Booth who would kill Lincoln forty-one days later. Far below him, among the hoi-polloi of ordinary citizens, are five of the men who would be involved in that assassination. Spookily, a fingerprint on the original plate has obliterated Lincoln's head as he stands at the podium to speak. Wilkes, of course, shot him in the back of the head. When he was arrested after the assassination, Booth said, 'What an excellent chance I had to kill the President if I had wished, on inauguration day.' With his accomplices Lewis Powell, George Atzerodt, David Herold, John Surratt and Edmund Spangler feet away, had that been an actual plan? And did something go wrong?

You couldn't miss William Taft. He stood 6ft tall and weighed over 300lb. That said, were there any real attempts on his life at all? Mel Ayton in the scholarly and readable *Plotting to Kill the President* (2017) makes the point that the most powerful man in the world is naturally a target for any number of deranged individuals and causes. Some were taken seriously at the time; some were not and the widespread carrying of firearms in the United States under the Second Amendment to the Constitution has not made life any easier for presidential protection squads.

With the assassinations of Lincoln, Garfield and McKinley, a Secret Service was formed to guard the man in the White House, but even then, successive presidents have been far from safe.

William Howard Taft was the twenty-seventh president and the only one to have served as chief justice. Seen as a supporter of Teddy Roosevelt (see below) his politics became increasingly different once Taft's administration gained its own momentum. He was a middling sort of president, unexceptional and the three attempts on his life, however half-hearted, say more perhaps about American society than Taft himself. What is extraordinary is that there were two assassination attempts in the same month, October 1909. In the first, 27-year-old Arthur Wright of Lowell, Massachusetts, travelled to Portland, Oregon to shoot Taft as he rode in a parade. He was arrested by a policeman before he could fire and his motive was never made clear. The second attempt was more serious, at least in the setting and implications. On 16 October, Taft met President Porfirio Diaz of Mexico on the Chamizal Strip, a neutral zone between El Paso in Texas and Cuidad Juarez in Mexico. The relationship between the two countries had always been tense and remains so today; both presidents faced death threats and it was the first time that an American president had set foot on Mexican soil.

By the standards of the day, security was high. Apart from the nascent Secret Service, there were Texas Rangers and US Marshals, not to mention the Mexican Army. A man in the crowd at the ceremony was seen behaving oddly and was arrested by an observant Texas Ranger. He had been carrying a pistol. Online today, neither the would-be killer nor his motive would have any coverage at all.

The attack on President Theodore Roosevelt, the Bull Moose, was not only far more serious; it nearly came off. A larger-than-life character, the twenty-sixth president was a war hero, having led his Rough Riders up San Juan Hill in the Cuban War of 1898. His friend, the poet Rudyard Kipling, wrote *The White Man's Burden* especially for him; to others, he was that 'damned cowboy', prone to making embarrassing speeches about the greatness of America long before Donald Trump took over the mantle. Famously, he summed up his policies as 'speak softly and wield a big stick' and his imperialism, though fitting for his own time, would find far less support today. In 1912, the Republican Party was in disarray. Its more liberal element, headed by Roosevelt, was termed the Progressive Party, while William Taft's old guard were more traditional. Both men were on the campaign trail, but Roosevelt was a 'national treasure' who had already served two terms as president and was straining the Constitution by going for a third. He was just leaving the Gilpatrick Hotel, Milwaukee, Wisconsin, on 14 October when a shot rang out.

Roosevelt was standing in an open-topped car, waving to crowds when John Flammang Schrank blasted him at close range with his .38 calibre Colt Police Special revolver. It is not clear from photographs of the weapon taken later whether this was the 1896 pattern with its 4½in barrel or the modified 1905 pocket variant, whose shorter barrel (2½in) and rounded butt made it easier to hide in a pocket.

There was, of course, instant hysteria. Roosevelt recoiled, but did not fall and his secretary, Elbert E. Martin, grabbed the gunman, while a member of the crowd, Czech immigrant Frank Bukovsky, grabbed the gun. The president-wannabe's bodyguard, the former Rough Rider A.O. Girard, plunged in too. There were immediate demands for a lynching, as anybody who could reach Schrank hit him with whatever came to hand. Roosevelt's aide, Harry Cochens, checked that the victim was all right. A shaken but nonetheless rock-solid Roosevelt said, 'He pinked me, Harry.'

Realizing that Schrank was in some danger, Roosevelt called out, 'Don't hurt him. Bring him here. I want to see him.' He held the pinioned would-be killer's face between both hands, looking him in the eyes. 'What did you do it for?' There was no response, so Roosevelt said, 'What's the use? Turn him over to the police.' Then he looked again at Schrank. 'You poor creature. Officers, take charge of him and see there is no violence done to him.' Roosevelt had tackled police corruption in New York City years before and knew at first hand how 'over-zealous' America's finest could be. To boos and hisses, Schrank was taken into the hotel and handed over to the local police in the kitchen.

Insisting that he was unhurt, Roosevelt went on to the Milwaukee Auditorium and delivered an eighty-four-minute speech. Towards the end of it, his voice tired and he had some difficulty breathing. As a child, he had had bad asthma and this was nothing new to him. Blood seeping through his shirt, however, was another matter. He knew he had been hit by Schrank's bullet, but as he was not coughing blood knew that his lungs were not impaired. Towards the end, he said, 'Ladies and gentlemen, I don't know whether you fully understand that I have just been shot, but it takes more than that to kill a Bull Moose.' The crowd, recovering from the shock of the announcement, were on their feet in a standing ovation and instantly the Bull Moose became *the* symbol, both of Roosevelt and his Progressives.

In fact, it was that Progressive speech – and his spectacles case – that had saved Roosevelt's life. He was carrying the fifty-page speech, folded over, in his inside jacket pocket, so that it had something like the thickness of a telephone directory. Schrank's bullet bounced off the metal case, thudded through the folded pages, Roosevelt's waistcoat, shirt and skin and lodged in the muscles of his chest. When he finally let doctors examine him, they X-rayed his chest and decided that it was safer to leave the slug where it was than to try to remove it. Former experience had shown the way. Even modern surgery could not have saved Abraham Lincoln, with a bullet lodged in his brain, but both Garfield and McKinley had died several days after being shot and *some* of that can be labelled as medical malpractice. Accordingly, Roosevelt carried the bullet around for the rest of his life, all seven years of it. 'I do not mind it,' he told a friend, 'anymore than if it was in my waistcoat pocket.' Within two weeks of the shooting, he was back on the campaign trail.

John Schrank was a Bavarian, born in Erding, who had moved to the United States when he was 9. When his parents died, he was brought up by an aunt and uncle who ran a bar in New York. When they died, Schrank sold the business for a tidy sum and wandered the east coast. His girlfriend had been killed in a shipping disaster in 1904 when the PS *General Slocum* blew up in New York Harbor. The loss of two sets of 'parents' and the girl he loved may have led to a breakdown. Certainly, Schrank became a religious obsessive, writing rambling poetry and wandering the streets of New York at night.

He had been stalking Roosevelt for weeks and exactly why he should have targeted him is not clear. Having interviewed the man, the judge believed a trial to be unnecessary; Schrank was pleading guilty and a string of doctors testified that he suffered from 'insane delusions, grandiose in character'. He was committed for life to Central State Hospital for the Criminally Insane in Waupun, Wisconsin, 'not guilty' of shooting Roosevelt 'by reason of insanity'. In hospital, Schrank wrote long letters as rambling as his poetry to his doctor, Adin Sherman, and these have survived. Unfortunately, they shed no light on the assassination attempt. John Schrank died of pneumonia in September 1943 and his body was donated to Marquette University.

Teddy Roosevelt was probably the only assassination target to confront his would-be killer and ask him to his face why he did it. He got no answer. And even, in later years, when answers were sometimes forthcoming, they rarely made sense.

Chapter 7

Killing Hitler

Georg Elser was a carpenter, electrician and odd-job man. He was also a chain-smoker and a Communist. And he could make a bomb. After these brief facts, truth and the man who nearly killed Adolf Hitler begin to part company.

One version runs like this. Loathing Nazism and believing, as many did, that the Fuhrer's generic war with most of Europe would end in disaster for Germany, Elser got a job working on refurbishment of the Burgerbraukeller in Munich. This beer hall had iconic status in the Third Reich. From there, on 8 November 1923, Hitler and his infant Nazi Party had begun their putsch to take over Munich for National Socialism. Germany, after defeat in the First World War, was split between Fascist and Communist groups, each vying with the other for the heart and soul of the country. Hitler's procession, badly organized and badly timed, met a fusillade of bullets from the police and the future Fuhrer was one of the first to run. Sixteen of his followers died in the street battle and they instantly became martyrs to the cause.

Ten years later, the Nazi Party was the only one permitted in Germany and Hitler, quite literally, called the shots in what was a gangster state. Every year, to mark the failed putsch, the party faithful would meet at the Burgerbraukeller to worship at a building that had become a shrine.

Elser's bomb was fitted with an eight-day alarm clock mechanism and a gadget that enabled it to be detonated by an electronic switch. It was set so that Hitler and several cronies would have been in the building. The usual pattern of the ceremony was for speeches to be made, especially by the Fuhrer, and everybody hung around, congratulating themselves on their political success and reliving the early days. The anniversary in 1939 would be different. There was a war on (Britain had declared war on Germany eight weeks earlier) and the Fuhrer was a middle-aged man in a hurry. His usually lengthy speech abruptly terminated after only a few minutes and he and his entourage left the building. Elser's bomb, hidden inside a pillar behind Hitler's podium, duly went off, killing seven and wounding sixty-three more. The Fuhrer himself put all this down, publicly, to providence (he avoided the word 'God' whenever he could because he wanted the German people to see deity only in him).

The next day, however, the Nazi newssheet, the *Volkischer Beobachter*, carried a very different slant on the bombing, giving the second version of events. The assassination attempt had been the work of the British Secret Service and behind them, their duplicitous prime minister, Neville Chamberlain. In fact, although no one outside the corridors of power knew this, the Secret Intelligence Service was in complete turmoil in these weeks, with agents being pulled out of Europe and embassies closing down in the chaotic days of the 'phoney war'.

On 9 November, in what was one of the most bizarre incidents of the war, two British agents, Major Richard Stevens and Captain Sigismund Payne Best, were kidnapped at Venlo on the Dutch-German border and dragged into the Third Reich. They had been lured there by Walter Schellenberg, an SS officer infinitely smarter than they were, on the orders of his boss, Heinrich Himmler, head of the SS. These hapless Englishmen spent the rest of the war in prison and appear to have told Schellenberg whatever he wanted to know.

The story that Hitler's government did not want put about was that the whole Burgerbraukeller bombing was a fake assassination attempt, designed to blacken the British and to boost the Fuhrer's popularity. This certainly worked. Shops and houses all over Germany put up photographs of the leader, along with swastikas and in various German churches, priests and pastors thanked God for the Fuhrer's salvation. In this version, Georg Elser was already doing time in Dachau concentration camp for his left-wing leanings and the SS made him an offer he could not refuse. He was given a postcard photograph of the Burgerbraukeller interior, access to the building and tools to do the job. He was, of course, supervised during all this. In exchange, he was to be given a cushy life in Dachau until 8 November, with decent food, clothes and the cigarettes that were essential to his life. On 8 November, he would be taken to the Swiss border (Switzerland was neutral throughout the Second World War) with enough cash for him to live on happily ever after. Not unnaturally, Elser went along with it.

All went well, but when his guards dropped him at the appointed spot near the border, he was suddenly arrested by the Gestapo, still carrying his damning photograph of the bomb scene. The idea was to mount a show trial, at which Elser, Stevens and Best would admit their part in trying to kill Hitler at the behest of the British government. For whatever reason, this trial never happened.

Elser spent the rest of the war in Sachsenhausen concentration camp on the outskirts of Berlin and it was here that he met Best, to whom he told the version you have just read. Best survived the war, which is why we have Elser's version at all; Elser did not. He was murdered on 16 April 1945 by the Gestapo, who maintained that his death occurred as a result of an Allied air strike.

How much of Elser's story is true can be judged, perhaps, by the fact that he was tortured by the SS using drugs and hypnotherapy. Walter Schellenberg, who was allegedly involved indirectly in the scheme, interrogated Elser over a period of time and believed implicitly that the bomb plot was real and it was only the Fuhrer's famous good luck that led it to fail.

In fact, it transpires that luck had little to do with it. On 3 May 1942, Hitler recorded a monologue (his usual MO when having 'discussions' with subordinates) at the Berghof, his headquarters in Bavaria. He can be heard saying:

> I quite understand why 90 per cent of the historic assassinations have been successful. The only preventative measure one can take is to live irregularly – to walk, to drive and to travel at irregular times and unexpectedly ... As far as possible, whenever I go anywhere by car, I go off unexpectedly and without warning the police.

In America, in particular, the dates and times of presidential appearance have always been – and still are – reported widely in the media.

'There can never be absolute security,' he went on, 'against fanatics and idealists ... If some fanatic wishes to shoot me or kill me with a bomb, I am no safer sitting down than standing up.' It was grimly prescient in terms of John F. Kennedy's take on things the day he was killed in Dallas in 1963 – 'Jackie,' he said to his wife, 'if somebody wants to shoot me from a window with a rifle, nobody can stop it, so why worry about it?'

As to the motivation for assassinations, Hitler went on, 'The only really dangerous elements are either those fanatics who have been goaded to action by dastardly priests or nationalist-minded patriots from one of the countries we have occupied. My many years of experience make things fairly difficult even for such as these.'

While the Allies came to the conclusion that assassinating Hitler would achieve nothing – behind him were Himmler, Goering, Goebbels and countless others who could simply take over the Reich – the only real anti-Hitler movements were happening inside the gangster state itself. A soldier, Hans von Herwarth, told a doctor in

Munich in 1942, 'There were quite a lot of people who were willing to kill Hitler, but there was no possibility to bring them into contact with him.'

That was the Allies' problem too. The Fuhrer was protected by vast squads of troops, his own black-shirted SS fanatically loyal to him and his various headquarters were designed to be impregnable. The Berghof high on the Obersalzburg was certainly targetable from the air, but access on the ground was very difficult. The Wolf's Lair at Rastenburg near the Eastern Front was a military base, with trenches, barbed wire, guns and minefields. As the war went on, Hitler spent less and less time in Berlin, a city he did not like anyway. While the British held off from assassination attempts in Germany, American involvement (they had joined the war after the Japanese attack on Pearl Harbor in December 1941) considered 'eliminating' their arch-enemy, Emperor Hirohito of Japan, as being more important. General Henry 'Hap' Arnold wrote 'Not at this time' on a memo suggesting it in December 1942. He was concerned with reprisals on American prisoners of war.

There had always been elements in Germany who were opposed to Hitler and as the war began to go badly, their numbers grew. The problem was that most of Germany, the rank-and-file civilians, were loyal to him. They ignored the concentration camps, the systematic subjugation of women, the removal of Jews – all this, Nazi ideology told them, was how it was meant to be. Even eugenics, ethnic cleansing to create the perfect Aryan race, had its following and not just in Germany. While clinics in Berlin's Tiergartenstrasse 4 were carrying out euthanasia on 'life unworthy of life', popular 'philosophers' like George Bernard Shaw backed at least some of what the Nazis were doing.

If an actual attack on Hitler were to happen, it could only come from the Wehrmacht, the army. Like all armed forces and the police, soldiers in the Third Reich had been hijacked by the Nazis, even swearing an oath of allegiance to Adolf Hitler personally. Many generals despised him. Several of them were literally the 'old guard', noble families who had ruled the multiplicity of states before German unity in 1871. Hitler on the other hand was 'the Bavarian corporal' who scarcely knew one end of a rife from the other; it galled the generals to have to take orders from him.

Several of the officers' attempts involved the political removal of the Fuhrer, not his murder, and as long as this dichotomy existed, formulating a successful plan was difficult. A case in point was Field Marshal Erwin Rommel, the 'desert fox', one of the most famous and dazzling of Hitler's generals. He was never a committed Nazi and eventually lent his name to a plot to overthrow him; but he drew the line at assassination.

The first practical attempt to kill Hitler took place in March 1943. Because of the pyramidal nature of the Nazi state, executing the Fuhrer would not be enough; there would have to be a coup (in effect a revolution) to seize Berlin and remove all the key figures in the government. The actual hit would take place outside the capital and the Reserve Army (a sort of pumped-up Home Guard) would take Berlin, with tanks, and carry out whirlwind arrests. Replacements for key officials were posited and they in turn would announce Hitler's death and begin negotiations with the Allies. At this stage, of course, there had been no effective landing in the west (that would be D-Day in June 1944) and the Russians were still fighting on their own soil.

At one stage, Colonel Freiherr von Boeselager was put in place as commander of a cavalry unit ready to machine gun Hitler as he and his staff arrived. The order – the call sign was Operation Flash – had to be given by Field Marshal Gunther von Kluge, but he lost his nerve and no order was sent. A back-up to Flash was the placing of a bomb on Hitler's plane, to make it look like an accident. The German-made bombs the plotters experimented with were no good, giving out a tell-tale hissing noise. British versions were to be used instead. Twice, on the afternoon of 13 March, plotters tried to set the bombs and twice they failed. During the process, one of them, Fabian von Schlabrendorff, noticed the outsize hat that Hitler was wearing; it was lined with 3½lb of steel!

The bomb was to be smuggled aboard the plane hidden in a parcel carrying two bottles of brandy from another plotter, Major-General Henning von Tresckow, to an 'innocent' recipient, General Hellmuth Stieff. There was no clockwork in the device. Von Schlabrendorff pressed a button inside the parcel which broke a small bubble, releasing a corrosive chemical that ate through a wire. When that happened, the detonator would strike and the bomb would go off. Hitler was on his way to the Wolf's Lair but after half an hour, as the plane was over Minsk, it would disintegrate, killing everybody on board.

Furious telephone calls darted back and forth. There was no news, no sign of an explosion. Von Schlabrendorff flew out the next day and inspected the dud package. 'The mechanism had worked,' he wrote to his co-conspirators, 'the small bottle had broken; the corrosive fluid had consumed the wire; the striker had hit forward; but the detonator had not fired.'

Rattled, but determined, the conspirators tried again. Heroes' Memorial Day, *Heldengedentag,* was on 21 March and all the Nazi elite would be present in Berlin. Colonel Freiherr von Gersdorff was chosen for the mission, which would involve his suicide. He stayed at the hotel in the capital and was given two bombs, one for each trench coat pocket, by von Schlabrendorff. The fuses had ten-minute timers, but March was unusually cold that year and that might double the detonation time. The next day, Hitler duly turned up, Gersdorff stood close to him, but before he could set his timers, a change of plan was announced. The Fuhrer would spend less than ten minutes (rather than the anticipated half an hour) inspecting Russian war trophies and then he left. Operation Flash was getting nowhere.

By October, General Stieff, to whom the brandy had been sent earlier in the year, had joined the conspiracy and had bombs planted at the Wolf's Lair to go off at Hitler's daily meeting with his chiefs of staff. Stieff got cold feet and did not set the fuses. The bombs were quietly removed before they could be discovered. The following month, 24-year-old infantry captain Axel von dem Bussche was modelling a new army coat for Hitler's approval. In his pocket were two bombs, German this time, with only a few seconds delay before detonation. Von dem Bussche, like von Gersdorff, had volunteered his life.

The day before all this was due to happen, an Allied air raid destroyed the models and von dem Bussche was recalled to his unit on the Eastern Front. By December, he was back with new models and new bombs, but the Fuhrer changed his plans and left to spend Christmas at the Berghof. An action replay took place on 11 February 1944. Von dem Bussche had been badly wounded at the Eastern Front and was replaced by Heinrich von Kleist. On that day, Hitler did not show up. Military dictators do not have to give reasons.

Although they abandoned the whole idea later in the war, the 'black operations' men of Britain's SO1 *did* have a plan to assassinate Hitler. The first idea was to hit his special train, *Amerika* (renamed *Brandenburg* after the United States' entry into the war in December 1941). The train was deliberately destroyed in April 1945 by Julius Schaub but we still have the specifications for it. Hitler was the first leader of his country to fly (as was Chamberlain in Britain) but he used *Amerika* frequently, especially for short distances. It had two locomotives and an armoured flat-bed mounted with anti-aircraft guns manned by Luftwaffe Regiment No. 9. There were two dining cars, a baggage car and accommodation for twenty-two guards and household staff. The Fuhrer had his own personal quarters; there was a bathing car, two dining cars, a conference room and press accommodation for Hitler's communication chief Otto Dietrich.

The problem with hitting the train is highlighted by Hitler's own comments of May 1943. His journeys remained closely guarded secrets and he frequently changed his mind about times, days and even directions. No doubt infuriating to his staff, this policy kept the man alive. A side plot to contaminate the train's water supply was found to be impracticable because of the need for an inside man.

Operation Foxley abandoned the train idea completely and focused on the Berghof, as the less well-protected of Hitler's favourite headquarters. The plan emerged in the summer of 1944, but the tightness of the date structure throws at least some of it into doubt. An unnamed prisoner captured in Normandy (by definition this had to be after D-Day, 6 June) was found, under interrogation, to have been a guard at the Berghof and told SIS that the Fuhrer routinely took a half-hour walk, alone, in the Berghof grounds, shortly after ten o'clock each morning. He usually ended up in the Teehaus, a café in Berchtesgaden on the Mooslahnerkopf.

SOE would drop two killers into nearby Salzburg where they would be sheltered by a local anti-Nazi with the codename Heidentaler. Both men would be issued with Wehrmacht mountain uniforms to blend in with most of the troops in the area. They would know that Hitler was at the Berghof because the Teehaus flew a swastika whenever he was in residence. One of the pair was a German-speaking Pole and the other a British sniper who was training with a Kar98k Mauser rifle, the standard Wehrmacht issue. He would also be carrying a 9mm Luger, complete with silencer. This gun is now on display in the Combined Military Services Museum at Maldon, Essex.

The ideal time, it was decided, was 13–14 July. This 'window' means that very little time could have been given. It could only have been weeks, perhaps days, since the Berghof guard had been captured. Churchill was all for it, as was General Gerald Templer of the general staff. Lieutenant Colonel Ronald Thornely, head of SOE's German Directorate, had his doubts, however. If Hitler were killed, a more able strategist would take his place – and Germany had a lot of those. Rather than causing chaos in the Reich, Hitler would become a martyr and a rallying cry for Germany, on the ropes but not yet out of the fight. So Foxley never happened.

Ironically, Adolf Hitler left the Berghof on 14 July and would never return.

The last and most famous attempt on the life of Adolf Hitler was code named Valkyrie, made into a movie starring Tom Cruise in 2008. The brains behind it and the hit man rolled into one was Claus Schenk, Count von Stauffenberg, who, like several conspirators, was descended from the 'greats' of the Prussian general staff who had faced Napoleon. He was highly intelligent, good looking and quick thinking, but war wounds made him slower and more vulnerable than he would have liked. In April 1943, his car hit a landmine in Tunisia and von Stauffenberg lost his left eye, his right hand, two fingers of his other hand and had wounds to his left ear and knee. It was during convalescence from this that he became an anti-Hitler conspirator. 'I feel I must do something now to save Germany,' he wrote to his wife. 'We General Staff officers must all accept our share of the responsibility.'

Von Stauffenberg was very persuasive and got a small number of generals on side to co-ordinate moves in Berlin. The hit would happen at the Wolf's Lair, from which all telephone and radio communication would be cut and the Reserve Army would arrest Nazi leaders and, effectively, take over Germany. There would be immediate overtures to Stalin, as leader of the Red Army and General Dwight Eisenhower, commanding the Expeditionary Force that had landed in Normandy the previous month.

The timing of the operation was vital. Berlin was inundated with the SS, but the police were prepared to back the plotters once Hitler was out of the way. They and the Reserve Army would occupy the city's two radio stations, telegraph and telephone exchanges, the Reich Chancellery, the various ministries and the headquarters of the SS. All this must be done in twenty-four hours and similar activities must be taken in Paris. The only officer with the clout to order Valkyrie to go ahead was General Friedrich Fromm and he was shaky from the start. To that end, a number of documents ordering movement were pre-printed with his forged signature at the bottom. Discussing revolution, putsch and assassination was one thing behind closed doors and over a glass of schnapps; actually carrying it out was something else. What few of the plotters realized was that some of the news had leaked and they were being shadowed by Himmler's Gestapo.

Von Stauffenberg's promotion to colonel at the end of June meant that not only was he working directly under Fromm but that he was a bona fide and regular visitor to the Wolf's Lair. In fact, the staff officer's first opportunity came, not there, but at the Berghof, on 11 July. The attacks by the Russian Red Army were taking a terrible toll on the German Eastern Front and Fromm would have to provide men from his Home Army to plug the gaps. Von Stauffenberg's liaison was vital in this and he turned up that day with English-made bombs. Goering and Himmler would be there as well and it was a heaven-sent opportunity to strike.

Himmler pulled out at the last minute and conspirator generals Ludwig Beck and Friedrich Olbricht told von Stauffenberg to delay until all three were there. The colonel was now determined to go ahead. His principal target was Hitler; the others could wait. On 14 July, von Stauffenberg turned up with his bombs to be told that there was a crisis at the Eastern Front and the Fuhrer had flown to the Wolf's Lair to be nearer operations. He was now conducting the war by himself rather than leaving it to his generals and he was clearly out of his depth.

The next day, von Stauffenberg flew to Rastenburg carrying a briefcase with a bomb in it. At eleven o'clock that Saturday morning,

Olbricht issued the Valkyrie order, ignoring the still-dithering Fromm, for the Reserve Army to march on Berlin and the tanks from the Panzer school at Krampnitz to back them up.

Von Stauffenberg entered Hitler's conference room, absented himself to make a vital phone call and checked with Olbricht that all was well. He then returned to the room to set the timer, only to find that Hitler was not there. Von Stauffenberg rang Olbricht again and Valkyrie was cancelled, the troops returned to barracks. Olbricht thought on his feet – if anybody asked him what was going on, he would claim that it was a manoeuvre as a precaution against a Russian attack on the capital. The whole thing had clearly rattled Olbricht. For it to happen again, he had to be sure that Hitler was dead.

On 17 July, news came through that Erwin Rommel had been hit when Allied aircraft strafed his car; he was out of the plot for good, although once his part was known, he was given the choice – a public court martial exposing him or suicide. He chose the latter.

At a little after six o'clock on Thursday, 20 July, von Stauffenberg and his adjutant, Lieutnant Werner von Haeften, left bomb-battered Berlin for the Wolf's Lair. In his briefcase, von Stauffenberg carried a time bomb wrapped in a shirt. It was the same timer that had failed to explode in the brandy package, but this time the wire was finer and the bomb would explode in ten minutes. From the airport, the hit man flew on a plane made available by another conspirator, which had instructions to wait, engine gunning, for a return flight later that day. A staff car took the staff officers to the thickly wooded Wolf's Lair, with its electrified fences and constant patrols by the SS.

Von Stauffenberg met General Fritz Fellgiebel, chief of signals. His role would be vital in the minutes ahead. He was to shut down all communication with the Wolf's Lair so that no one outside a tiny circle would know what was happening. The hit man then went to Wilhelm Keitel's post to be told that the meeting with the Fuhrer would be short; Benito Mussolini was coming to tea! There had been a time when Il Duce was seen as the senior partner in the Pact of Steel, the alliance between their countries, but a dismal military showing by the Italians had led to a revolution against Mussolini and the country had pulled out of the war. Mussolini himself had been rescued by a daring commando mission carried out by the SS.

Von Stauffenberg seized a quiet moment to set the bomb, using a pair of tongs because of his disabled hand. In ten minutes, the thing would blow. On his way into the conference room, with its 18in-thick concrete walls, he told a telephonist that he would have to nip out to make an urgent call, the same trick he had used before to stay in touch with Olbricht. The room was 30 by 15ft and all the windows were open because the day was stiflingly hot. Everybody was standing around a solid table in the centre, made of thick oak and supported by blocks rather than legs. Himmler and Goering were not there, but the Fuhrer was, fiddling with a magnifying glass now that his eyes were not so good.

The man with the briefcase stood a few feet to Hitler's right. He casually put his briefcase on the floor *inside* the table's supports where the explosion would have most impact. From there, he noted, it would take the Fuhrer's legs off. It was now less than five minutes before impact. General Adolf Heusinger, Deputy Chief of Staff of the Army, was droning on with more bad news from the Front. Colonel Heinz Brandt, his aide, leaned over to see the map more clearly and felt von Stauffenberg's briefcase in the way of his feet. He could not kick it aside so he reached down and moved it to the far side of the support. That unconscious act undoubtedly saved Hitler's life.

Meanwhile, von Stauffenberg was not a suicide bomber. In fact, an essential part of the job was that he report on the mission's success by phone before flying back to Berlin to take part in the putsch. He had made his excuses and left the conference room.

'If our army group around Lake Peipus is not immediately withdrawn, a catastrophe ...' But Heusinger never finished his sentence. At 12.42 the bomb exploded, shattering windows, collapsing the table, blowing bodies and body parts into the air.

A couple of hundred yards away, von Stauffenberg was standing with Fellgiebel, both men waiting for the moment they had planned for so long. The explosion sounded like the roar of a 155mm shell and von Stauffenberg knew that no one in that room could have survived.

He now had to get out to take the good news to Berlin. Obviously, with the explosion, the whole area of the Wolf's Lair was alerted. Von Stauffenberg bluffed a phone call in the first check point and he was waved through. The duty officer even wrote it down in his log – '12.44. Col. [von] Stauffenberg passed through'. The second check point was not so easy and a jobsworth named Kolbe insisted on some kind of clearance. Von Stauffenberg rang the camp's adjutant, claiming that General Fromm was waiting for him at Rastenburg airport (Fromm was, of course, in Berlin). It worked again and the bomber was on his way.

There had been a second bomb, carried by von Haeften in *his* briefcase. On the journey, this was dismantled and thrown on to the roadside. The Gestapo found it later. The flight to Berlin took three hours and during it, because of the technology of the time, von Stauffenberg had no contact with the outside world; not with the Wolf's Lair or Berlin. He just had to hope that Hitler was dead and that Valkyrie was underway.

From Rangsdorf airport, he rang Olbricht. What had happened? Nothing. Fellgiebel had contacted Berlin a little after one o'clock, but the transmission was bad and nobody knew whether Hitler was dead or not. So Valkyrie had been put on hold. Unwilling, because of the failure last time, to act too quickly, Olbricht had let three vital hours slip away. No troops had moved.

At the Wolf's Lair, Hitler's hair had been singed. His eardrums had burst, his legs were burned and his right arm temporarily paralysed. Two men had been killed; two others died later of their wounds. Three more were injured, but all in all, von Stauffenberg's bomb had failed to deliver. Arguably, the highest profile casualty was Field Marshal Alfred Jodl, seriously wounded in the explosion. He was Hitler's chief adviser in the army high command and a committed Nazi. He sanctioned the bombing of civilians and signed orders which led to the shooting of commandos and prisoners of war. He was executed after the Nuremberg trials but, unaccountably, exonerated by a Munich court in 1953 on the grounds that he was not a 'major offender'.

It was two hours before the wild rumours stopped – it was an air raid, it was builders working on the site – and then somebody remembered the sudden disappearance of 'the one-eyed colonel'. It was assumed that the man had flown somewhere behind the Russian lines and that he was acting alone, not the spearhead of a vast conspiracy.

Hitler and Mussolini went on to have tea as planned, the last time they met. It must have been a surreal couple of hours. The pompous, strutting ex-journalist was now a gaunt and defeated wreck; the shell-shocked ex-artist, nursing a damaged arm, deaf as a post and probably suffering from quite advanced Parkinson's disease. They both decided, however, that providence had spared the Fuhrer (again!) and that the end would be triumph for them both.

During this weird tête-à-tête, the German high command were screaming at each other. Admiral Doenitz, who would replace Hitler briefly after his suicide, turned on the army. Goering, head of the Luftwaffe, backed him up and in turn pitched into von Ribbentrop, the foreign minister, for his useless policies, calling him a 'dirty little champagne salesman'. 'I am *still* the Foreign Minister,' he reminded him, 'and my name is *von* Ribbentrop.'

In the middle of it all, Hitler vowed revenge.

We have seen various aftermaths to assassination and attempts in this book, but the Nazis were past masters at it. After Heydrich's murder, the entire town of Lidice was wiped out. In the case of the 20 July Bomb Plot, the net was cast as widely as possible. It quickly became apparent that von Stauffenberg was not a lone agent; his return to Berlin to galvanise the putsch proved that.

General Fromm rang General Keitel at the Wolf's Lair, unaware that Keitel was sitting there with his hair still smoking. 'What has happened at General Headquarters?' Fromm asked. 'Wild rumours are afloat in Berlin.'

'What should be the matter?' Keitel asked. 'Everything is as usual here.'

'I have just received a report,' the increasingly hysterical Fromm said, 'that the Fuhrer has been assassinated.'

'That's all nonsense,' Keitel told him. 'It is true that there has been an attempt, but fortunately it has failed. The Fuhrer is alive and only slightly injured.'

And, almost as an afterthought, he said, 'Where, by the way, is your Chief of Staff, Colonel Count [von] Stauffenberg?'

Von Stauffenberg had been ringing frantically, assuring everybody that Hitler was dead; no one could survive a blast like that. In fact, he said, to bolster the waverers, he had seen his body carried out of the conference room on a stretcher. Fromm now showed his true colours. Always a shaky conspirator, he threw in his lot wholly with the other side, confronting von Stauffenberg and Olbricht and demanding their arrest. Von Stauffenberg and Olbricht demanded his. In the scuffle that followed, Fromm was bundled into an anteroom and the conspirators put a guard around their building.

But nothing else happened. There was no march of troops on the city, no tanks in support. Josef Goebbels' Ministry of Propaganda, the most powerful man in the Reich in the absence of Hitler, Himmler and Goering, was left unmolested and free to set up communications with the Fuhrer who broadcast to the nation over the radio that he was well. Men on the verge of joining the conspiracy melted away like ice in fire. Hitler named von Stauffenberg in his radio message and promised, 'This time we shall settle accounts with [the conspirators] in the manner to which we National Socialists are accustomed.'

Von Stauffenberg, his adjutant von Haeften, General Olbricht and General Erich Hoepner were taken outside the Nazi headquarters building and shot. There was no trial, no attempt to gather evidence. Von Stauffenberg's last words were, 'Long live our sacred Germany!'

A series of kangaroo courts met over the next few days and weeks as the plotters were rounded up. The judge in all cases was Roland Freisler, described by the American journalist William Shirer as a 'vile, vituperative maniac'. All the defendants had been tortured by the SS and shambled into court with their trousers without belts and their shirts spattered with blood. They had not shaved for days. 'Why didn't you join the Party?' Freisler asked Count Peter Yorck. 'Because I am not and never could be a Nazi,' he told him.

On 8 August, the first batch of conspirators was executed. At Ploetzensee prison, eight of them were stripped to the waist in a small room. Piano wire nooses were tightened around their necks and they were hung from meathooks 'borrowed' from local butchers' shops. Their trousers fell down as they writhed, strangling slowly and one of Goebbels' state-of-the-art movie cameras recorded the whole thing. The 'poison dwarf', watching the ghastly event, had to cover his eyes. The reel was sent to Hitler later that day. The film of the trial has survived; that of the executions has not. It was shown to army recruits in the last weeks of the war to bolster morale – most soldiers refused to look at it. At the cadet school at Lichterfelde, they walked out as the reel began.

The total death toll was 4,980 and it included General Fromm, accused of 'cowardice' in not stopping the plot. He was shot by firing squad on 19 March 1945.

But perhaps, after all, there was a God. On 3 February 1945, Fabian von Schlabrendorff, one of the earliest plotters, was stepping into a courtroom to face judge Freisler when an American air raid smashed the building, blowing Freisler to pieces. Von Schlabrendorff lived to tell the tale. Much of what you have read in this chapter comes from him.

Chapter 8

All the President's Men (and Five Women)

'We're nothing but sitting ducks in a shooting gallery.'
Jacqueline Kennedy, 22 November 1963

There was never a more apposite comment than that of Jackie Kennedy on the day that someone murdered her husband in Dallas, Texas. It was a day all of us alive at the time remember and the First Lady's summation of the situation says all we need to know about the targets presented by American presidents – and indeed most of the victims in this book.

The president of the United States is the single most powerful individual in the world and while that was not true of Andrew Jackson, anyone, arguably, from Herbert Hoover onwards fits the bill. James Monroe (president 1817–25) was so concerned for his own safety that he positioned sharpshooters in the trees on the White House site and built an iron wall around it in 1818.

John Tyler (1841–45) had a morbid fear of bombs, not helped by the accidental explosion on board the navy's USS *Princeton*, which blew up in full view of the president and his entire cabinet on the Potomac River. As there was no Secret Service until Teddy Roosevelt's incumbency, Tyler commandeered the Washington Metropolitan Police as an unofficial bodyguard in 1844. When a mysterious package arrived at the White House addressed to the president, trembling aides opened it carefully to discover – a cake!

Andrew Johnson (1865–69) was one of America's most contentious presidents. He had a hard act to follow in that he had been vice president to Abraham Lincoln. Today, he routinely ends up near the bottom of popularity polls for presidents, largely because, as a Southerner, he was seen as too soft on the ex-Confederate states of the South. He was staying at the Indianapolis Hotel in that city when a gunman fired at him. No one was hurt and no arrests were made.

William Meyers may be unique in the annals of would-be assassins because of his motive. When he fired at Rutherford Hayes (1877–81) during his inauguration ceremony on 4 March, it was because *he* wanted to be president instead. There is no doubt that Hayes was deeply unpopular, the media of the day openly calling him 'His Fraudulency' and 'Rutherfraud Hayes' after irregularities in his election. Meyers was literally in a world of his own, however, and spent the rest of his life in institutions.

Chester Arthur (1881–85) was targeted twice. 'Chet' was fired at in the opening months of his administration, or rather, he was not. A deranged gunman mistook a reporter from *The Cincinnati Enquirer* for the president and missed him into the bargain. The second attempt could have been altogether more serious. In 1881, Dr John Noetling of Colesville, Pennsylvania, turned up at the White House and asked to see the president. Such an act would be highly suspicious today and security would mean that such an audience would be impossible, but in 1881, despite the recent assassination of James Garfield, things were rather more laid-back. Noetling was searched, however, and was found to be carrying a seven-bullet revolver with all chambers loaded. Since the carrying of firearms was permitted under the Constitution, there was no proof that Noetling had anything nefarious in mind. Washington DC was as dangerous after dark as any eastern seaboard city. The authorities, satisfied that he was harmless, let Noetling go.

Benjamin Harrison (1889–93) received death threats in the post. He was aloof and too connected to the rich and powerful in the 'Gilded Age' of the Carnegies, Astors, Rockefellers and Vanderbilts. He also made reforms on behalf of Black people, never a popular move south of the old Mason–Dixon line. White House aides covered up the anonymous letters and saw that none of them reached the press, for fear of 'cranks' and, as we would say today, copycats.

There was a similar cover-up in the case of Grover Cleveland (1885–89 and 1893–97). During his second incumbency, Cleveland was having dinner with a friend, Dr Joseph Bryant, at an upmarket New York restaurant. A recently arrived German immigrant barged his way in and pointed a .44 calibre revolver at the president. The gun jammed. When the would-be killer was overpowered, the police were told to 'forever keep your mouth shut', because the incident was 'likely to stir up a large crop of cranks'.

In the incumbency of William Taft (1909–13), as the president was due to travel by Southern Pacific Railroad near Santa Barbara, a routine check of the track found sticks of dynamite. No one was ever linked with this particular attempt.

Woodrow Wilson (1913–21) is revered today as the man who not only brought the United States into the First World War, but created the League of Nations in an attempt to keep lasting peace in Europe. It was not his fault that the project failed. Today, however, his track record in domestic politics is far less impressive. He believed in racial segregation, at a time when such a policy was becoming taboo, and openly enjoyed 'darkie' jokes. There were three attempts to kill him while he was in office. John Rogofsky was declared insane after the first one, but the second, a plot by fourteen men from Hoboken, was regarded as a genuine anarchist outrage; it came to nothing. The third was the oddest of all. In 1918, twenty inmates of Leavenworth prison drew lots to decide who should kill Wilson. The 'lucky' man was Pietro (Sam) Pierre, 'lucky' because the agreement was that if he failed in his task, he would, in turn, be assassinated! Pierre was caught, tried, found guilty and served three and a half years, which for a man intent on murdering a president is laughable. Having failed to kill Wilson, it is not recorded whether Pierre died in mysterious circumstances.

Calvin Coolidge (1923–29) was a difficult man to get to know. 'Silent Cal' was as taciturn as it was possible for a president to be. Journalist H.L. Mencken summed the man up – 'His ideal day is one in which nothing happens.' The attempt on his life, however, took place not on American soil but in Cuba, always a hotbed of intrigue (see Chapter 9). In 1924, during a state visit, two assassins, Spaniard Claudio Bonzon and Russian Noske Yaleb, took rooms in a hotel opposite the president's. The authorities were suspicious and arrested them, but there was virtually no publicity and no trial. In accordance with the Cuban regime's strategy, they were summarily executed by orders of President Gerardo Machado. Both would-be killers were Communists and 1924 was the year in which Vladimir Lenin set up the Union of Soviet Socialist Republics in what would be a long and protracted war between East and West.

Author Mel Ayton has written two books on presidential assassinations and attempts, but the problem with the subject is that it is a fertile ground for lunatic conspiracy theories. In 1861, Abraham Lincoln was riding alone in Washington DC when his stove pipe hat blew off. He assumed it was a gust of wind. When the hat was discovered later, however, a bullet hole was found in it. Lincoln believed it was a freak hunting accident. Much more likely is that it was a stray shot from infantrymen training in the capital. During the American Civil War, Washington DC looked like one huge army camp. Our view of the incident is inevitably coloured by what happened at Ford's Theatre four years later; it *had* to be an assassination attempt.

In the past, everybody, from common-sense White House aides to a media far more responsible than today, looked at such things differently. As an aide told a *Boston Evening Transcript* reporter in September 1901, 'Of the larger number of seemingly suspicious cases, whether alarming or not, are nipped in the bud, little is ever known.'

Herbert Hoover was a target even before his inauguration. In November 1928, he embarked on a goodwill tour of Latin America. Hoover would go on to be a failure as a president because he (along with every other head of state, it should be pointed out) had no clue how to solve the recession into which the world was thrown after the Wall Street Crash of 1929. Before that, however, people had high hopes and as president-elect he made all the right noises. Relations between the United States and Mexico were poor and most South American countries regarded the US with suspicion.

The previous year, two Italian-American anarchists, Nicola Sacco and Bartolomeo Vanzetti, had been executed by order of the Federal government. Their crime, the murder of a guard and theft of a payroll in 1920, was never adequately proven and someone else confessed to it. Nevertheless, the pair were executed in what became a cause célèbre around the world.

One sympathizer determined to do something about the injustice was Severino Di Giovanni, an Italian anarchist who had emigrated to Argentina. Di Giovanni was a force of nature, with a rap sheet of 'activism' as long as anybody's arm. He was a staunch opponent of Fascism, at a time before that phrase was applied to anybody in power, and was arrested in June 1925 for distributing anti-government literature at a state celebration and shouting (ironically) 'Assassins! Thieves!' when the police grabbed him. In May of the following year, he bombed the American embassy in Buenos Aires on hearing of Sacco and Vanzetti's executions. Arrested and tortured, he gave nothing away and was released for lack of evidence. Believing in 'propaganda by the deed' (effectively his battle cry) he blew up a statue of George Washington in Buenos Aires and bombed a Ford factory. When he hit the Bank of Boston in the Argentine capital, he killed two people and injured twenty-seven more. Amazed at the rise of Benito Mussolini in his home country, he bombed the Italian embassy too. His last outrage came just a month before Hoover's visit when Di Giovanni killed newspaper editor Emilio Lopez Aranjo.

In December, as the president-elect's trip continued, the Argentine police uncovered a plot. *Time Magazine* reported it, but mainstream media remained oddly quiet, perhaps because the Hoover administration wanted to keep relations with South America as sweet as possible. Two men and two women were found in an anonymous Buenos Aires slum with bombs, guns and railway maps. President Hipolito Yrigoyen accompanied the Hoovers on much of their visit in an attempt to save their lives. This turned out to be rather ironic as Yrigoyen was himself the target of a failed assassination on Christmas Eve 1919 prior to his regime being overthrown.

The hitman responsible for the would-be attack on Hoover was Alejandro Scarfo, who was jailed for the attempt. Di Giovanni's plan to rescue him failed. What bothered Hoover most in those weeks of terrorism was that his wife Lou (probably the most intelligent First Lady in American history) should not get wind of the anarchists' plots. On one occasion, he tore the front page from a local newspaper so that she missed the headlines (she was a fluent Spanish speaker).

While Scarfo was released from prison in 1935, Di Giovanni was arrested for his bombing campaign and executed by firing squad on 1 February 1931. As he heard the rifle bolts lock, he shouted, 'Viva l'anarchia!' (Long live anarchy).

Several years later, information was unearthed about a second plot to kill Hoover. On 9 November 1932, the president was travelling home to Palo Alto in California by train. In the early hours, security forces had found two men acting suspiciously near the Southern Pacific Railroad track at Palisade, Nevada. A railway engineer noticed several sticks of dynamite and they opened fire in the darkness. Whether they had any links with anarchists or Di Giovanni is unknown.

With hindsight, Franklin Delano Roosevelt (FDR) was one of the best American presidents, routinely coming third after Lincoln and Washington in opinion polls of presidential ratings. He brought in the New Deal, bringing economic security to millions affected by the Slump and stoically led the United States into, if not quite out of, the Second World War. For a man paralysed with polio since his twenties, his success and work rate were astonishing. In his own day, however, not everybody saw things that way. To make the New Deal work, Roosevelt had to ride roughshod at times over state sensibilities, to the extent that both Hitler and Mussolini, the Fascist dictators, publicly congratulated him on his high-handed approach. They were doing much the same in their respective countries.

Just as there was an assassination attempt on Hoover before his inauguration, so there was with FDR. On 15 February 1933, he came back after a twelve-day vacation off Florida aboard the yacht of his friend Vincent Astor. He went ashore on his way to the railway station and stopped off to make an impromptu speech at Bayfront Park, Miami. Just how impromptu this was is anybody's guess, because the local papers carried news of it and at least 10,000 people turned up.

Giuseppe (Joe) Zangara turned up too. He was an unemployed bricklayer who, having served his country in the First World War, emigrated to the United States in 1923. In his pocket, he carried a second-hand revolver that he had bought days before from a pawn shop for $8. As he told a court later, his original plan had been to kill Hoover, whom he blamed, as did many people, for the Recession. The general election had changed all that and Zangara, of course, had no idea how much the new president was going to be a friend of the people.

Roosevelt stood up in the back of his open-topped green Buick. It had specially adapted rear seats so that he could raise himself easily without the aid of crutches or sticks. He gave a short speech and in doing so recognized a face in the crowd. It was Anton (Tony)

Cermek, the mayor of Chicago, who was holidaying in Florida. As Roosevelt invited him over and shook his hand, Zangara fired. The assassin was only 5ft tall and had brought along a rickety collapsible chair to give himself a better shot. His first bullet hit Cermek in the stomach and as he fired the other five, Lilian Cross, a middle-aged woman standing on a bench beside Zangara swung her handbag and knocked the man off balance.

'Too many people are starving!' the killer shouted, as he was engulfed by Secret Service men and the crowd. The panic at that moment was caught on newsreel, the floodlights (it was 9.30 pm) flashing on people surging in Zangara's direction. In accordance with presidential protocol, the Secret Service climbed all over FDR in his car and ordered the driver to get out of there. Roosevelt would have none of it and told the driver to stop, ensuring that Cermek was in the car too. The president-elect held the man in his arms all the way to the hospital.

Despite his height restrictions and the rickety chair, five of Zangara's bullets found their mark, except that none of them was in Roosevelt. One of the women injured died from her injuries, days later.

There was virtually no discussion about insanity. In prison and at his trial on 20 February, Zangara gave lucid answers to police and the press. He had nothing, he said, against FDR personally, but he hated all presidents and anyone who was rich. At Dade County courthouse, the judge sentenced him, once he had been found guilty on four counts, to eighty years in prison. Since he was already in his thirties, that meant life. 'Oh, judge,' he joked as he heard the sentence, 'don't be stingy. Give me a hundred years.'

In fact, it got worse for him. Despite managing a smile for the newsreel cameras from his hospital bed, Tony Cermek died from his injury on 6 March, two days after FDR had been sworn in as the thirty-second president. There was a retrial, because the murder charge demanded it and this time Zangara got the electric chair. Zangara faced the moment stoically, annoyed that movie cameras were not allowed into the death chamber. 'Go ahead,' he said to his executioner. 'Push the button.'

There had always been the whiff of conspiracy around assassinations, even when it appeared that a killer operated alone. In the year of the attempt on FDR there were rumours of a plot to stage a military coup which would, years later, become the basis of the Burt Lancaster and Kirk Douglas thriller *Seven Days in May*. Today, most historians doubt that such a conspiracy ever existed, but that fact that it was Tony Cermek who died was not lost on the natives of Chicago, a city notorious for its organized crime in the era of prohibition. Al Capone, the hoodlum most feared in the city, was in prison on tax evasion charges, but his empire was run by his 'enforcer', Frank Nitti. Almost by definition, the mayor of Chicago would be Nitti's enemy and a likely target for a mob hit. Zangara, however, rejected this entirely; Roosevelt was his target and he was only sorry that he had missed.

'A number of cream-coloured envelopes, almost eight by six inches, arrived in the White House, addressed to the president and various members of staff,' Margaret Truman told the press. More terrifyingly, the president's daughter added, they contained 'powdered gelignite, a pencil battery and a detonator rigged to explode the gelignite when the envelope was opened'.

It was 1947 and the United States was setting up the Marshall Plan and the North Atlantic Treaty Organization, which committed President Harry S. Truman's country to the role of world leader and an assurance that the American isolation of the 1930s would never happen again. It was also the year when the Office of Strategic Services morphed into something altogether more disturbing in the world of assassination – the Central Intelligence Agency.

The letter bombs were believed to be the work of a deranged group of fanatics, Lehi (Fighters for the Freedom of Israel), formed by Avraham Stern in 1940. The ideology of the Zionist movement was so confused that they believed Nazi Germany was less of a threat to Jews than Britain. They wanted to set up a state of Israel with Germany as an ally. Although letter bombs were part of their methodology, it is not clear what the Stern gang, as it was known, had to gain from killing Truman or why they tried it.

The second attempt, on 1 November 1950, was altogether more obvious and more public. During October, terrorists working on behalf of the Puerto Rican National Party had targeted American officials in Puerto Rico in a co-ordinated attack in six towns. There was instant retaliation by the US military, especially in Jaynya, the home town of Griselio Torresola, who promised revenge. Together with Oscar Collazo, the pair took a train from the Bronx to Washington DC, dressed as tourists in smart-casual suits. In their waistbands, under their jackets, Collazo carried a Walther P.38 pistol with an 8-round magazine and Torresola a Luger, also with eight rounds. This was the assassin's weapon par excellence and Torresola, unlike Collazo, was a crack shot.

The pair had stayed overnight in a hotel near Capitol Hill and took a cab to the White House. It is not clear whether they knew that the president was not at home. Extensive refurbishment meant that the Trumans effectively spent the second term at Blair House, a couple of streets away. They got there at about 2.15 pm, by which time, the president was having his customary afternoon nap on the second floor. There were four guards on duty, all White House policemen part of the Secret Service group that protected presidents.

Collazo got behind one of the guards, Donald Birdzell, and fired at him. The gun jammed. His second shot grazed the guard's knee before a fusillade from the front door pumped bullets into Collazo's chest and he went down. On the east side of Blair House, Torresola put three bullets into Leslie Coffelt, who collapsed still holding his gun. The killer emptied his clip into two other guards, then had to reload. As he did so, a bewildered Harry S. Truman stuck his head out of his bedroom window, demanding to know what was going on. The policemen shouted at him to get down, but had it not been for Torresola's reloading, it is highly likely that the president would have died. As it was, Coffelt still had the strength to fire a shot, hitting the assassin in the head and killing him instantly. Leslie Coffelt died from his wounds hours later. His funeral was attended by the president and he remains today the only Secret Service agent to die in the defence of an American president.

Collazo's death sentence was commuted by Truman to life imprisonment and Jimmy Carter reduced that still further during his presidency to time served. Collazo died in Puerto Rico in 1994.

Truman told reporters that it was 'all so unnecessary for a thing like that to have happened', but, amazingly, attempts on his life continued after he left office, in all cases by individuals with personal (and unreasonable) grudges against the man. It led Lyndon B. Johnson in 1965 to extend Secret Service protection for life for ex-presidents, their widows and children under the age of 18. Bearing in mind that in 1950, and as a direct result of the Colazzo-Torresola attack, the powers of the Secret Service were greatly extended, it did not achieve all that much, as six seconds in Dealey Plaza were to prove.

In the list of disgraced presidents, Richard 'Tricky Dicky' Nixon ranks high. An unpleasant oaf in his personal life, he forever destroyed his reputation by not only instigating the Watergate bugging operation, but covering it up and lying about the cover-up. Ironically, the motive given for his attempted murder had little to do with him. Failed businessman Samuel Joseph Byck believed that Nixon was embarked on a campaign to keep America's poor poor. In fact, a number of the president's social welfare bills had been rejected by Congress.

Byck was born to Jewish parents in Philadelphia and dropped out of high school. He served honourably in the army, married and had four children, but in 1972 it all began to go wrong for him. His wife divorced him and he started having blackouts and depression as various business projects failed. He spent two months in a psychiatric clinic and sent threatening tape-recordings to a number of minor politicians, CEOs and the composer Leonard Bernstein. He also tried to join the Black Panthers, who politely pointed out that he was the wrong ethnicity!

Byck was regarded as harmless by the Secret Service, who had often seen him parading with the ever-present string of protestors outside the White House, once in a Santa outfit.

All that changed on 22 February 1974. He had already made a bomb out of two cans of gasoline and taped himself during its production. He intended to kill Nixon by hi-jacking a plane and sending it crashing into the White House. He believed he would be regarded as a hero once the deed was accomplished. It may be that the bizarre stunt by soldier Robert K. Preston in landing a stolen UH-1B Huey helicopter on the White House lawn on 18 February influenced him, just as it is possible that Al Qaeda's attack on New York's Twin Towers was inspired by Byck's work (or at least, his idea) twenty-seven years later.

Byck drove to the Baltimore/Washington Airport and shot and killed Maryland Aviation Administration policeman George Ramsburg. He then jumped on to waiting DC-9 Delta Airlines Flight 523 bound for Atlanta a little after seven o'clock. Holding his .22 rifle to the heads of pilots Reese Loftin and Fred Jones, he told them to take off. They played for time and while Byck was closing the plane's door, radioed the control tower for help. When they came out with excuses for why they could not take off, Byck shot them both. Then he grabbed a terrified female passenger and ordered her to fly the plane.

Airport police fired at the aircraft's tyres, but the .38 calibre Smith and Wesson bullets failed to pierce the rubber. In the ensuing shootout, patrolman Charles Troger fired four bullets from Ramsburg's fallen .357 Magnum, two of which hit Byck. He went down inside the plane and shot himself in the head before the police had time to reach him.

Clearly, Nixon, miles away and unaware, was never in the line of fire and the incident was dryly noted as one of several routinely listed by the Secret Service, albeit a potentially dangerous one. Reese Loftin survived the shooting and carried on flying but Fred Jones died within minutes. In 2004, a movie was produced, *The Assassination of Richard Nixon*, starring Sean Penn as Byck.

Gerald Ford has a reputation for stupidity that will probably never go away. Lyndon Johnson famously summed him up with – 'nice guy, but he played too much football with his helmet off'. In a rather more vicious mood, he claimed that Ford could not 'fart and chew gum at the same time'. He was the only president other than Joe Biden to fall up the steps of Air Force One, the presidential jet. He was briefly vice president to Richard Nixon who said to a White House aide in the Oval Office, 'Can you imagine Jerry Ford sitting in that chair?' His performance as part of Earl Warren's Commission into the Kennedy assassination was lamentable. He said little, but went along with what any sane American recognized as a whitewash. And on 5 September 1975, someone tried to kill him.

He was walking through crowds in the park surrounding the California State Capitol building in Sacramento, shaking hands and waving to the crowd, when 26-year-old Lynette Alice Fromme, dressed in red, poked her hand between people in front of her and fired her M1911 pistol at Ford from less than 20 feet away. People heard a loud click and Secret Service agent Larry Buendorf grabbed gun and girl, forcing Fromme to the ground. 'It didn't go off!' she shouted. 'Can you believe it? It didn't go off!' The Secret Service were all over Ford, to the extent that he had to ask them to put him down and went on to a planned meeting with California's governor, Jerry Brown. He did not mention the assassination attempt.

It turned out that Lynette Fromme had 'previous'. A high school dropout who became hooked on drugs as a teenager, she left home and drifted to San Francisco in 1967, the 'summer of love'. She met a social misfit and ex-jailbird, Charles Manson, with whom she became (along with several other young people) obsessed. Manson was fifteen years older than most of his acolytes and posed both as Jesus and the Devil, playing bad rock music and living the hippy commune life at the Spahn Ranch, an old Hollywood movie set in the desert. Manson was a racist and misogynist of epic proportions, 'prophesying' that the world was about to undergo 'Helter Skelter' when a race war would break out between Blacks and Whites. The women at the ranch, like Fromme, were menials, cooking, cleaning and scavenging for food in supermarket dumpsters. They also had to do Manson's bidding and be ready for sex at any time.

The whole weird world came crashing down in 1969 and 1970 with the Manson 'Family's' murder of the actress Sharon Tate and her friends while her husband, film producer Roman Polanski, was away. Fromme was not part of this murderous group of four who butchered the residents of the villa in Cielo Drive, but it is incredible that she did not know about it, at least as an accessory after the fact.

During Manson's trial for the Tate–LaBianca murders, Fromme camped outside the courtroom with other Family members, with a cross carved into her forehead. After the killers' imprisonment, she acted as a go-between and served time in 1971 for tampering with the evidence given by Barbara Hoyt, another Family member.

The attack on Ford was, according to her, all about the environment. Manson had called her 'Red', both because of her hair and her love of the giant California Redwoods (which explains her scarlet outfit on 5 September 1975). She wanted to highlight California's appalling smog problem and the effects of pollution on wildlife. She must be one of the most disturbed eco-warriors on record. During her trial, she refused to co-operate in any way and threw an apple at the district attorney who was prosecuting her. She was sentenced to life.

Subsequently, Fromme claimed to have had no intention of killing Ford, but it is far more likely that she did not understand the mechanism of her Colt-Browning M1911 which explains her shouts when it did not fire. She was certainly capable of violence; witness her attack on a fellow inmate in prison in 1979 and the fact that she was released over the murders of James and Lauran Willett in 1972 only because of lack of evidence.

Lynne Fromme, known as 'Squeaky' among the family, was paroled in 2009 and wrote a book on her experiences, published nine years later. There is no doubt that it was the 'Helter Skelter' years that formed the narrative of her life, not her attack on the president. When asked in a television interview in 2019 whether she had been in love with Charlie Manson, she said, 'Yeah. I still am.'

No doubt it was Fromme's notoriety and the fact that a *woman* had become an assassin, that led a copycat to turn up seventeen days after the first attack. Ford was in San Francisco for a World Affairs Council, walking along Post Street to his limo and just passing the St Francis Hotel when two shots rang out. One bullet hit the wall about 5 inches above the president's head, the other slammed into the groin of John Ludwig, a taxi-driver waiting for a fare. San Francisco police captain Timothy Hettrich leapt on the assassin as the Secret Service bundled Ford into his car with Secretary of State Donald Rumsfeld lying across him. Alongside Hettrich was bystander Oliver Sipple, whose reactions were even faster than the policeman's.

The would-be killer was an unlikely assassin. She was 45-year-old Sara Jane Moore, a former nurse who had four children and had been married five times. She had become obsessed with Patty Hearst, of the immensely rich press family, who had been kidnapped and had 'gone native' by taking part in her captors' raids on banks. She had obtained a .38 calibre Police Special revolver and this was the gun she used on Ford. Sentenced to life, like Fromme, Moore claimed that she wanted to bring about change in America through violent revolution. She was paroled in 2007. Gerald Ford's one concession to security after these two hits was to wear a special bulletproof overcoat in public.

Who would want to kill President Jimmy Carter? The quick answer is: no one. The president made mistakes as they all do and he served only one term, but there was little in his administration, either domestic or foreign policy, which could be seen as particularly contentious.

In 1979, shortly before Carter was due to speak at a Cinco de Mayo festival at Los Angeles' Civic Centre Mall, Secret Service agents arrested a suspicious-looking drifter who was standing 50 feet from Carter's podium. He was carrying a .22 calibre gun and had seventy rounds of ammunition. The problem was that it was a harmless starter pistol, of the type used on an athletics track. The other problem was the gunman's name – Raymond Lee Harvey. He was 35, from Ohio and had a history of mental illness.

In custody, he confessed to being a decoy. He would first fire his fake gun at Carter while two real hitmen, staying in a nearby hotel, would do the actual killing. And that led to a second name problem – 21-year-old Osvaldo Ortiz was detained by the police and admitted to testing the starter pistol with Harvey the night before the planned shooting.

The authorities checked every possible angle but could find no believable motive other than a wicked sense of humour and the need in some people to find fifteen minutes' worth of fame.

The names said it all. At least half the world in 1979 still believed that it was Lee Harvey Oswald who had killed John F. Kennedy in

Dallas in November 1963. That was the most shocking presidential murder in history and America still vividly remembered it in the Carter administration. Whether Raymond Lee Harvey and Osvaldo Ortiz were the pranksters' actual names was never verified.

The odd thing about the Carter assassination attempt that was not is that he really did pass within feet of a man who intended to kill him but the assassin changed his mind and went to shoot another president instead. His name was John Hinckley Jr and his eventual target was Ronald Reagan.

Reagan came to be regarded as a joke president, a former Hollywood B-feature Western star often referred to by his enemies as 'the *acting* President of the United States'. In fact, he was a lot shrewder than many believed, a tough, hard-line conservative whose policies chimed very well with those of Margaret Thatcher in Britain. When he began to show signs of dementia, he passed actual decision-making to his three secretaries of state and continued to make speeches, as suave and Brylcremed as ever.

John Hinckley Jr did not have a political motive to kill either Carter or Reagan. He did it for love. Or at least, that is the polite way of putting it. Journalist Simon Heffer calls him an 'erotomaniac', obsessed as he was with the Hollywood starlet Jodie Foster, who played a 12-year-old prostitute in Martin Scorcese's *Taxi Driver* (1976) while still at school. Robert De Niro plays a hitman obsessed with killing a president, a persona based on Arthur Bremer who had shot and crippled George Wallace, the racist governor of Alabama, in May 1972.

As has become a pattern in this book, Hinckley was a drifter with a complicated psyche and too much time on his hands. He was the son of an oil executive, and was 25 years old on 20 March 1981 when he fired at Reagan. His family had given him everything and ironically, he had been brought up in what most of the world saw as the shrine of assassination, Dallas, Texas. He attended Texas Tech University intermittently but never qualified. Bored and listless, he toyed with joining the National Socialist Party of America, a Neo-Nazi outfit of misfits generally too young to understand the implications of Adolf Hitler's regime (see Chapter 7). Ironically, the party had kicked Hinckley out on account of his 'violent temper'.

In October 1980, Hinckley was in Nashville, Tennessee, during a visit by Jimmy Carter. Routine airport surveillance discovered that he had ammunition and three handguns in his luggage. Those were confiscated and he was given a $62.50 fine. No further action was taken and once again, we face the mindset of American authorities in obeisance to the Second Amendment of the Constitution – the right to bear arms. Nowhere in that document does it give citizens the right to shoot presidents, but the mere carrying of a weapon is a very minor crime, if a crime at all. Four days later, Hinckley was back in Dallas buying two .22 calibre guns in 'Rocky's' pawn shop. For the technically minded, what would become a potential murder weapon was a snub-nosed 'Saturday night special', a Rohm RG14 22LR revolver (see Appendix).

The killer's infatuation with Foster is a matter of record. She was a very intelligent girl, attending Yale University, and Hinckley wrote to her at least four times. Somehow, he got her phone number (in the days before mobiles) and we still have their conversations on tape. He tells her he loves her and she is icy cold, firm and polite, telling him to leave her alone. It must have been a terrifying experience for an 18-year-old but one perhaps that Hollywood starlets have to live with.

One letter, dated 30 March 1981, 12.45 read:

Dear Jodie. There is a definite possibility that I will be killed in my attempt to get Reagan. It is for this reason that I am writing to you now ... although we talked on the phone a couple of times, I never had the nerve to simply approach you and introduce myself ... Jodie, I would abandon this idea of getting Reagan in a second if I could only win your heart and live out the rest of my life with you, whether it be in total obscurity or whatever. I will admit to you that the reason I'm going ahead with this attempt now is because I just cannot wait any longer to impress you. I've got to do something now to make you understand ... that I'm doing all this for your sake. By sacrificing my freedom and possibly my life, I hope to change your mind about me.

This letter was found in Hinckley's apartment after the events that took place less than two hours after he wrote it. Like the Kennedy assassination, caught on film by Dallas dressmaker Abraham Zapruder, Hinckley's attempt on Reagan was caught on at least three television cameras. He was walking, with aides and security around him, out of the President's Walk, from the Washington Hilton hotel when shots rang out. One moment, the president was waving to the crowd, the next he was down, Secret Service agents with drawn guns shielding his body with their own on the pavement. One of the clichés used in the scripts of umpteen cop dramas, British as well as American, is, 'It all happened so fast.' Because of that, no one was certain how many times Hinckley fired, anything between four and six.

In fact, he fired all six shots in an estimated 1.7 seconds. The first bullet hit James Brady, the president's press secretary, in the head. The ammunition was of the Devastator type, 'dum-dum' bullets that exploded on impact, causing maximum damage. The shot hit Brady above his left eye, shattering his brain cavity. It was the only one of the six bullets to explode as it was supposed to. Astonishingly, the pressman survived, but he never walked properly again and was hospitalized for months. The second shot hit Thomas K. Delahanty in the neck, just as he was turning to the sound of the first. He fell on to Brady, mumbling, 'I'm hit.' Alfred Antenucci, a harbour official from Cleveland, pummelled the shooter in the head and dragged him down, but not before all six rounds had been fired. Shot number three hit the wall above Reagan's head. Number four punctured the lung and diaphragm of Secret Service agent Timothy J. McCarthy, who leapt into Hinckley's line of fire to save the president's life. The fifth shot hit 'Stagecoach', the Secret Service code for the presidential limousine, as did the sixth, but it was this bullet, ricocheting off the metal, that hit 'Rawhide' (Reagan).

Secret Service agent James Parr pushed the president into Stagecoach so hard that Reagan thought the pain in his chest was caused by the shove. As they roared away from the scene, it became obvious that the president had been hit. The bullet had smashed a rib, entering under his left armpit and he was having difficulty breathing. A quick-thinking Parr re-routed the car to the nearest hospital, George Washington Memorial, four minutes away.

When they got there, there were no stretchers available, so Reagan walked in unaided. Inside he collapsed on to one knee. Close behind him was his doctor, Daniel Ruge, who thought the 70-year-old was having a heart attack. Unaccountably, some of the hospital staff did not recognize Reagan until he gave his address as 1600 Pennsylvania Avenue! He complained about the medics who set about cutting him out of his $1,000 suit. His blood pressure was 60, as opposed to the 140 it should have been, but as he was being prepared for surgery, he was able to quip with medical staff. He passed a note to a nurse, quoting one of his favourite lines from comedian W.C. Fields – 'All in all, I'd rather be in Philadelphia.' When his distraught wife Nancy (code named Rainbow) arrived from the White House, he delivered another quotation, this time misquoting the boxer Jack Dempsey – 'Honey, I forgot to duck!' When faced with a line-up of masked doctors and nurses, he said, 'I hope you are all Republicans.' Dr Joseph Giordano, a Democrat, replied, 'Today, Mr President, we are *all* Republicans.'

Outside events at the George Washington, an unseemly row broke out between Vice President George Bush and Secretary of State Alexander Haig as to what should happen next and who should run the country. Technically, it was Bush, but he was in Texas at the time and Haig was in the White House. For a whole day, he gave interviews and press releases until Bush was in place.

Americans who remembered Dallas in 1963 and Martin Luther King and Bobby Kennedy in 1968, were shocked all over again. There was superstitious talk in the media of the 'curse of Tippecanoe', a reference to an obscure battle against the Native Americans in William Harrison's administration (1840–41). The legend ran that the Shawnee chief Tecumseh put a curse on Harrison and any other president sworn in in an '0' year. Harrison himself died of pneumonia. Lincoln (1860), Garfield (1880) and Kennedy (1960) were all assassinated. Harding (1920) was a near-victim.

Jodie Foster pulled out of Yale for a term and had a bodyguard for the rest of her time there. She spoke of Hinckley rarely during her subsequent film career, occasionally refusing interviews when the subject came up. Hinckley faced trial on 21 June 1982, the prosecution believing him sane, the defence otherwise. In the event – and to the outrage of most of America – he was declared 'not guilty by reason of insanity'. The old M'Naghten defence still ran 140 years after it was laid down, but several states amended it in their own legislations and three refused to accept it altogether. In 1988, against the advice of the Secret Service, Hinckley was due to be released into his mother's custody, subject to strict scrutiny. It was discovered, however, that he was in correspondence with Ted Bundy, the serial killer awaiting execution and the process was delayed until 2006.

As for Reagan, he continued in office until 1989 and today ranks high in the list of presidential popularity, credited (a little generously perhaps) with ending the Cold War which (in theory at least) makes assassinations less likely.

George H. Bush is possibly unique in presidential annals as the only incumbent of the White House to face an assassination attempt *after* he left office, and the plot itself was mired in controversy. On 14 April 1993 (Bush left the top job in January), the ex-president was due to visit Kuwait for a celebration of the Gulf War victory. The previous day, Kuwaiti authorities foiled a three-pronged attack using bombs. The first phase of this was a series of devices planted in cars at Kuwait International Airport and if they failed, another car bomb was to go off at Kuwait University, where Bush was to be given an honorary doctorate. If that failed too, the third phase was that most devastating killing mechanism, the suicide bomber.

As we saw in Chapter 3, the most dangerous assassins are those who have no fear of being caught. To Islamic fundamentalists in particular, death is merely part of a bigger process, by which the killer will be rewarded in paradise. What was extraordinary about the attempt on Bush was that sections of Iraqi Intelligence were involved, rather than a religious sect. Fourteen defendants faced trial and all but one were convicted, but that was not enough for President Bill Clinton. On 26 June, he ordered the firing of three Tomahawk missiles from USS *Peterson* to hit Iraqi Intelligence Headquarters building. The place was destroyed, along with several civilian casualties.

When it comes to the presidency of Bill Clinton himself (1993–2001) we have entered what I call the age of hysteria, where millions of the easily offended take umbrage at the most innocuous of circumstances and believe that there is a conspiracy lurking behind every corner.

The first of two attempts on Clinton was traditional and straightforward, but it was what lay behind the shooting that proves that the world has gone mad. On 29 October 1994, 26-year-old ex-soldier Francisco Duran was mingling with the usual crowd of protestors outside the grounds of the White House that fronted on to the North Lawn. It was six weeks since Frank Corder had deliberately crashed his Cessna aircraft into the South Lawn, more or less to prove that it could be done.

A group of men in suits emerged from the White House and stood talking on the gravel. Duran was sure that one of them was Clinton and he whipped out his SKS semi-automatic rifle from under his trench coat and opened fire. Three others in the small crowd leapt on him and beat him to the pavement as Secret Service agents hurtled across the lawn to arrest him. At no time was the president in danger; he was watching a football game on television inside.

At the trial that followed, Duran faced four counts, including the attempted murder of the president and assault on Secret Service officers. The defendant, born in Albuquerque, New Mexico, had enlisted in the army to avoid imprisonment for offences as a teenager. An unremarkable soldier, he was dishonourably discharged in 1990 for a drunken brawl with civilians and served two and a half years in gaol. In common with the vast majority of would-be assassins we have met in this book, Duran pleaded not guilty by reason of insanity. He had been trying to save the world by destroying an alien mist attached by an umbilical cord to an alien in the Colorado Mountains. The prosecution produced sixty witnesses who testified that Duran had repeatedly criticized the government and Clinton in particular. The jury took less than five hours to find Duran guilty and he was sentenced to forty years; his release date will be 2029.

Almost immediately after the shooting, the trolls of conspiracy theory came out from under the bridge with what they called the Clinton Body Count. According to this proposition, both Bill Clinton and his wife Hillary are guilty of the murders or attempted murders of at least fifty political opponents. Currently these include: John F. Kennedy Jr, who died in a plane crash; Jeffery Epstein, the paedophile who hanged himself in prison; Shito Abe, the prime minister of Japan; and Her Majesty Queen Elizabeth II! Since this collection is made up of people who were not the Clintons' political opponents and since the list has continued to grow even after Clinton left office, we can see that the Body Count conspiracy is total nonsense. Needless to say, Donald Trump mentioned it to the press during his presidential campaign against Hillary Clinton.

The second attempt on Bill Clinton's life happened on 24 November 1996, although details were not revealed until 2009. The president was on a visit to Manila, due to speak to the Asia-Pacific Economic Co-operation Forum and his motorcade was running late. Lew Merletti, in charge of the Secret Service detail, heard a garbled, crackling radio message in his headphones. He made out the words 'bridge' and 'wedding'. There was at least one bridge on the motorcade's route and 'wedding' was the code name for assassination. After a few heated, expletive-ridden words with Clinton, the motorcade took a different route and all was well. Explosives were found under the Jones Bridge, enough, it was calculated, to destroy the whole entourage. No one took responsibility but it was decided that the group most probably responsible was Osama bin Laden's Al Qaeda terrorists.

In the clash between Clinton and Merletti, law (and common sense) was on Merletti's side. It is one of the very few instances when a security chief can legitimately override the will of the American commander-in-chief.

There were three attempts on the life of George W. Bush, although given the lightness of the sentences dished out against the perpetrators, it is difficult to know how seriously anybody took them (see Obama below). On 7 February 2001, Robert W. Pickett fired several shots with a Taurus .38 special revolver 'in the general direction' of the White House. He was shot in the knee by a Secret Service agent and arrested. He was charged with discharging a firearm in public, which carries a ten-year sentence, but this was far below the recognized level of attempted murder of the president. The United States has the disgraceful legal nicety of the Alford plea, which means that a defendant does not admit guilt, but accepts that in a court, the weight of evidence would find him guilty. Interestingly, military courts do not accept this mitigation; neither do the states of Indiana, Michigan and New Jersey. This was the plea deal that Pickett took, serving three years in the Federal Medical Centre in Rochester (specifically for those with healthcare issues) and a further three years' probation.

Four years later, an attack was made on Bush in Freedom Square, Tbilisi, Georgia, where the president was making a speech. Vladimir Arutyunian, a native Georgian, threw an RGD-5 hand grenade at Bush's podium. It bounced off a girl in the crowd and landed 20 feet away. Because it had been wrapped in a handkerchief as concealment in the crowd, it failed to detonate. The would-be killer got away, but was caught later and given life imprisonment after his trial.

Perhaps the most bizarre attempt in this book took place on 14 December 2008 when Muntadhar al-Zaidi threw both his shoes at Bush during an Iraqi press conference. Both shoes missed, but one hit the American flag. Al-Zaidi was sentenced to three years in prison but he was released by order of an Iraqi court in September 2009 because he had no previous criminal record.

Social media had come of age by 2008 and bizarre and ill-informed comments flooded the Internet, to be turned into 'truth' by the gullible and deranged. One Facebook comment said, 'Let's kill Bush with Shoes'. Another spoke of 'The Shooing of the President'.

In the case of Barack Obama, who took office in January 2009, there are so many incidents that not only do we have to categorize them according to seriousness, but we have to decide where a threat ends and a genuine assassination attempt begins – and that is by no means easy.

Threatening the president is a federal felony under US Code Title 18 Section 871. It covers 'knowingly and wilfully' mailing or otherwise making 'any threat to take the life of, to kidnap, or to inflict great bodily harm to the President of the United States'. That in itself is vague to the point of inanity and scores of overpaid lawyers in America have quibbled over the exact meaning of 'knowingly' and 'wilfully' for years. There are hundreds of such threats every year, all of them investigated by the FBI or the Secret Service. The motivation behind them, as one federal executive put it, is that 'sometimes they disagree with his policies, but most often just because he is the president'.

With Barack Obama, the causation was almost always racial. He was the first African American to be elected to the White House in history. And no Black man in America has ever been accorded so much prestige and so much power. This alone was enough for the rednecks of the white supremacy movement to want him dead. As person said on Twitter, 'The next American with a clear shot should drop Obama like a bad habit.' Another seemed more concerned about policy. 'As I promised in a previous post, if the healthcare reform bill passed, I would become a terrorist. Today [2010] I became a terrorist.'

Has the man who objected to a fair, rational and humane change in America's crypto-criminal healthcare program actually carried out a terrorist act? Has he tried to kill Obama, who brought in the legislation? We cannot know, because of the imbecilic anonymity of the Internet.

One thing is disturbingly true, however. Of the hundreds of such threats a year that can be properly investigated, 75 per cent of them are made by people who are mentally ill. As, I think, were the couple from South Carolina my wife and I met on a holiday recently. We were discussing healthcare problems and what Britain has done since 1948 with the creation of the National Health Service. At one point, the South Carolinian said, horrified, 'You love Obama!' Before we could answer, his wife dropped to her knees – 'Then we're gonna pray for you!'

As we saw in a previous chapter, in various countries and at times of national insecurity, casual bar-room/locker room banter becomes a treasonable offence carrying severe penalties. It was like that in Oliver Cromwell's England in the seventeenth century, Winston Churchill's Britain and Adolf Hitler's Germany, both in the 1940s. The administration of Barack Obama was a peaceful one, although it was, perhaps, a little odd that the man should be given a Nobel Peace Prize while his country was involved in not one but two international military operations.

At the bottom of the heap in the sense of the least actual risk to the president comes from Scranton, Pennsylvania in October 2008. Sarah Palin was leading a rally and when (inevitably) she mentioned Obama's name, someone yelled, 'Kill him!' No one was arrested. On 19 September 2014, an Iraqi War veteran, Omar Gonzalez, jumped over the White House fence and was stopped by Security Services at the front door. He was carrying a knife, but investigation revealed no solid motivation and he was charged with carrying a concealed weapon, which many saw as far too lenient. Another military veteran, this time from the air force, made threats over the phone in April 2017. He was 59-year-old Stephen Taubert from Syracuse, New York and he rang his senator, Al Franken, threatening to hang Obama. In court, he apologized for the foul language. 'That's all it was. It does get me upset when I listen to the news and they attack President Donald Trump. He's a good person …' As the judge pointed out before sentencing Taubert to forty-six months in federal prison, 'Racial threats to kill present and former public officials are not protected free speech, but serious crime.'

Possibly in the same category, but with an altogether nastier streak in it, was the threat made by a terrorist only known as Lee, a Korean who posted letters on the White House website in July 2015, promising to kill Obama, the South Korean ambassador Mark Lippert (who had already been injured in an actual shooting), and to rape Obama's younger daughter, 14-year-old Sasha. Lee was arrested in July 2016, but four years later, the Supreme Court of Korea overturned his sentence on the incomprehensible grounds of 'insufficient evidence'.

Arguably in the more dangerous category of offences came seven cases between 2008 and 2015. On 15 July 2008, a couple sitting in the North Carolina Waffle House in Charlotte, NC, overheard an extraordinary conversation involving Jerry Blanchard, a local accountant, who said, 'Obama and his wife are never going to make it to the White House. He needs to be taken out and I can do it in a heartbeat.' Interviewed by the Secret Service, Blanchard denied any such pronouncement, but admitted that he thought Obama was the Antichrist. Clearly, the accountant was very talkative because customers in Charlotte's Crown Plaza Hotel heard him planning to kill Obama with a sniper's rifle he intended to buy from Hyatt's gun shop in the town. Mr Hyatt told the Secret Service agents that Blanchard had indeed visited, but had bought nothing. In June 2009, because there was no evidence of 'furtherance of a crime', the accountant was given a gaol sentence of one year and one day and slapped with a $3,000 fine.

Later that month, Raymond H. Geisel made threats against Obama during a training course to become a bail-bondsman in Miami. 'If he gets elected, I'll assassinate him myself.' Despite the Secret Service finding ammunition, an axe, tear gas, body armour and a loaded 9mm pistol in Geisel's possession, he took a plea bargain in August and got a mere three years supervised probation.

October proved to be a busy month for those with a grudge against President Obama. A much bigger conspiracy was uncovered by the Secret Service on 22 October when two white supremacists, Paul Schlesselman and Daniel Cowart, were arrested for a plot to kill eighty-eight African Americans, intending to decapitate fourteen of them, at an unspecified, predominantly Black, high school in

Tennessee. At the end of this spree would come the murder of Obama. The pair bragged of firing shots at a Black church in Brownsville in the state (the scene of racial violence since the 1890s) and with a 66 per cent Black population. Both were sentenced to fourteen years in federal prison.

The title of this chapter refers to five women, proving that assassination and attempts are largely male crimes. Two of the five were those who shot at Gerald Ford; Kristy Lee Roshia was a third. The 35-year-old had a history of making threatening calls to the Secret Service before 10 November 2009 when she rang the Boston office. She planned to 'blow away' the entire Obama family while they were holidaying in Honolulu for Christmas, plus any US Marines who got in the way. She had made similar threats against George W. Bush. She was apprehended 2 miles from the Obama residence in Hawaii, resisting arrest and smashing a Secret Service agent in the face. She underwent a mental competency test in February 2010 and was sentenced in January 2012. There, she disappears from the public record.

The same cannot be said of Mitchell Kusick, who was arrested by the Secret Service in October 2012 after his therapist reported that his client had been tracking the president with intent to kill him. He was diagnosed with 'severe mental illness' and served nine months in a psychiatric facility before being released into the custody of his parents, both psychotherapists!

Three more would-be killers who have vanished from the record were arrested in a plot to kill Obama in February 2015. All from New York, their leader was Abdurasul Juraboev from Uzbekistan. Their plan was to hijack an aircraft, à la the notorious attack on the Twin Towers fourteen years earlier, drop bombs on Coney Island, the seaside attraction outside New York and to kill the president. Their aim was to join Islamic State (ISIS) and turn themselves into martyrs. The Obama administration at first downplayed the lethal capabilities of this group, but they clearly meant business. A video was sent to the White House the previous year showing a British jihadist holding a knife to the throat of Steven Sotloff, an American journalist, with the chilling commentary, 'The life of this American citizen, Obama, depends on your next decision.' The president did not get tough until 2014 when he promised on television, 'We will degrade and ultimately destroy [ISIS] through a comprehensive and sustained counter-terrorism strategy.' To some, he was signing his own death warrant. There appears to be a blackout on news of these three, as nothing is available online.

Threats of an altogether more dangerous kind began in August 2008 when three men came to Denver, Colorado, to kill Barack Obama at his Democratic Party acceptance rally. Tharin Gartrell, Shawn Adolf and Nathan Johnson had a truck loaded with weapons and drugs. All were agreed that Adolf was the instigator, but the authorities believed that an assassination attempt was unlikely to succeed, so the three were charged with weapons and drug offences.

Towards the end of the year, a vicious criminal element got involved. In what appeared to be a typical 'domestic', one of hundreds handled by law enforcement officers in the United States, Amber Cumings shot and killed her abusive husband James in Belfast, Maine, on 9 December. In a routine search of the marital home, local police found child porn on Cumings' computer, links to the United States National Party, a neo-Nazi operation and, most disturbingly of all, the makings of a 'dirty' bomb. Further investigation by the FBI uncovered a plot to kill Obama during his inauguration ceremony (traditionally held outdoors). Given the wealth of evidence against Cumings, who had been abusing his daughter as well as his wife, the judge gave Amber a suspended sentence 'due to extenuating circumstances'.

In an attempt at assassination that would never be accepted by a television drama producer, Glenn Crawford and Eric Freight of upstate New York were arrested in June 2013 in a plot to kill Muslims and the president using a 'death ray' machine which would release deadly doses of radiation. The FBI had sent an undercover agent to work with Crawford and they uncovered links to the Ku Klux Klan, only too keen to eliminate Muslims. Crawford had also been in touch with local synagogues to help the pair eliminate 'Israel's enemies'. The response from the synagogues was less enthusiastic, to the point of the correspondence being passed to law enforcement. The death ray machine itself would probably not have worked, but the authorities took this conspiracy seriously and sentenced both men to thirty years in federal prison.

A month earlier, the nerve agent ricin had appeared in letters sent to the president and other White House staff. Enter the fourth and final woman in the list of presidential assassins. She was television B-feature actress Shannon Richardson, best known perhaps for her minor role in *The Walking Dead* series and was going through a messy divorce. She at first claimed that her husband had sent the ricin letters, then that he had forced her to send them. The letters themselves referred to the 'God-given' (i.e. constitutional) right to bear arms. Richardson is currently serving time in Fort Worth, Texas, under a plea agreement and is due for release in 2028.

On 11 November 2011, Oscar Ortega-Hernandez was sitting in his car parked in Constitution Avenue when he poked his Cugir semi-automatic rifle through the window and fired seven shots, all of them spraying the walls of the White House. Obama was not there at the time and no one was injured. Ortega-Hernandez was arrested five days later in Indiana, Pennsylvania. As with Jerry Blanchard, the would-be assassin claimed that the president was the Antichrist and the Devil. In an astonishing piece of brass neck, even by American legal standards, Ortega-Hernandez's lawyers objected to 'terrorism enhancement' included in the indictment, even though, as part of his plea agreement, the would-be killer had admitted to that. Again, the charge ended up as damage to property and the discharging of a firearm. He was sentenced to twenty-five years in prison on 31 March 2012.

In some ways, the most dangerous potential attack on Obama came in 2012, when four soldiers from Georgia plotted to kill the president. Umpteen examples exist throughout history of military men acting as assassins, often in the elite bodyguard of a ruler. They have the training to kill, a familiarity with weapons and often a warped antipathy to those who give them orders. During the Vietnam War, a number of officers were blown sky high by 'fragging', disturbed members of platoons rolling grenades around army barracks. Privates Isaac Aguigui, Michael Barnett and Christopher Salmon, along with Sergeant Anthony Peden had joined a terrorist group within the army called FEAR (Forever Enduring, Always Ready). Their plan was to take over their base, Fort Stewart, bomb various targets and kill Barack Obama.

By the time the plot was uncovered, the group had already begun a murderous campaign. Michael Barnett had killed ex-soldier Michael Roark and his girlfriend Tiffany York in 2011 because they knew too much about FEAR. Isaac Aguigui had already strangled his wife Dierdre, claiming that the murder was a result of a robbery gone wrong, and used the insurance money to set up FEAR itself. Had the four remained loyal, it would have been a difficult case to crack, but Michael Barnett was not 'forever enduring'; instead, he turned state's evidence against the others. He was given an eight-year sentence followed by forty years supervision and the others got life without parole.

The pattern of threats which *could* have escalated into assassination attempts continued under Donald Trump who took over the White House in January 2017. After the benign regime of Barack Obama,

Trump was a polarising whirlwind who made the jaws of the world drop in disbelief.

Like Obama, the threats began even before the election. On 18 June 2016, while 'The Donald' was making a speech at Treasure Island Hotel, Las Vegas, Nevada, a member of the audience, 20-year-old British student Michael Sandford, tried to grab the pistol of an on-duty policeman. He was duly arrested and handed over to the Secret Service. He admitted that he planned to kill Trump and would do so again, given the chance. He was sentenced to a year and a day in prison and deported on release back to Britain.

Three days before the election, Trump was speaking in Reno, New Mexico, when someone in the crowd screamed 'Gun!' This simple word is universal among security staff of all persuasions to leap into action and for bystanders to duck. Austyn Crites, 33, was whisked away by the Secret Service and was found to be unarmed. He represented the 'Republicans v. Trump' group, a reminder of how hopelessly divisive American politics has become. Another reminder was the hoo-ha made over this minor incident by the Trump camp, especially Donald Jr, who built it up in the media into a full-blown assassination attempt.

Gregory Lee Levingay was not playing around when he stole a forklift truck from an oil refinery in Mandan, North Dakota, in September 2017. His aim was to use the vehicle to ram the president's motorcade and flip his car. However, he could not get the forklift out of the refinery grounds. Suffering a 'serious psychiatric crisis', he was given a twenty-year sentence.

The last two threats/attempts of the Trump administration hang in the air with no resolution that I can find online. On 1 October 2018, envelopes containing ricin were posted to Trump and various Pentagon staff. All were labelled 'Jack and the Missile Bean Stock Powder'. Two days later, 39-year-old William Allen III, a navy veteran from Utah, was arrested and charged. He pleaded not guilty and there the story ends.

Perhaps it is fitting that the last terrorist/assassin in this chapter should be a woman. Her name was Pascale Ferrier and she was a 53-year-old Canadian. On 20 September 2020 it was found that she had sent Trump a ricin-laced letter telling him to pull out of the election race. She called the president an 'ugly tyrant clown' and in court faced eight counts relating to biological weapons and inter-state threats. The last report on her online is that she is looking at life imprisonment.

There is no doubt that the number of threats and possible assassination attempts on American presidents has increased over the past twenty years. We have come a long way from the unbelievable shock felt worldwide over the murder of John F. Kennedy; conversely, *all* of the attempts discussed in this chapter have failed, partly due to the vigilance of the Secret Service and partly to the ineptitude of would-be assassins. We can only hope that that situation prevails.

Chapter 9

The Man They Could Not Kill

Everybody was agreed. Historian Arthur Schlesinger wrote of Cuba in the late 1940s, 'The corruption of the government, the brutality of the police, the government's indifference to the needs of the people ... is an open invitation to revolution.' Playwright Arthur Miller said that Cuba was 'hopelessly corrupt, a Mafia playground [and] a bordello for Americans and other foreigners'.

The largest island in the Bahamas, only 90 miles from Florida, it was discovered by Cristoforo Colon (Columbus) in 1492 and was for years the world's foremost supplier of sugar cane. Because of its geographical proximity to the United States, it invariably became associated with American political ambitions. In 1898, the warship USS *Maine* was blown up in Havana harbour and America declared war on Spain, who had ruled the island for nearly four centuries. Cuba became an independent republic in 1901 but its democratic structures very much echoed the American system, with a senate and a house of representatives and a president who had to be replaced every four years. An exceptional amount of power was allotted to the president, however, giving him the right to intervene in almost every aspect of life.

Enter Ruben Zaldivar, better known as Fulgencio Batista. He rose to prominence as an army sergeant for his part in a coup against President Machado in 1931–32. Elected president between 1940 and 1944, he carried out the same coup in 1952, kicking out President Prio Socarras and putting himself in power. Since there were no other presidential candidates, Batista was now a full-blown dictator. Photographs of him from the 1930s follow a stereotypical pattern – he wears the medals associated with Benito Mussolini and an outsize cap as worn by Josef Stalin and other members of the Soviet politburo.

Batista's regime, described by Schlesinger and Miller above, was every bit as dissolute as that of his predecessors. The American government backed Batista because Cuba was the United States' dirty secret. Prostitution, gambling and drugs were the lifeblood of the island, rather than sugar, and by the mid-1950s it had become the 'hedonistic playground of the world's elite'. There were an estimated 270 brothels in Havana, the city which exported its expensive cigars to the world's great and good, including Winston Churchill.

Hand-in-glove with Batista was the diminutive Jewish hoodlum, Meyer Lansky. Nor was he alone. Mafia bosses who operated out of Miami included Sam Giancana and Santo Trafficante, who would both be implicated in various assassination plots in the 1960s.

Since the Batista government was so corrupt and the Cubans themselves so poor, no one can have been surprised by yet another military coup in 1959. Batista was kicked out, hiding out in the nearby Dominican Republic and was replaced by Fidel Castro backed by his brother, Raoul. Both boys were from a relatively affluent background, but while studying law at Havana University, the most high-profile centre of learning in the Caribbean, Fidel became a full-blown Marxist.

This, of course, sent shock waves through post-war America. The Second World War had seen a fake friendship between East and West against the common enemy that was Hitler. Now that it was over, Stalin's USSR seemed bent on the domination of Eastern Europe and perhaps, even, the world. That, at least, had been the avowed aim of the Trotskyites and the fact that Stalin had had his rival Trotsky assassinated in 1940 did not reduce the importance of the idea. Territory that the Russians gained, they did not want to give back. Consequently, Eastern Europe became the Eastern Bloc, countries behind the invisible 'Iron Curtain' that Churchill warned about as early as 1946, completely under the thumb of Moscow. Even Berlin, firmly in the geographical Western camp, had its Communist Eastern half, as the Soviet building of a wall between the territories proved.

During the 1950s, America had become obsessed with 'Reds under the bed'. Socialism had never really caught on in the United States; the 'huddled masses' who had emigrated there wanted freedom and above all, money. Marx's Utopian mish-mash offered neither. Nor could a revolution of the proletariat work in a wealthy country. It *could* work, however, in a poverty-stricken area like Cuba, especially if that revolution was organized by a hard-nosed realist, prepared to use force to achieve his goals. In every state that adopted Marxism, such a situation was only ever achieved by force of arms – China and Russia were living examples of it.

While Joe McCarthy, the senator from Wisconsin, ranted about the Red terror in every aspect of American life, and Hollywood A-listers lined up to report 'leftie' colleagues to the House [of Representatives] Unamerican Activities Committee, Castro booted out the Mafiosi bosses, froze their assets and closed their casinos and brothels. So the battle was not merely ideological; Castro had hit capitalist America where it hurt – in its wallets. Castro had to go.

According to Fabian Escalante in 2006, there was a total of 634 assassination attempts against 'El Comandante', the last one as recently as 2000. All this began under Dwight D. Eisenhower, in the White House at the time of Castro's coup, during which thirty-eight attempts were made. As with some of the attempts described in Chapter 8 of American presidential shootings, it is unlikely that all these were genuine. The important distinction, however, is that these were government-inspired attempts, not the work of deranged loners. They were termed 'Executive Action', as we saw in Chapter 3, and, in the written and oral records, used vague euphemisms to disguise what was actually planned murder. All this became more obvious in the Kennedy administration (1961–63). Five days after Kennedy's inaugural address, William King Harvey, a CIA executive, made notes at a meeting with the new president. The killing process was 'the magic button' in Harvey's notes, 'a last resort beyond last resort and a confession of weakness'. As if to clarify the vagueness of these phrases, he wrote 'never mention word assassination'.

Harvey, often referred to as 'America's James Bond' had been kicked out of the FBI for breaching protocol and joined the CIA out of spite. He prepared lengthy reports from the point of view of Intelligence readying everyone for an invasion of Cuba that would end in disaster in the Bay of Pigs.

For fifteen years, various pressure groups had been trying, under the American Freedom of Information Act, to find out what actually went on in these frantic months. Rather like the assassination of Hitler, merely killing Castro would not be enough; he had a perfectly competent brother and the people of Cuba were firmly behind him. The whole regime would have to be dismantled, but that could not be done by an overt act of war on the part of the United States; the world would not tolerate it.

When the information finally came to light in declassified documents released in 2007, the full extent of the assassination plan was revealed. The invasion was dreamed up under Eisenhower, although how far the president himself was involved remains infuriatingly unclear. It would be implemented by Kennedy, although he had serious reservations about it. Kennedy wanted Castro overthrown for ideological and political reasons. The Mafia wanted him out because he had stolen their highly lucrative business empires; as usual with Cosa Nostra, it was all about money. That led to an unholy alliance; the young, vigorous, apparently saintly president in bed with some of the shadiest characters in American history. Literally in bed, because the gorgeous brunette Judith Exner was sleeping with both Kennedy and Sam Giancana.

In September 1960, according to the documents known as the 'family jewels' from the 1959–73 CIA archives, available from 2007, Robert Maheu, a CIA 'cut-out' (intermediary) who had run millionaire Howard Hughes's PR for years, contacted Mafioso boss 'handsome Johnny' Roselli with a plan that came to be known as Operation Mongoose. Roselli had worked under Al Capone in Chicago since the early 1940s and exerted huge influence in Hollywood and Las Vegas. Maheu also recruited Sam Giancana, Capone's ultimate successor, and Santo Trafficante, whose Mafia empire covered Florida and (until 1959) Cuba. Trafficante admitted all this in 1978, adding that Maheu kept to the CIA protocol of fake names; Giancana was 'Sam Gold', Trafficante was just 'Joe'. Both these men were on the FBI's 'most wanted' list.

At a meeting on 14 September, Maheu offered Roselli $150,000 to 'remove' Castro (note the continued use of euphemisms). Giancana, at the same meeting, was offered the same amount and suggested the means – pills containing a botulinum toxin placed in Castro's food or drinks. For anyone who expected the Mafia's usual solution – a bullet to the head or machine guns and a hail of such bullets – this clearly would not work. Neither the CIA nor the Mafia used those methods in the 1960s and the murder of Castro (rather like the murder of Kennedy three years later) had to remain shrouded in mystery.

The CIA's Technical Services Division could and did make such pills and they were given to Juan Orta, a Cuban government official and mole with access to Castro. Orta was typical of Cubans who privately resented Castro's coup. While many of them left the island, mostly for Florida, and formed the basis of the Bay of Pigs invasion, some of them stayed to sabotage the brave new world that Castro was trying to create. Orta had done well out of the Mafia; now his funds were running low.

But Orta got cold feet, like other assassins we have come across in this book. He was carrying three of the deadly capsules given to him by Roselli, but they were never used and he hid in the Venezuelan embassy. As Richard Belfield says in *The Secret History of Assassination*, if Orta had gone to the media with his story, who would have believed him? '[He] had been recruited by the Mafia to assassinate Fidel Castro on the orders of the president of the United States, using poison pills made by the technical services division of the CIA.' It all sounded like one of the weaker plots of a James Bond movie and one which would have been laughed out of court by every newspaper editor in the West.

A second attempt was made by Giancana, Roselli and Trafficante, this time making use of the Cuban exiles. Manuel Antonio de Varona was leader of the grandly named Cuban Revolutionary Council and had been prime minister of Cuba between 1948 and 1950 and president of the Senate until 1952. The idea this time, via de Varona's contacts, was to use the poison pills, placing them into a meal at Castro's favourite restaurant in Havana. When this was set up, the dictator suddenly changed his plans and never used the place again. Before a similar plot could be set up using another restaurant, the Bay of Pigs invasion took place and everything was put on hold.

In April 1961, at the end of the second phase in the attempted removal of Castro, a force of Cuban guerrillas landed on the beaches of the Bay of Pigs ready to strike inland to take Havana and topple the dictator. Any thought of this as another D-Day, which took place seventeen years earlier, was quickly dissipated. Kennedy knew of the plan and approved it, which he admitted to the American people on television days later. But he was not prepared to provide the necessary back-up of aircraft, artillery and other materiel to make this work. Castro organized his military quickly and blasted the invaders, pinning them down to their beachhead. By 24 April, 742 men had been captured. There was widespread international outrage, as Kennedy knew there would be, and the rebels had made so little headway that discussion about actually killing Castro did not have the chance to come up. Kennedy took the flak, although most Americans were happy that at least someone had tried to do something about a Communist state in America's backyard. 'There's an old saying,' Kennedy told the nation, 'that victory has a hundred fathers and defeat is an orphan.'

Eighteen months later, with Soviet missiles standing on Sagua La Grande, Cuba, and with all cities of the American seaboard well within range, some people took this as a sign; Kennedy should have backed the Bay of Pigs and the missile crisis would never have happened. Others took the opposite view – the Bay of Pigs triggered Castro's anti-American response in the first place.

As for the president's dealings with the CIA, there was a dichotomy. On the one hand, he and his closest adviser, his brother Robert, threatened to blow the CIA 'into a thousand pieces' because their schoolboy naivety and abject failure had caused all the trouble. On the other hand, the Kennedys did not follow through on their threat and plots to kill Castro continued, forty-two of them altogether during JFK's administration. Journalist Jack Anderson, referred to by some as a founding father of modern investigative journalism, uncovered five CIA teams sent undercover into Cuba after the Bay of Pigs, the last one caught by Castro's agents on a rooftop within rifle range of the dictator's private apartments.

Two Cuban soldiers were recruited by the CIA and the Intelligence organization almost immediately regretted their decision. Major Rolando Cubela and Major Ramon Guin were selected but Cubela's group leaked like a sieve. The pair were issued with a 7.62 FAL rifle with telescopic sights, grenades and other bombs. All this was discovered by Castro's men at Cubela's house. There was a trial, which America dismissed as Communist propaganda, like the notorious show trials of Stalin's USSR in the 1930s and both men were condemned to death. Castro commuted this to thirty years without parole.

The problem with all this plotting by the CIA, and the presidential backing that went with it, was twofold. First, the CIA was fast becoming a maverick organization, originally under Allen Dulles, its first director and then under his successor, Richard Helms. Both men seem to have had ideas above their station and to pander to ever more ludicrous 'wheezes' to achieve their goals. The hopelessly inadequate Bay of Pigs is an example of this and led to Dulles' dismissal, but it is not the only one. And there is a precedent for it. In the 1940s, Churchill set up the Special Operations Executive (SOE), part of which was concerned with 'black' propaganda, designed to confuse the German people and to lower their morale. They tried to bombard Hitler with pornography in order to drive him mad (?) although how this was to work on a man notoriously disinterested in sex is difficult to say. When rumours abounded that Heinrich Himmler, head of the SS, was angling for the Fuhrer's job, SOE printed thousands of postage stamps with Himmler's head instead of Hitler's to fool the Germans into believing that a coup was underway. It did not work.

So too with the CIA. Crafty, rather intelligent men plotted in dark corners, probably with too much Bourbon in their glasses and dreamt up ever-more idiotic schemes against Castro. If actual assassination was a problem, how about propaganda? 'El Comandante' always appeared in public wearing combat fatigues and cap and sporting an enormous beard. The beard was a sign of 'machismo' and had been for centuries in Spain. The eleventh-century hero Rodrigo Diaz, El Cid, was described as having a 'splendid' beard. The CIA appear to have believed in all sincerity that making the hairs of his beard fall out would reduce his status in the eyes of his people! Various depilatory drugs such as thallium were tried and tested. None was used.

Then, there was the poisoned pen. Long gone were the days of quills and ink that Robert Cecil could have fallen back on in the days of the Gunpowder Plot, but a 1960s Papermate could be modified into a syringe filled with Black Leaf 40 (nicotine). The prick would be so slight that the user would assume he'd been scratched by an over-starched shirt.

And of course, someone reasoned that Castro's hobby of scuba diving could well prove his undoing, but if the bends did not get him, how about making him a present of a specialist diving suit contaminated with tuberculosis? The effect would not be immediate (in fact, he could last for years) but there would be no way of differentiating this from natural causes. Another variant was the use of a conch shell placed on the seabed where he swam which would be packed with explosives. The problem here was that the exotic conch chosen was not native to the Caribbean and an experienced diver like Castro would notice it at once and become suspicious. Neither could the technical wizards of the CIA come up with an explosive powerful enough to do much damage except at *very* close range.

The 1960s was, of course, the decade of psychedelic drugs and LSD or its equivalent would make Castro a laughing stock if he fell victim to it in public. The CIA hatched ideas to spray a recording studio with something that would turn his regular radio broadcasts into a pantomime of incoherent drivel (there were, of course, some hard-line rednecks who said that was what he spoke all the time anyway). Cigars were another obvious way forward. Castro smoked prodigiously and smoking was, after all, the recreational pastime of millions. Why not lace a gift sent from an admirer? Throughout, the CIA was experimenting with a variety of toxins, designed either to disable or to kill. Dr Gunn fed one variant to his guinea pigs who ate it and asked for more; they were immune to that particular poison. Monkeys died by the dozen, but nobody believed for a minute that a head of state, more than alert to the threats against him, would be so easily taken in.

Taking a leaf out of SOE's postage stamp ploy, the CIA planned to distribute thousands of leaflets, dropping them from aircraft, offering cash incentives to inform on or even kill named individuals in government. The price went up to $20,000, an astronomical sum for a Cuban at the time, but only a paltry $0.02 for killing Castro. The message was simple; the dictator is not worth a plugged nickel. And the Cubans were supposed to fall for that! Needless to say, the scheme never got off the ground.

Seventy-two attempts on Castro were carried out by the CIA during the presidency of Lyndon B. Johnson, 184 under Richard Nixon. Then, they stopped – for a while. The Senate Select Committee to Study Government Operations with Respect to Intelligence Activities, mercifully known today after its chairman, Frank Church, as the Church Committee, was set up in 1975. That was three years after Richard Helms had categorically denied that assassination was a tool of government, even though it had been since the Eisenhower administration. Church uncovered eight plots against Castro to that date sanctioned by various presidents. What he could not discover was who authorized them. Richard Helms was at his most evasive in front of the committee.

One witness who was due to testify but never did was Sam Giancana. In 1966, he had fled to Mexico to avoid searching questions from a grand jury about his activities. Eight years later, he was arrested by Mexican police and deported back to the United States. He was under police protection at his home at Oak Park, Illinois, when someone entered the basement of his house. Giancana was about to testify days later to the Church Committee. That night, at about eleven o'clock, he was alone in his kitchen, frying some sausages and peppers for a late-night snack when a bullet smashed into his head. A further six bullets were fired in a neat circle around his mouth. The message was clear – keep your mouth shut. The gun was a .22 calibre fitted with a silencer. Neither the police guard nor Giancana's wife heard a thing.

No one was ever charged with this murder. Suspicion fell on a Mafia rival, Dominic 'Butch' Blasi or Santo Trafficante who had been in an on and off war with Giancana for years. It also fell on the CIA, especially the ever-tricky William King Harvey, who was himself facing demotion within the organization. True to form, former CIA director William Colby said, 'We had nothing to do with it.'

Johnny Roselli had already appeared twice before the Church Committee but they wanted to see him a third time. The problem was that he had gone missing at the end of July, about a month after Giancana's death and no one knew where he was. On 7 August, fishermen found him floating in a 55-gallon oil drum in Dumfoundling Bay off Florida. The medical examiner ruled that he had been asphyxiated. The FBI believed he had been murdered by Mafia associates from Chicago, but it was an extraordinary coincidence that two of the three men employed by the CIA to kill Castro should end up murdered within a month of each other, just as they were about to spill the beans.

As a direct result of the Church Committee, President Gerald Ford issued Executive Order 11905 the following year – 'No employee of the United States government shall engage in or conspire in, political assassination.' And that should have been the end of it. There should have been no more attempts on Castro nor anyone else. But that flew in the face of realpolitik. If Russia's KGB were still at it, the USA would have to step up to the plate too. Under Jimmy Carter, there were a further 64 attempts on Castro; under Ronald Reagan (a man, of course, who had taken an assassin's bullet himself) 197, the highest of all. And then, as Castro's personal power waned and he passed the reins over to his brother, numbers dropped to sixteen under George H. Bush and twenty-one under Bill Clinton. The buck passed to Raoul.

The last assassination attempt on Castro that involved Cuban exiles took place on a visit to Panama. Ninety kilos of explosives were placed under the podium on which he was to speak, but the bomb was discovered by his security team before he arrived. Commenting on it later, Castro said, 'If surviving assassination attempts were an Olympic event, I would win the gold medal.' The dictator died peacefully in his bed in 2016, aged 90.

In 2006, Britain's Channel 4 screened a documentary entitled *638 Ways to Kill Castro*. A number of people were interviewed, including Eugene Olivares, who was probably the first hitman to try, in 1960. Appearing too was Felix Rodriguez, involved in training the commandoes for the Bay of Pigs. Antonio Veciana, leader of the exile group Alpha 66 tried to kill Castro three times. Possibly unique in the annals of Castro-killing was the testimony of the man's ex-lover Marita Lorenz. They met in 1959, the year in which Castro seized power, but the relationship soured and she agreed to smuggle a jar of poisoned cold cream into his bedroom. Somebody tipped 'El Comandante' off and he confronted Marita, even offering her a loaded pistol to do the job properly. She could not go through with it.

There was an interesting fall-out from the programme. Outrage was caused in some circles when Ileana Ros-Lehtinen, Miami congresswoman, said, 'I welcome the opportunity of having anyone assassinate Castro and any leader who is oppressing the people.' The comment did her own political career no harm at all.

So how did Fidel Castro become the man they could not kill, the most Teflon world leader of all time? The resources of the CIA were formidable and despite the 'plausible deniability' of successive presidents, the will was there. Because Castro kept so much to himself, we do not have Hitleresque long ramblings about assassinations, as about everything else, so we do not know how he adapted his life to stay alive. He undoubtedly had an efficient, alert security team able to second guess would-be killers, but equally, he probably had a lot of luck on his side.

But there is one figure in the unlikely story of Fidel Castro who has rather fallen by the wayside. He is the third of the triumvirate recruited by the CIA in 1960, the only one who did not die by a murderer's hand – Santo Trafficante. He was in the perfect position – more of a cut-out than Maheu ever was – to play both sides against the middle. It was Trafficante who had Cuban contacts, shady men prepared to use violence to get 'their' island back. And these men, time after time, came up against problems and sheer bad luck. Poison capsules may never had got further than Trafficante's own toilet. We only have his word that fast boats were shot out of the water by Castro's coastguards. Money, radios, weapons of all sorts, all of it funded by the CIA, never got anywhere near Castro's island.

Did Trafficante do a deal with Castro, informing him of the latest CIA ruse, giving the dictator plenty of advance warning? Is that why he changed restaurants for no explicable reason? Is that how he found out about Marita's cold cream? Both men are dead now and we will probably never know.

But the CIA did not get either of them.

Chapter 10

Wolves and Jackals

'On Friday, August 30th,' wrote Robert Hamilton Bruce Lockhart, the British agent:

> Uritsky, the head of the St Petersburg Cheka, was murdered by a Russian Junker [nobleman] called Kannegeisser. The next evening a Social-Revolutionary, a young Jewish girl called Dora Kaplan, fired two shots [*sic*] point blank at Lenin as he was leaving Micheson's factory ... One bullet penetrated the lung above the heart. The other entered the neck close to the main artery. The Bolshevik leader was not dead, but his chances of living were at a discount.

These two assassination attempts, one successful, one not, unleashed what came to be known as the Red Terror in Russia, where the death penalty, which had been abolished, was restored and over 800 social revolutionaries were executed in the months that followed. The problem with researching this attempt on Vladimir Ilyich Ulyanov (Lenin) is that the whole period of Russian history is riddled with misinformation, what Donald Trump calls 'fake news', that it is now – and probably was then – impossible to get to the truth. It is 'another of the many mystifications of Bolshevik history' as one historian has put it.

In 1917, the Romanov family had been ruling Russia for 300 years. A number of the tsars had been assassinated and there had been serious attempts at revolution, the most serious in 1905. Russia was a vast, desperately poor empire stretching from the frontiers of Poland in the West to Siberia in the East. The tsar was an autocrat, only nominally interested in change and highly suspicious of democracy. The fact that Nicholas II was suave, cultured, speaking and writing fluent English and with a host of English relatives did not help. He was not very intelligent, reminded some people of a turnip farmer and was stubborn to a ludicrous degree.

While Russia was famous for its culture, the ballet and the arts, the middle class was actually tiny, while industry was struggling to make headway in what had always been a peasant-ridden agrarian economy and the people had only just (in 1861) emerged from actual serfdom. The minor changes made by the Duma, the Russian parliament, had little effect on a desperately poor and unhappy state.

Into this mix floated the deranged ideas of Karl Marx, a German Jew who, in 1848, had written *The Communist Manifesto*. It was a slim and one-track book. The rhetoric sounded good – 'The proletarians [working class] have nothing to lose but their chains. They have a world to win. Workers of all countries, unite!' – but outside the confines of an undergraduate debating chamber, the prospect was fraught with difficulties. The bottom line was that Marx and his co-writer Friedrich Engels did not specify *how* this revolution of the masses should take place. It could never have worked in a successful capitalist state like Britain (where Marx worked and died) nor America, nor indeed any Western country. Russia, however, was perfect. It already had class hatred of the type that Marx espoused and what, indeed, did a starving Russian peasant have to lose?

One of several men who had the unenviable job of making Marx's simplistic notions work was Vladimir Ilyich Ulyanov. He chose the name Lenin – 'of the Lena' (a river) – because he was a dissident watched by the Russian authorities and they all took assumed names. Lev Bronstein, who organized the Red Army from 1918, became Leon Trotsky to make him sound less Jewish in a country as anti-

Semitic as most. Iosif Dzhugashvili became Josef Stalin, 'man of steel' because who could not be impressed with a moniker like that? The problem was false identities, false beards, false promises and lies became a way of life to these men. They had to persuade Russia's downtrodden masses that the Marxist-Leninist way was better and Lenin promised them 'peace, bread and land'. Of the three, he only gave them peace – and that came at a price.

In March 1917, the tsar was overthrown by a provisional government of democrats under Alexander Kerensky. Had matters ended there, Russia might well have become another modern democracy along British, French and American lines. But Kerensky made the mistake of trying to continue the First World War against Germany and things went from bad to worse. Whereas the Russian Army made some headway against the Austrians (it was the biggest army in the world in 1914) it habitually lost to the Germans.

This led to a second revolution in November (October in the Russian calendar) led by revolutionary groups like the Social Revolutionaries and above all the Bolsheviks (the majority) led by Lenin. The Orthodox Church was swept away. Councils of workers – the Soviets – called the shots. Opposition was stamped out. Lenin negotiated the 'robber peace' of Brest-Litovsk with Germany, by which Russia lost huge swathes of the land he had promised to give to the people.

And even peace did not come to Russia until 1921 because the Tsarist forces launched a comeback – a White Russian Army, bolstered by maverick units from Britain, the United States and elsewhere, challenged the Red Army of the Bolsheviks. Life under the Soviets was no better and was probably worse than under the tsar, who was murdered, along with his family on Bolshevik orders at the House of Special Purpose at Ekaterinburg.

In that sense, Comrade Lenin was a target waiting to happen. The first attempt took place on 1 January 1918 when shots were fired at him in the back of an open-topped car. Nothing had been learned from the experience of the emperor-to-be Franz Ferdinand in Sarajevo four years earlier. In fact, despite the existence of a vicious secret police force, the Cheka, security measures in the new Bolshevik state seemed rudimentary in the extreme. Years later, Prince Dmitry Shakhovskoy claimed that he had orchestrated this hit and had put half a million roubles at the disposal of the actual assassins. One of the gunmen was probably Nikolai Nekrasov who left Petrograd in a hurry after the attempt, changed his name to Golgofsky and hurried to Kazan. He was arrested by the Cheka in March 1921 and taken to see Lenin in person. Typically, in the topsy-turvy world of Bolshevik history, he was released without charge or reason. In the shooting itself, Friedrich Platten, a Swiss Communist, was riding beside Lenin and undoubtedly saved his life. Platten was the man who had engineered Lenin's return from exile to Russia in a sealed train 'like a plague bacillus' in Winston Churchill's words, to cause havoc in Kerensky's war effort. Platten got away with a grazed hand and Lenin was totally unhurt.

Two weeks later, there was another attempt, although how genuine it was is uncertain. A soldier named Spiridrov admitted to Mikhail Bonch-Bruyevich, an aristocrat turned Bolshevik, that he was a hitman ordered to kill Lenin by an organization calling itself the Union of St George's Cavaliers. On 22 January, a number of conspirators from this group were rounded up by the Cheka at 14 Zakharyevskaya Street in Petrograd and given a choice – the Lubyanka prison and a bullet in the head or the Eastern Front. Not surprisingly, they all chose the Front. At least two of them later defected to the Whites.

Behind these ham-fisted attempts to remove Lenin was an altogether more serious effort that came to be known as the 'Lockhart Plot'. Robert Bruce Hamilton Lockhart was the 'boy ambassador' to Moscow, sent by the British prime minister, David Lloyd George, to negotiate with the new regime – Britain was the first nation to recognize the new Soviet Union as it emerged by 1924. He realized, having met the leading protagonists and seen the state of war-torn Russia for himself, that there would be no Tsarist revival. Bolshevism would morph into Communism and that would remain the case for the foreseeable future. Of his first meeting with Lenin, Bruce Lockhart wrote, 'He looks at first glance more like a provincial grocer than a leader of men. Yet, in those steady eyes ... he was impersonal and almost inhuman.' If plotting meant that Bruce Lockhart wanted to keep the Bolsheviks – and Russia – in the First World War, then he was guilty, but the suggestion that he was involved in an assassination plot does not hold up.

The real instigator of all this, for which Bruce Lockhart was imprisoned and later given a death sentence, was Sidney Reilly, the British 'ace of spies' who would be the subject of many books and be the hero of a television series in the 1980s starring Sam Neill. He was not British and his name was not Reilly. He was actually Sigismund Rosenblum, a Jew from Odessa. Personally charming and bent as a corkscrew, 'Reilly' (he actually did have British citizenship) was almost certainly a double or even triple agent, playing fast and loose with some of the most dangerous people on the planet. It may be that Reilly was in cahoots with Felix Derzinski, the sinister head of the Cheka in Moscow, whose eyes, said Bruce Lockhart, 'blazed with a steady fire of fanaticism. They never twitched. His eyelids seemed paralysed.' Between them, the pair concocted a plot in which Lenin would be assassinated in order to discredit the British government, not yet ready to back the new regime.

We are really nowhere nearer the truth of the Lockhart Plot now than we were in 1918, but a trial took place in Moscow on 25 November. By this time, both Lockhart and Reilly had wisely left the country but if they ever returned, they would be shot.

On 30 August of that year, as we saw at the beginning of this chapter, Moisei Uritsky, head of the Petrograd Cheka, was shot dead.

His killer was a disillusioned military cadet, Leonid Kannegeisser, whose family had been Tsarist supporters until recent events had made this increasingly unlikely. Despite this, Lenin travelled to the Hammer and Sickle plant of the Michelson factory chain without an escort, into a building that had no security at all. Speeches were routinely made to workers in situ, strengthening the 'man of the people' image of Lenin, Trotsky and the others and emphasizing the importance of hard, physical work. Typically, Lenin ended with a rousing 'We will win or we will die.' And he went outside, nearly doing that very thing.

Lenin was getting into his car, talking to a woman who approached him from the crowd. As he was about to take his seat, a second woman came forward. She was Feiga (Fanny) Haimovna Kaplan, often called Dora, and she interrupted, insisting that Lenin answer a complaint she had about bread being held at railway stations. Warehousing of bread had happened often under the tsar and since Lenin had offered bread as part of his 'election' promise, it touched a chord. Before he could answer, Fanny Kaplan drew her FN Browning M1900 pistol and fired three times, virtually at point-blank range. If the magazine had been full, she still had five bullets left, but clearly assumed her work was done.

What happened next has remained controversial. As Lenin slumped in his car, his driver, Stepan Gil, chased after the killer and grabbed her. In another version, it was Deputy Commissar S.N. Batulin who overpowered her. In a third variant, she was chased down the street by schoolchildren, stopped and waited to be arrested. Whatever the truth, she ended up in the Lubyanka prison in the grim Cheka headquarters where Bruce Lockhart had already spent some time.

The first bullet had blasted a hole in Lenin's open coat and done no damage. The second hit him in the neck, just below the jaw, nicked a lung and lodged near the right collarbone. The third hit Lenin in the left shoulder. Gil drove like a maniac through the hysterical crowd to the Kremlin, the most secure building in Moscow. Lenin refused to leave in case of further attempts, fearing that this may be part of a bigger coup and was drifting in and out of consciousness. So the doctors came to him and, unable to perform surgery properly, had to leave one of the two bullets in place.

Under interrogation (which, from the Cheka, was not exactly a walk in the park) Fanny Kaplan made a statement:

> Today I shot Lenin. I did it on my own. I will not say from whom I obtained my revolver [this is a mistranslation. The FN1900M is a semi-automatic with a magazine clip in the butt; it does not have revolving chambers]. I had resolved to kill him long ago. I consider him a traitor to the Revolution. I was exiled to Akatny [a Siberian prison camp] for participating in an assassination attempt against a Tsarist official in Kyiv. I spent eleven years at hard labour. After the Revolution, I was freed. I favoured the Constituent Assembly and am still for it.

The Constituent Assembly was another attempt to establish a genuine people's government after Kerensky's was overthrown. It lasted just thirteen hours before the Bolsheviks closed it down by force and made it illegal.

The exact spelling of Kaplan's name is uncertain. She was Jewish and had become a revolutionary at the age of 16. Her actual part in the planting of a bomb to kill the mayor of Kyiv is unclear, but during her years in Siberia, she became completely blind (how is not known) and had only regained partial sight by the time she shot Lenin. She suffered periodic blindness after being given her freedom, and chronic headaches. Since there was no doubt about her guilt, she was taken two days later to one of two sections of the Alexander Gardens outside the Lubyanka and was shot in the back of the head (the standard Russian execution method) probably by P.D. Malkov, commander of the Kremlin, under orders from Yakov Sverdlov, the 'dark man' who had shot dead all members of Tsar Nicholas's family six weeks earlier.

Unnerving questions remain over Kaplan's attempt on Lenin. Luck played a part in keeping the dictator alive but had Fanny Kaplan actually fired the shots? No one at the scene had specifically seen her do it and her eyesight, even at close range, was defective. She would implicate no one else, but the gun and ammunition must have come from somewhere. Most mysteriously of all, according to some accounts, the bullet extracted from Lenin's neck did not come from a Browning semi-automatic – 'another of the mystifications of Bolshevik history'.

As for Lenin, he was doomed to suffer Fanny Kaplan's repeated headaches. He found sleeping difficult and his wounds may have contributed to the strokes he suffered before his death in 1924.

The Day of the Jackal was one of those iconic movies of the 1970s, based on an equally iconic novel by Frederick Forsyth. In it, the French police are facing a huge problem. They know there is likely to be an assassination attempt on President Charles de Gaulle, but they do not know where or when; above all, they do not know by whom.

The answer is debonair Englishman Edward Fox, whose name we never discover, but who uses a number of aliases. He speaks perfect French, has a state-of-the-art rifle made which can be hidden in a metal leg-brace and, disguised as a disabled war veteran, takes his shot during a military parade. Then, the unthinkable happens. One of the tallest men in France suddenly bends over as Fox fires and the shot misses. He does not get a second as the police close in on him. I am sorry if this has spoiled a film you may not have seen but watch it anyway, because the tension is racked up superbly. As to the split-second miss, even by a superlative marksman, such is the nature of assassination attempts. It really does happen like that.

The Day of the Jackal is based on events on 22 August 1962 which were far clumsier and less urbane than the film version. There were indeed foreigners involved, but no Englishmen and there was no 'Jackal'; merely the one who got away who had the nickname 'The lame woman'.

Charles André Joseph Marie de Gaulle was born in Lille in 1890. Serving with distinction as an officer in the First World War, he survived the hell-hole of Verdun and spoke for the new generation of soldiers who wanted to revolutionize the French Army, still hopelessly hidebound to the days of Napoleon and '*la gloire*'. In 1940, when the blitzkrieg he had been warning against swung west to destroy France, de Gaulle ran to Britain as head of the 'Free French' and was an almost constant irritant to everybody, especially the prime minister, Winston Churchill. After the war, de Gaulle rose rapidly in politics to become president of the Fifth Republic in 1958.

One of the burning issues with which he had to contend was Algeria. The North African territory had been a French colony since the 1840s but over a century later, a different mood prevailed and reform was in the air. Prime Minister Harold Macmillan talked about a 'wind of change' blowing across Africa and de Gaulle spectacularly changed tack. Whereas earlier, he had happily backed the *pieds noirs* (black feet), the Europeans who essentially ran Algeria, he now began to advocate genuine Algerian independence. This did not please right-wing elements in French society and some of them decided to make a point.

A turning point came in 1954. With the French defeat at Dien Bien Phu, de Gaulle pulled out of Vietnam, leaving the Americans to continue their own dogs' breakfast. That same year, fighting broke out in Algeria between native Muslim forces and the Organisation de l'Armée Secrète (OAS) who were trying to hold the empire together. De Gaulle's insistence on a three-year ceasefire merely underscored his weakness in the OAS's eyes.

Attempts on de Gaulle's life made him blasé. Although he could not reach the ridiculous heights of Fidel Castro, there were at least thirty-one efforts to kill him. On 8 September 1961 the OAS exploded a bomb containing 50kg of plastic explosives and 15l of napalm at the side of the road outside the president's home. The Citroen was nearly blown off the road, but its specially armoured tyres kept going and de Gaulle simply drove through the smoke and flames. No one was hurt.

One of those waiting for the president on the morning of 22 August 1962 was Jean-Marie Bastien-Thiry. He was an air force colonel and his father had known de Gaulle personally in the 1930s, before the Free French came into existence. Bastien-Thiry was waiting as lookout in the Petit-Clamart district on the outskirts of Paris and saw the motorcade in the distance. The streets were relatively narrow, the weather clear and all looked promising. The black Citroen DS, with the flags fluttering on its wings, gleamed in the morning sun. This was the revolutionary design that was described to the world as like something from outer space with its broad 'frog' mouth and 'proud' headlights.

Bastien-Thiry signalled to his three hitmen positioned nearby. They were: Lieutenant Alain de la Tocnaye, like Bastien-Thiry a disgruntled right-winger; Jacques Prevost who had fought in Vietnam when it was still French Indo-China; and Georges Wati, the 'lame woman' because of an old war wound. All three men had been practising with their sub-machine guns and they opened up now.

Glass shattered in a hail of bullets. People screamed. De Gaulle's car was hit fourteen times, the bodywork punched repeatedly. Twenty more shots had destroyed the frontage of the Café Trianon past which the car purred. When police counted later, there were 187 spent shell cases lying on the pavement and road.

De Gaulle glanced at Yvonne, his wife. She was unhurt. He brushed broken glass off his sleeve, commenting to his wife and chauffeur, 'They shoot like pigs'. Two of the Citroen's tyres had been blown out, but the driver put his foot down and the suspension got them through. The assassins melted into the back streets before everyone got up from wherever they were crouching in stunned silence. The only casualty was a Monsieur Fillon, who had been driving past with his young family when the killers opened up. His hand was grazed.

The Sûreté immediately went into action. It was not known how many shooters there had been and no doubt, eyewitnesses interviewed would have come out with the television cop show cliché – 'It all happened so fast'. Even today, some accounts give as many as twelve hitmen squeezing triggers in all directions.

Any known members of the OAS and the FLN (the National Liberation Front) were rounded up and interrogated. One who had his collar felt was particularly helpful. He was an army officer, Antoine Argoud, a member of the OAS who had been suspected of earlier attempts on de Gaulle. He had been tried twice, once *in absentia* because he was on the run and had been sentenced to life after his second trial. Argoud had been found hiding in the Eden-Wolff hotel in Munich and had been captured (illegally in fact) by French security forces and brought back to France. One of the names he mentioned under interrogation was Jean-Marie Bastien-Thiry. The airman had just returned from a training liaison course in Britain (which he no doubt hoped would distance him from the de Gaulle shooting) and was arrested on his return.

Bastien-Thiry was born in 1927, had attended the Ecole Nationale Superieure de l'Aeronotique and had joined the air force, specializing in air-to-air missile technology. He was married with three daughters. There was no doubt that before 1960, Bastien-Thiry had been a Gaullist, but the U-turn over Algeria had driven him away and he contacted both the OAS and the FLN. He never admitted to joining either group.

A military tribunal was held between 28 January and 4 March 1963 which was chaired by General Roger Gardet. Bastien-Thiry had a high-powered four-man defence team, including Jean-Louis Tixier-Vignancour, who would go on to run for president in the years ahead. The accused's defence was interesting. He claimed that the murder of de Gaulle was justifiable homicide because the president was, in effect, a war criminal. Especially relevant was the Oran massacre of July 1962 in which many of the *pieds noirs* were killed in an orgy of slaughter by Algerian Muslims. Figures are estimated at between 95 and 365 deaths, many of them women and children whose throats were routinely cut. Today's right-wing groups, led by Marine Le Pen, claim that this figure could be as high as 7,000.

Bastien-Thiry contended, however, that he did not intend to kill de Gaulle, but to kidnap him and hand him over to a war crimes tribunal. When the prosecution asked how he intended to prevent the president from escaping before such a trial, the accused said he would merely take away his spectacles and braces. One of his defence counsel turned to another and murmured, 'He has just signed his death sentence.' De Gaulle was insufferably vain and would not forgive a comment like this. It is just as well that he did not live to see René Artois (Gorden Kaye) in the British television series *'Allo! 'Allo!* refer to him contemptuously as 'the one with the big 'ooter'.

The psychiatrists who examined Bastien-Thiry agreed that he was perfectly sane and he and the two shooters caught with him were found guilty. As president, de Gaulle had the right to commute sentences and he did so for Prevost and de la Tocnaye, giving them life imprisonment instead. As for Bastien-Thiry, he rejected this on the grounds that an innocent civilian (his wife) was in the line of fire; another civilian, Fillon, had been hurt; and above all, that, acting as a lookout, he had not had the nerve to pull the trigger himself.

The execution was carried out with almost indecent haste before the Court of Appeal could be galvanized. There was actually a plot to spring him, led by OAS officer Jean Cantelabre, but the huge police presence – 2,000 officers and 35 vehicles – made such a plan unworkable.

Jean-Marie Bastien-Thiry, villain to many, hero to just as many, faced a firing squad at the Fort d'Ivy prison in Paris on 11 March 1963. He declined a blindfold and was the last man in France to be executed in this way.

That night, President de Gaulle threw a dinner for high court judges, including General Gardet who had sentenced Bastien-Thiry. Of that particular case, de Gaulle said, 'The French need martyrs ... I gave them Bastien-Thiry. They'll be able to make a martyr of him. He deserves it.'

According to the historical record, seven popes have been murdered while in office in the holiest of Sees. Because of their status as spiritual heads of the Catholic Church, they can all be classified as assassinations, even though the motivations in many cases were more personal. John XII, for instance, holding St Peter's chair between 955 and 964 was found in bed with a mistress (*strictly* against everything His Holiness stood for, of course) and was dispatched by the lady's husband. Whether he was strangled or thrown out of a window, the record does not make clear.

When I began this section on the attempted assassination of Pope John Paul II in May 1981, I thought it would be a simple, rather touching story of atonement and forgiveness. In fact, the motivation of the would-be assassin is so complicated, it makes Dan Brown's *Da Vinci Code* story look like a *Mr Man* book!

Part of the problem is that John Paul's background was mired in controversy and although the man himself seems to have been above reproach, they would not let him forget his origins. Karol Josepf Wojtyla was born in Wadowice, Poland, in May 1920. His father was an army officer and Karol himself had recently enrolled in Krakow University, studying languages, when Hitler and Stalin split Poland between them in the Nazi–Soviet pact, top-secret at the time, and the Wojtylas moved east to avoid the German occupation. Finding that eastern Poland was overrun by the Russians, they came back to Krakow and carried on as best they could, while Germany in particular tried to destroy the Polish state.

Karol, along with many young Poles, joined the Resistance, hoping to smuggle Jews out of the country before the roaming *Einsatzgruppen* hanged then from lampposts or shot them in the street. During this, he was hit by a tram and badly hurt by a German tank which damaged his posture permanently. This near-death experience persuaded him to join the church and he visited an underground Catholic seminary (officially banned by the Nazis) as the Germans put down the Warsaw uprising with appalling violence, and Oskar Schindler set up his metalwork factory in Krakow in an attempt to save as many Jews as possible. By 1941, Karol was the only surviving member of his family.

After the war, his church career was meteoric. Ordained in 1946, he was the youngest bishop in Poland by 1958, archbishop of Krakow six years later and a cardinal by 1967. He was ordained pope, the white smoke billowing out of the Vatican's chimneys, in August 1978.

Because of his background, John Paul was heavily involved in politics. He was professor of moral theology at the universities of Lublin and Krakow and travelled widely, even as a cardinal, preaching in a variety of countries. He attacked apartheid in South Africa and was opposed to capital punishment. As the first non-Italian pope for four and a half centuries, he had no difficulty opposing the Mafia either and he supported the group of Polish freedom fighters called Solidarity, determined as it was to break away from Soviet rule.

On the way, John Paul made enemies and one, perhaps two of them, were waiting for him in the late afternoon of Wednesday, 13 May 1981 in St Peter's Square, Rome. The position of pope as head of the Catholic Church remains as fixed as ever (although there had been a time when there had simultaneously been *three* popes!) but the physical domain of what the English contemptuously called 'the bishop of Rome' in the sixteenth century, had shrunk. The Papal states had spanned central Italy for centuries, but now, it had shrunk to the Vatican, a city within a city, centred on the basilica of St Peter, accredited with being the first pope. Like many other parts of Rome, St Peter's is a popular tourist trap, made all the more so by its spiritual connections and it is a security nightmare. Like other popes before and since, John Paul was protected by a 'Secret Service' style bodyguard and by the official Swiss Guard, carrying halberds and wearing the breastplate and helmets of their sixteenth-century counterparts.

Oral Celik was a Bulgarian hitman waiting in the crowd that always thronged St Peter's, especially when the pope came and went. Like other heads of state who had to be seen by their people in the open policy of the West, it was widely publicised that John Paul was to return to the Vatican late that afternoon.

At about 4.30 that happened. Celik was supposed to set off a bomb in the square, not to kill anybody but to cause chaos, during which a second assassin would actually carry out the hit. This was a professional assassin, Mehmet Ali Agca, who had already murdered his fellow Turk Abdi Ipeka, the editor of the newspaper *Milliyet* the year before. Agca was no shadow lurking in the shadows. He had openly vowed to kill the pope if he ever showed his face in Turkey, referring to him as 'the masked leader of the crusades' and 'the incarnation of all that is capitalism', at once giving two possible motivations for murder.

Agca had been dotting around the Mediterranean for months prior to the hit, on the run as he was from Turkish authorities. They knew that he was a member of the Grey Wolves, a neo-Fascist organization notorious for terrorist attacks on a number of individuals and institutions in the 1970s. Rather like the fictional Edward Fox 'Jackal' in the film of the same name, Agca went by a number of aliases and used different passports to evade would-be captors. He reached Rome from Milan by train on 10 May and met three accomplices, a Turk and two Bulgarians, one of whom was Celik.

Agca found a seat in the square in the early afternoon and sat quietly in the sun writing postcards as the crowds assembled. In his pocket he carried a 9mm Browning Hi-Power semi-automatic pistol, with a 13-round magazine. As the pope passed him in his open-topped car, waving to the people, Agca fired four times. He then ran, pushing people aside, and threw the gun under a truck before being grabbed by a number of people, including Camillo Cibin, the pope's bodyguard, and a nun!

Two bullets had hit John Paul, one smashing the index finger of his left hand, the other hitting him in the chest, miraculously missing any major organs. Two other people were hit, both Catholic tourists on holiday. Ann Odre from Buffalo, New York, was shot in the chest and Rose Hall was hit in the arm. Both recovered. Of Oral Celik and his diversionary bomb there was no sign. Today, there is a small marble plaque at the site of the shooting, engraved with the date and the pope's personal coat of arms. He suffered severe blood loss from the chest wound, but rallied and was back at work as soon as he was able.

Agca was tried and sentenced to death in July, but the pope intervened to persuade the president, Carlo Ciampi, to pardon him. In 1983, John Paul met his would-be killer at Rome's Rebibbia prison, a centre well known for rehabilitation and seen as a 'soft' gaol. Agca kissed the pope's ring and they had other meetings. John Paul was also in regular touch with Agca's mother and brother.

In 2000, Mehmet Agca was extradited to Turkey to stand trial for the murder of the journalist Ipeka back in 1979 and for two bank raids in Istanbul. Found guilty, he was paroled and finally released from gaol in January 2010, having spent twenty-nine years behind bars. By then, he had converted to Catholicism.

This is the simple story of atonement and forgiveness I spoke of earlier, but it is the theories relating to motivation that make the tale so tortuous.

We have to start – and perhaps end – with Agca himself. He told so many versions of what happened and what motivated him, even writing his own book about it (as did the pope) that it is unlikely that the truth will ever come out. His original vitriol against John Paul, that he was the 'masked leader of the crusade' and the worst example of capitalist greed, throws us into confusion at once. By definition, popes since at least 1099 have been the leaders of Christianity against Islam. Some of them, like Urban II and Innocent III, were active advocates of crusade, urging Christians to take back the Muslim-conquered Holy Land for Jesus. By the twentieth century, however, this ideology had long gone, although presumably, there are still Muslims who believe it. The Grey Wolves' ideology is unclear, but the group seems to have no particular anti-capitalist leanings. Formed in the late 1960s, the Grey Wolves claim that they are a cultural organization, rather like the Irish Republican Brotherhood in the nineteenth century, and do not participate in terrorism or assassination. If anything, they are far Right, not far Left.

So what are the theories swirling around Mehmet Agca's attempt on Pope John Paul? In the 1980s, American historian Michael Ledeen joined forces with crime and assassination buff Claire Sterling to put forward the claim that the whole thing was sponsored by the KGB in Moscow using the Intelligence networks of both Bulgaria and East Germany. We have to remember that the 1980s was the height of the Cold War, with President Ronald Reagan squaring up to Moscow that, at the time, looked frightening. Everybody's Intelligence services were trying to outwit everybody else's. Behind that was the pope's outspoken support for Lech Walesa's Solidarity which was undermining the status of Russian Communism in Eastern Europe.

In 1988, Noam Chomsky and Edward S. Herman countered this with *Manufacturing Consent*, which claimed that Ledeen and Sterling had no evidence to substantiate their claims. Since both Chomsky and Herman were internationally known intellectuals and social commentators, such views were taken seriously. The British newspaper *The Independent* went further, that the Ledeen/Sterling theory was 'one of the most successful cases – certainly the most publicized – of disinformation'. While all this may be true, it gets us no closer to what made Mehmet Agca tick.

The assassin's stories kept morphing during his years in prison. As Italian lawyer Antonio Marini wrote, '[Agca] has manipulated all of us, telling hundreds of lies ... forcing us to open tens of different investigations.' For instance, Agca's claim that he had joined the PFLP (Marxist Popular Front for the Liberation of Palestine) was met with a flat denial – they had never heard of him.

Then, Agca made it known that his various trips to Sofia in 1980 had been made in order to meet up with Sergei Antonov, who ostensibly worked for Bulgarian Airlines, but was actually a government agent working for the KGB. This led to Antonov's arrest and a three-year trial ending in 1989 which fell apart due to lack of evidence.

In a subtle variation, Agca claimed that the Bulgarian secret service and the Turkish mafia had offered him 3 million Deutsche Marks to kill the pope. Since this assertion was made after interrogation by SISMI, the Italian military Intelligence organization, it was taken with a pinch of salt. Investigations by judges Severino Santiapechi and Franco Ionta found evidence that SISMI had fabricated Agca's story. Conversely, the Senate's Intelligence Committee quoted former CIA agent Melvin A. Goodman in September 1990 as saying that the CIA's own investigation into this had itself been falsified.

What of the Grey Wolves? Its leader, Abdullah Catli, a 'hitman for the state' (*anybody's* state, for the right money), asserted in court in 1985 that the BND (West German Intelligence working with the CIA) offered him DM3 million. The sum involved stayed the same, but those prepared to pay it wavered in all directions. Catli himself was killed in a car crash in 1996. The BND and the CIA, Catli had maintained, were trying to subvert Russian and Bulgarian secret services.

In March 2006, the Mitrokhin Commission was set up in Italy by Silvio Berlusconi, the prime minister, to investigate links between the KGB and the ever-fluid Italian political set-up. In the course of this, photo-computer analysis established that Sergei Antonov, whom Agca had mentioned as his KGB handler, was actually in St Peter's Square at the time of the shooting. The previous year, the pope's own account of what happened appeared in his book *Memory and Identity*. His conclusion? 'Someone else masterminded it and someone else commissioned it.'

The story of the attempted assassination of Pope John Paul took a bizarre twist on 22 June 1983. Fifteen-year-old Emanuela Orlandi, the daughter of a Vatican employee, vanished into thin air on her way to a flute lesson. The police were called and an investigation was soon underway. Umpteen sightings of the 'Vatican girl' were reported. She had run away and was mixed up in drugs; she was living under an assumed name – the usual barrage of 'fake news' whenever a teenaged female goes missing. There were several phone calls from someone with an American accent, but on 8 July, there was a call to one of Emanuela's friends from someone with a Middle Eastern accent. The caller said that he was holding the girl captive and the authorities had just twenty days for an exchange to be arranged between her and Mehmet Agca. When Agca was confronted with this, he told the authorities that the girl was indeed still alive, had been kidnapped by the Grey Wolves and was hiding in a convent somewhere in central Europe. Some people assumed that this, in turn, was the work of East German Intelligence, who had taken the girl and set up the alleged Agca connection to throw everybody off the Bulgarian/East German assassination theory. There were also rumours that Emanuela's disappearance had nothing to do with assassination, but that she was a victim of a perverted sexual cult operating out of the Vatican (which is very much Dan Brown country). In January 2023, Pope Francis announced an official enquiry into the disappearance.

All this pales into insignificance alongside the Three Secrets of Fatima. In 1917, three teenagers, two of them shepherds, living in Fatima, Portugal, had heavenly visitations from Our Lady of Fatima, a local version of the universal Virgin Mary. Shepherds, children, astral voices; these have been the standard stuff of Catholic spiritualism from the Children's Crusade of 1212, through Joan of Arc in the fifteenth century to the miraculous appearances at Lourdes in our own time. The Fatima children somehow acquired information called the Three Secrets of Fatima, which were kept under lock and key by the Vatican until 2000, when the Curia decided to release the Third Secret. The first two dealt with Hell and both world wars, but the third related to the apocalypse, which is still to come, but which was heralded by Agca's assassination attempt on the pope. John Paul himself had always been impressed by Our Lady of Fatima and expressed the belief that she had been watching over him on 13 June 1981 in St Peter's Square. Mehmet Agca was said to be obsessed with the Lady and very much believed in the second coming, which may explain his conversion to Catholicism in 2007. The bullet extracted from the pope's chest was later placed in the crown on the head of the Lady at the Fatima shrine. Two days before John Paul died, in April 2005, Agca was said to be writing a detailed account of the attempt, hinting at a conspiracy and an 'inside man' – 'The Devil,' he said cryptically, 'is inside the Vatican's Walls.' In his 2013 memoirs, however, he was passing the buck to the Iranian government and specifically, the Muslim cleric Ayatollah Khomeini.

How much of this is fact and how much the ramblings of conspiracy theorists, you will have to judge for yourself.

Chapter 11

'Dead at 4.30 pm'

In his book *The Secret History of Assassination*, author Richard Belfield lists more than fifty-eight assassins. The exact number is obscured by the fact that within the listings are murderous societies and cults, like the *Arab* Black Septembrists in the 1970s, the KGB throughout their existence, the Sicarii of ancient Rome and of course the Hashashin themselves. Carl Sifakis in his colossal *Encyclopedia of Assassinations* (1993), covers over 300 such murders and admits, depressingly, that this is only the tip of the iceberg.

None of this is surprising, if Jonathan J. Moore is right in *Shot, Stabbed and Poisoned* (2018) when he claims that assassination is the second oldest profession in the world, after prostitution!

Less prodigious however are the *failed* assassinations, the ones that went wrong. We have looked at several of these in this book, but can we draw any conclusions from these failures? Most of it is down to human frailty, the moral complications a killer faces when he is planting a bomb, wielding a knife or is about to fire a gun. Assassination, after all, is murder and the complexities of a murderer's mind are (perhaps mercifully) a mystery to most of us. Motivations for murder vary wildly; there is a world of difference between the anonymous Whitechapel murderer, roaming the streets of London's East End in search of prostitutes to butcher, and the actor John Wilkes Booth who put a single Derringer ball into the head of President Abraham Lincoln in Ford's Theatre, Washington DC.

This book is about 'what ifs'. What if Thomas Knyvet had not discovered Guy Fawkes lurking in the vaults under St Stephen's

Hall in November 1605? What if the spy George Edwards had not infiltrated Arthur Thistlewood's Cato Street gang in 1820? What if Margaret Thatcher had still been working on her speech late at night in Brighton's Grand Hotel? The irony is that we will never know what difference any of this would have made. With James I dead and his government destroyed, would England have become Catholic again, as the plotters hoped? Highly unlikely. Younger members of the Stuart family would have inherited the crown and new men, Protestants all, would have filled dead men's shoes. With Lord Liverpool and his cabinet shot down at Lord Harrowby's house in Grosvenor Square, would Britain have become a fair and balanced society, run by the people, for the people? Hardly. The army had made no move on the part of the Cato Street conspirators and without them, insurrection was doomed to failure. And had Margaret Thatcher been blown sky high in Brighton, would all Ireland now be Eire and Protestantism just a distant memory in 'John Bull's other island'? I doubt it. The authorities would have doubled down (to use twenty-first-century speak) on the IRA and the atrocities would have got worse.

Counter-factual history – what if – was a popular trend a few years ago but it was merely a vaguely interesting cul de sac. Who can say what would have happened, because it did not. Historians should concern themselves with what *did* happen. *Dodging the Bullet* is different, because it forms a bridge between what was and what might have been. Non-achievement, a lack of success in an enterprise, is as interesting and important as achievement and success.

Where do we start? In this book, we have come across over 100 would-be assassins. The vast majority were men and reflects absolutely the pattern of murderers – most of them are men too. The 'Squeaky' Frommes and the Fanny Kaplans of this world are rare birds indeed and a psychologist would have a field day with both of them. Fromme was a runaway involved in the druggy, hippy culture of America's West Coast. She may not have been involved in the

Tate–LaBianca murders but she lived with and was fond of those who were. Her claim that she did not intend to kill President Gerald Ford rings very hollow. Kaplan lived in a time so different from ours that we cannot readily understand the political motivation of a teenaged girl in the violent, desperate Russia of the early twentieth century. She lost her sight in the hell-hole that was a Siberian prison camp and after all her hopes and aspirations, the man she thought was her saviour – Comrade Lenin – let her down. He let down millions of others too, contributing in no small measure to the creation of the pariah state that Russia is today.

Most of the assassins in this book have been dysfunctional. If we put to one side for the moment the professional hitmen employed by governments and look at the 'lone nuts' we realize that they are called that for good reason. It is not a very sophisticated psychological profile, but it conveys the problem.

Margaret Nicholson, who tried to kill George III with a fruit knife, was clearly deranged, if only because of the uselessness of the weapon she used on him in August 1786. 'Do not hurt her. The poor creature is mad,' was George's instant reaction and he was probably right. She claimed to be the queen, a virgin and a mother simultaneously and ended her days in an institution. James Hadfield, who also had a pop at George, this time with a pistol, was a war veteran who was almost certainly suffering from what today we would call post-traumatic stress disorder; he had taken eight sword cuts to his head in battle. He told his defence counsel in 1800 that by killing the king, he would be helping to bring about the second coming of Christ. When Edward Oxford fired at Queen Victoria, he could not handle his guns well and spent most of his trial bursting out into fits of laughter. Every time he told prison visitors the story of the assassination attempt, that story varied. A string of doctors concurred that the man was an imbecile.

Who knows what demons lurked in the mind of John Bean, the 'dwarf', ridiculed by his own siblings and by society at large whose gun was wrestled from him during his attempt on Victoria in July 1842 by a schoolboy? The newspaper headlines said it all – 'hump-backed boy of an idiotic appearance'. He could barely see over the rail in the dock of the Old Bailey and the hard labour he underwent in prison was sewing shirts. Robert Pate was raving. Dressed in flamboyant, over-the-top clothes, he skipped his way along pavements having been bitten by a rabid dog, some years before he tried to batter Victoria with his cane. Arthur O'Connor was descended from the ancient kings of Ireland and when he tried to shoot the queen, his gun was empty. He was dismissed as a 'crack-brained youth'. Roderick Maclean had been under psychiatric care for much of his life; he had tried to derail a train and to kill various members of his family.

Jaswant Singh Chail, about to fire at a different queen (Elizabeth II) and with a different weapon (a crossbow) assumed that the queen was guilty of involvement in a massacre in India that happened years before she was born. He also claimed to be a member of a monastic order from the *Star Wars* series of films.

Clearly, not *every* would-be assassin in this book suffers from paranoia and other illusions, but many do. In selecting hitmen, today's governments and institutions avoid such people like the plague. An assassin must blend in, be alert and quick-witted. He must be able to use the weapons he carries efficiently and be capable of thinking on his feet in the event of changes of plan on the part of his target.

Then, there is the choice of weapon. Wheel-lock and flintlock pistols, in the age of black powder, were notoriously unreliable. They jammed. They would not fire if powder was wet. Their range was limited, usually to 100 yards or less; a moving target was particularly difficult. Several of the would-be killers in this book could only afford second-hand weapons, often bought in pawnshops. The ammunition they used was just as often makeshift – wrong-sized balls, nails, even buttons which could be as dangerous to the shooter as to his victims. Even then, with a revolving chamber and, later, automatic guns, problems occurred. The German immigrant who shot at President Grover Cleveland in a restaurant in New York in the early 1890s should have got him but his .44 jammed. Giuseppe Zangara was only 5ft tall and fired on FDR from the top of a rickety chair to extend his height. There was nothing wrong with his gun, but he missed Roosevelt anyway. Then there was John Schrank, whose .38 calibre Police Special was fine too, but nevertheless, the bullet was partly deflected by Teddy Roosevelt's spectacle case and the thick wad of paper he was carrying in his pocket.

And then we come to that most unmeasurable complexity – plain good or bad luck, depending on whose side you stand. Had it not been for Colonel Heinz Brandt moving Colonel von Stauffenberg's briefcase to the *other* side of that table support in the Wolf's Lair, Valkyrie would have been a success and the Second World War might have ended several months before it actually did, saving who knows how many lives. If George III had been standing just a few feet further forward at the Theatre Royal, Drury Lane, on 15 May 1800, James Hadfield's bullet might have found its mark. Luck, of course, travels both ways. As far as Gavrilo Princip knew on 28 June 1914, Archduke Franz Ferdinand was already dead; he had heard the bomb go off. To his astonishment, the man suddenly passed him in his open-topped car, waving and smiling along with his wife. Princip could not believe his luck, opened fire and caused the First World War.

What looms large in the history of assassinations and failed assassinations is the incompetence of guards and security details. When the attempts failed, other factors explain that, but it does not minimise the irresponsibility of the security itself. Why, for example, did three American presidents die before a Secret Service unit was given training, money and wide powers to keep their charge alive? Why was John F. Kennedy's motorcade route published well in advance on 22 November 1963 for his journey from Love Field airport to the Dallas Trade Mart where he was due to give a speech? Look at a plan of Dealey Plaza, where Kennedy was shot, and you will see at a glance that there was no reason to turn right, then left on to Elm Street, under the windows of the Texas schoolbook depository, when the motorcade could and should have gone straight ahead. The problem for leaders of the free world in our own time is that they need to be seen. They deliberately 'go walkabout' among their people because, in a democracy, they need votes. Security forces therefore have a very difficult job. Motorcycle outriders in Dallas were actually useless in deflecting bullets. Kennedy's Secret Service detail were in the car behind him and only one of them – Clint Hill – had the presence of mind to dash forward on to the president's car, by which time, of course, it was far too late. There were rumours that the detail had been up partying the night before and were a little the worse for wear that Friday morning, their responses slow.

And there was a predictability about all this, not least from the assassin's target himself. George III loved going to the theatre, so he continued to do that even after he had been fired on in one. President after president in the United States travelled in open-topped cars, wide open to hitmen along their well-publicized routes. In no single instance of assassination – successful or not – have I come across a target wearing a bulletproof vest, before Gerald Ford's special coat. John F. Kennedy's back brace was not bulletproof and, in any case, the bullets that hit him found their mark well above it. Teddy Roosevelt's bulky spectacles case and speech notes were in his jacket by accident, not design. The bottom line is that world leaders, so often in the crosshairs of paid killers and lunatics alike, are far more than potential assassination victims. There are thousands of examples in which no known attempts have been carried out at all. If such people believed in the worst-case scenario, they would never leave their houses and today, thanks to keyhole bombing, even that safe haven is not guaranteed.

On 2 May 2011, Navy Seals, operating under orders from President Barack Obama, 'took out' the terrorist Osama bin Laden in his hiding place at Abbottabad, Pakistan. Two bullets were fired into his head by a Seal nicknamed 'Red' and several men pumped bullets into his body, just to be sure. The orders for Operation Neptune Spear were clear – 'to kill or capture bin Laden'. Former president George W. Bush, who had also tried to get the world's most wanted terrorist, underlined the point. 'There is an old poster out west, as I recall, that said, "Wanted – Dead or Alive".' The emphasis could not be missed.

Needless to say, bin Laden's death became the focus of conspiracy theories and hoaxes, which have been linked to several other examples in this book. Bin Laden was already dead before Abbottabad. He survived Abbottabad. Alleged photographs of his bullet-riddled corpse shown on Pakistani television were fake. There were stories of a burial at sea to prevent the creation of a shrine in a terrestrial burial place. The list goes on.

The two targets who most successfully avoided assassination were Adolf Hitler and Fidel Castro. Other factors contributed to their safety, as we have seen, but it was their uncanny ability to be unpredictable that saved their lives. Times, date, places were all changed, frequently and at short notice, to throw would-be killers off the scent. Faced with the prospect of an exploding cigar, Castro gave up smoking. He had at least twenty residences in Cuba and no one except his closest guards knew where he would be from one day to the next.

We have to be wary of the accounts left by Albert Speer, Hitler's architect and latterly munitions minister. He was the only senior Nazi at the Nuremberg trials in 1946 to admit responsibility and has come down to us as the marginally acceptable face of Nazism. According to *Inside the Third Reich* (1970), Speer decided very late in the day, that Hitler was committing treason against the German people by insisting that they all fought to the death. 'That night,' he wrote, 'I came to the decision to eliminate Hitler.' He considered poison gas as the best option, now that the high command were effectively trapped in the *Fuhrerbunker* under the shell-ridden streets of Berlin. Day and night they could hear the thud and rumble of the city's guns desperately trying to fend off Stalin's Red Army creeping forward from the east. Everybody was in a state of controlled hysteria, with the Fuhrer in complete denial, probably actually believing that he still had fresh armies he could summon out of the blue to break the stranglehold of the Soviets and even win the war.

Speer's plan was to use tabun, a gas that would be sent through the ventilation shaft into the bunker. He took Dieter Stall, his head of munitions production, into his confidence and asked him to get hold of the gas required. But there were technical problems. Tabun would only work, hidden in artillery shells, *after* an explosion and the explosion would destroy the ventilation ducts, so the gas would not spread. So Speer fell back on more orthodox gas and even persuaded his chief engineer, Johannes Hentschel, to remove the filtering system, on the grounds that it needed maintenance, prior to using the gas. To Speer's horror, the plan was thwarted. The air intake shaft, previously easily reachable at ground level, was now, suddenly, at the top of a new ten-foot chimney. It, as well as searchlights and SS guards, had been put in place on Hitler's order.

It is unlikely that the Fuhrer knew of Speer's intentions – the architect was afraid his guilt would show in his face – or Speer would have found himself dangling from piano wire. The building of the chimney, at a time of despondency in the bunker, was yet another example of the speed with which Hitler could change his mind and keep himself safe.

Arguably, one of the most deadly fields for assassination in the recent past was Northern Ireland, particularly Belfast, Londonderry, and the border with Eire. During the New Troubles throughout the 1970s, 1980s and well into the 1990s, terror attacks and killings of individuals were the order of the day as Republicans and Unionists fought a dirty, irregular war that involved sniper assassination and indiscriminate bombings. In 1975, the Northern Ireland security forces produced several posters, displayed among the political graffiti on every available wall. 'Don't Become a Murder Victim' the posters said and offered sensible advice:

> Make sure you know who is outside your front door before you open it. Vary your movements and times and routes [the Hitler/Castro method]. Make sure someone has a rough timetable of your movements [but keep it rough, so that men on the inside cannot take advantage]. Avoid going out alone at night. Watch out for suspicious cars. Avoid standing at street corners and under street lights.

A particularly chilling variant of this poster provides the title for this chapter. In a series of four identical photographs, a man is seen cycling along a quiet road. The first photograph is captioned 'Monday: Home at 4.30pm'. The second is 'Tuesday: Home at 4.30pm'. The third 'Wednesday: Home at 4.30pm'. The fourth 'Thursday: Home at 4.30pm'. The fifth photograph shows a bike lying by the roadside and its rider a corpse lying alongside it. The caption reads 'Friday: Dead at 4.30pm'. It was a graphic display to highlight the need for unpredictability, but man is a creature of habit and routine, imbued with the nonsensical denial strategy of 'It couldn't happen to me'.

In 1999, journalist Erik Durschmied wrote *The Hinge Factor*, the subtitle of which was 'How Chance and Stupidity Have Changed History'. Those two elements – the chance we cannot calculate and the stupidity of targets and those charged with keeping them safe – have conspired to explain everything you have read in this book.

As Carl von Clausewitz said in *On War* (1832), 'A plan which succeeds is bold; one which fails is reckless.' We have seen a great deal of recklessness in these pages, but it all came within a whisker of success. The depressing thing about assassination attempts is that they are just as likely to succeed if they are carried out by untrained amateurs as they are by professional hitmen. The most difficult attack to guard against is the mutiny/disloyalty of a bodyguard. Nobody has suggested that the Washington policeman who wandered away from his post on the night he should have been guarding Abraham Lincoln at Ford's Theatre was part of the assassination plot, but he must carry his share of the blame, nonetheless. Two of Indira Gandhi's bodyguard, both Sikhs, machine-gunned the woman they were supposed to be guarding on 31 October 1984. With 'friends' like that ...

What is common to all events in this book, the narrow misses, the ideas that never got off the ground, is the sense of shock once details were known. Shooting Pope John Paul II, like the murder of Mahatma Gandhi over thirty years earlier, horrified millions – and not just the supporters of those men in their different faiths. The shock is not as great, of course, if plots are foiled in advance. Appalling though it no doubt was to realize that there was a group of men prepared to blow up the king and most of his parliament in London in 1605, that was as nothing to the sense of grief, bewilderment and outrage had Fawkes' dynamite actually gone up. It is one of the clichés of the twentieth century that everybody remembers where they were when Kennedy was killed. As a 14-year-old in Britain, I was suitably annoyed that there was no television that evening (allowing for the time difference between lunchtime Dallas and mid-evening in the British Midlands) and I was going to miss my favourite Western, *Bonanza*. Seeing film footage later of people crying all over the United States as what had happened in Dealey Plaza sank in and put all that into perspective. Even more so years later, when Abraham Zapruder's amateur cine film became widely available and we all saw the president's head blown open by the shot from the grassy knoll.

Assassination is a bloody business and not just for those who are targets. Attempted assassination can be just as bloody. Does it change history? Yes, sometimes. Does it change history for the better? Never.

P.S.

The posters behind Trump said it all. 'You're fired!' they declared, in reference to 'the Donald's' former television show *The Apprentice* and his famous catchphrase. The point of the posters was that Joe Biden, the doddery octogenarian president of the United States, was supposed to be the one who was fired. He was too old for the job. Within minutes, it was Trump, only four years his junior, who was being fired at! As this book goes to press, Trump is poised to make a dramatic comeback in his bid to re-enter the White House. Assassination has made a comeback too.

And where there is an assassination attempt on a would-be President, accusations of laxity on behalf of the security forces are sure to follow and along with them, conspiracy theories without number. As I write, somebody somewhere is already writing a full-blown book on this attempt. All I can do, for reasons of time and space, is to scratch the surface.

Donald Trump is the most divisive President in American history. His 'colourful' career has meant that he is now a convicted felon with more charges to come, but such is the idiocy of the American political system that that does not diminish the likelihood of his success in the coming election. Missing death by inches will have done him no harm at all.

The following account of the shooting is hot off the press. No doubt, false assumptions have been made, as they always are by journalists hungry for a juicy story and racing to beat the other guy. More detail will emerge over the next few days and weeks and we will all know more by the time you read these words. For now, this is the story as we have it.

As part of his electoral campaign, Trump attended a rally at the Butler Farm Show in Pennsylvania. The great and the good of the Republican party flocked in through the security scanners at the gates at one o'clock in the afternoon, Eastern Daylight Time. The scanners could tell if anybody was armed. It was all clear. Saturday, 13 July was hot and sticky in Pennsylvania, with temperatures of 35°C (95°F) at midday. An estimated 30,000 Trump supporters, carrying the stars and stripes, with many wearing 'MAGA' (Make America Great Again) hats, waited for the great man to arrive.

Trump was due to start speaking at five o'clock but there was no sign of him. Like John Kennedy in Dallas in November 1963, the star attraction was late. Then, at 6.03, as the strains of Lee Greenwood's *God Bless the USA* were blasted over the sound system, he finally took the stage. He was wearing the trade mark blue suit without a tie and the red baseball cap with the MAGA logo above the peak. In accordance with the long-agreed protocol, the ex-President was flanked by his Secret Service detail, dressed like him but without the cap and bristling with sidearms.

At 6.11 there was a sound like firecrackers (witnesses in Dealey Plaza had said the same thing) as five shots rang out. Trump was talking about the rise in immigration under President Biden and turned his head to a chart on the huge 'jumbotron' screen behind him, showing a graph of the illegal border crossings from Mexico. 'Take a look at what happened,' he said and they could easily have been the last words he ever spoke. In November 1963, the assassination of Kennedy was filmed by an amateur cameraman, Abraham Zapruder, using a clunky home-movie camera. The Trump shooting in July 2024 was filmed by umpteen professional television cameramen. Trump moved his head imperceptibly, enough for the shooter to miss. Even so, the bullet hit the top of his right ear, spraying blood all over his face. On the film, we can see his hand come up as he feels the pain and the stunned reaction of the crowd on the podium behind him, several of them in the gunman's sights too.

The Secret Service were all over him in seconds, burly men with short haircuts and one woman, covering the wounded man with their bodies. The crowd were screaming and the Secret Service men had their mics still open. 'What are we doing? What are we doing?' can be heard clearly, which does not exactly inspire confidence and, in yet more seconds, armed officers in black tactical gear were on the podium, swinging from left to right, their rifles aimed in all directions. This was 'Hawkeye', the codename for the counter assault team assigned to protect the ex-President.

Less than a minute after the first shot, one of the team said, 'Shooter's down. Are we good to move? We're clear, we're clear, we're clear. Let's move.' In this situation, the job of the security forces is to get the target to safety as soon as possible. Trump was helped to his feet, clutching the cap that had been knocked off. 'Hold up,' an agent told him, 'your head is bloody.' Nobody at that stage could be sure of the exact extent of the wound. Incomprehensibly, Trump can be heard saying, 'Let me get my shoes. Let me get my shoes on.' They had been knocked off when he had been leapt on by his Secret Service detachment.

'I got you, sir,' another agent said, but Trump was determined to reassure his people, 'Wait, wait, wait,' and he turned to the crowd, his face streaked with blood and raised a fist to the heavens. 'Fight, fight, fight!' he yelled as the crowd roared back 'USA, USA, USA', ecstatic to find the man not only still alive, but able to walk *and*, whisper it, make capital out of the situation.

In minutes, Trump had been bundled into a bullet-proof Chevrolet Suburban. He raised his fist again before the door slid closed. The motorcade left the area in a hurry, flanked by Pennsylvania police cars. In the aftermath, Butler Farm looked like a battlefield. People had flattened themselves on the ground or the podium benches as the shots rang out, some holding hands, others covering bodies, everybody dazed and bewildered. Four people were wounded in the fusillade and one man was dead. He was 50-year-old ex-fire chief Corey Comperatore, hit in the head as he shielded his wife and two daughters from the bullets. The nephew of a congressman had his neck grazed and a woman was hit in the forearm. Both were recovering well at the most recent reports, along with two others, whose injuries were not specified.

If the assassin hoped to get away with his crime, he was mistaken. He was seen by a witness, Greg Smith, bear-crawling, army style, up a roof of a building fifty feet from his position. Smith could see a gun and spent three or four frantic minutes trying to find a police officer to raise the alarm. One of them climbed a ladder, but faced by the gunman's AR-15 semi-automatic rifle, scuttled back down to the ground. Within minutes, two Secret Service snipers shot and killed the assassin. When they reached the roof, they found a young man with long hair lying beside his rifle.

In the enquiries that followed, the FBI searched the killer's car and home. He was 20-year-old Thomas Crooks, a 'middle-class math geek' who had used his father's gun for the shooting. Explosive devices were found in his vehicle and he was not linked to any international terrorist organization.

What is uncanny about the Trump shooting is the similarity with the Kennedy murder. In both cases, the assassin struck in broad daylight in front of a large crowd. The murder weapon was a high-powered rifle. The Secret Service appear in Trump's case and certainly in Kennedy's, not to have checked the area adequately. The actions of the local police – in Dallas in 1963 and Butler today – were likewise below par. While many people now believe that the killing of JFK was part of a conspiracy, some still cling to the belief that Lee Harvey Oswald was a 'lone nut'; and Thomas Crooks fits that bill admirably.

Conspiracy theorists came out of the woodwork within minutes of the Trump shooting, thanks to the intrusive, ubiquitous nature of social media (a concept unknown in 1963) and, although even more bizarre theories are bound to follow, the obvious one is that Joe Biden's Democrats were behind the whole thing. Senator J.D. Vance said, 'The central premise of the Biden campaign is that President Trump is an authoritarian fascist who must be stopped at all costs' and it did not help that Biden himself said recently, 'Donald Trump is a genuine threat to this nation ... It's time to put [him] in the bullseye.' There have already been calls for Biden to be prosecuted for inciting violence against Trump. The other theory gaining ground is that this was a put-up job, carefully choreographed to strengthen Trump's position and turn him into a potential martyr. As one 'keyboard warrior' said within minutes of event, 'If you think this "shooting" at the Trump rally was an assassination attempt, you are in a cult. This is the most staged thing I've seen in a long time.'

No doubt the furore will continue, but one thing is certain. No one outside the United states is surprised about what happened, such is Trump's divisive front. What is, perhaps, surprising, is that Trump issued a statement after the shooting which said, 'It is incredible that such an act can take place in our country.'

Really? Perhaps I should send him a copy of this book.

Appendix

The Guns

'Only the monstrous anger of the guns ...'
Wilfred Owen, *Anthem for Doomed Youth*,
Autumn 1917

Although 'dodging the bullet' has become a phrase to mean avoiding trouble, whether by luck or judgement, most of the failed assassinations in this book have involved the use of firearms. It is not always possible, especially in the earliest incidents, to be accurate as to the type/make of the gun involved. In more recent incidents, we not only know these details, but have the actual weapon on display in a museum.

Gun laws vary, of course, all over the world. In Britain, the right to bear arms dates from the Assize of Arms in the reign of Henry II (twelfth century) and automatically passed to the ownership of firearms when they were invented. Interestingly, in 1584, after the assassination of William the Silent in Holland, Elizabeth I banned the carrying of wheel-lock pistols near her royal palaces. Under Charles II, a 1662 Act of Parliament allowed the authorities to seize guns that belonged to dubious characters. Under James II (1685–88) the whole issue became political (as it still is in the United States) in that the Catholic king removed firearms from his Protestant subjects (the majority of them). The Bill of Rights of 1689 reversed this so that once again, anyone could carry a gun. This was ratified in 1707 by William Blackstone, greatest of the English jurists, but, in a reversal of James II's stance, Jacobites (supporters of James's son and grandson) were forbidden to carry firearms after the rebellions of 1715 and 1745.

The 1820s saw laws brought in covering weapons used in the commission of a felony and in 1870, the Gun Licensing Act was a cynical ploy of Gladstone's government to raise revenue. No licence was required to buy a gun, but to take it off your property would cost 10 shillings, lasting for one year and the licence could be bought over the counter at post offices! A number of Acts were passed in the twentieth century, especially after the two world wars when guns were brought home as souvenirs by demobilized soldiers. Today, the United Kingdom's firearms regulations are the most restrictive in the world and the anti-gun lobby has even forced plastic toy manufacturers to put bright orange plugs in the muzzles of guns for children.

The United States is at the other end of the spectrum. The right to bear arms is enshrined in the Constitution as the Second Amendment and the gun lobby is led by the hugely influential National Rifle Association (NRA). Several presidents have tried in recent years to reduce legally available weapons and have constantly been defeated by Congress. None of this, in either Britain or America, deals with illegally owned firearms – in that criminals routinely ignore any laws they do not like.

It is not always clear what guns have been used in the failed assassination attempts on various people in this book. The list below is an attempt at clarity:

Jonathan Britain's attempt on George III (1770s). A flintlock pistol of unknown manufacture. Flintlocks had a snapping mechanism that struck a flint and caused a spark, thus igniting the black powder and expelling a ball cartridge. Such guns were notoriously unreliable and their range was limited to only a few yards with any accuracy. Reloading was slow and cumbersome.

James Hadfield's attempt on George III (May 1800). The actual flintlock pistol used is said to be in the possession of a family in

London's East End. It was acquired by Major Wright who had helped disarm Hadfield during the attempt.

Richard Lawrence's attempt on Andrew Jackson (January 1835). This was another flintlock pistol but the time of the year was not helpful to Lawrence. The powder contained in the pan was easily made useless by moisture and the attempt took place in a particularly hard winter.

Edward Oxford's attempt on Queen Victoria (June 1840). Oxford had bought a pair of second-hand flintlocks for £3 along with a powder flask (these were made of leather or brass). He practised shooting at various galleries which existed in Leicester Square and the Strand in London. He also bought fifty percussion caps and 3d worth of powder from an old school friend in Lambeth.

David M'Naghten's attempt on Robert Peel (January 1843). Two pistols, type unknown, but probably flintlocks.

John Francis's attempt on Queen Victoria (May 1842); **John Bean's** (July); **William Hamilton's** (May 1949) and **Arthur O'Connor's** (February 1872) all involved poor quality flintlocks. O'Connor bought his for 4 shillings.

William Meyers' attempt on Rutherford Hayes (March 1877). Unknown.

Anonymous gunman's attempt on Chester Arthur (1881). Unknown firearm.

Dr John Noetling's attempt on Chester Arthur (also 1881). Unknown firearm, but the gun fired seven shots.

Roderick Maclean's attempt on Queen Victoria (March 1882). Involved a Belgian pinfire revolver. The revolving cylinder, to allow a gunman to fire several times in quick succession, was being experimented with from the sixteenth century, but it was not perfected until the 1830s. The Belgian gun companies acquired an excellent reputation for manufacture.

Anonymous German immigrant's attempt on Grover Cleveland (1890s). A .44 calibre revolver. The best known of these were six-shot American weapons by Colt and Remington and became popular during the Civil War. They were widely exported.

Arthur Wright's attempt on William Taft (October 1909). Unknown, but **Julius Bergerson's** attempt two years later featured the unusual palm pistol, known in America as 'the Protector'. It was very small, designed to be hidden in the palm of the hand and therefore the perfect weapon for a close-range assassin. The gun was fired by squeezing the whole weapon in the fist and the very short barrel was inserted between the index and middle fingers. They were often nickel-plated to reduce the corrosive effect of skin on metal. Bergerson never got a chance to use his.

John Schrank's attempt on Teddy Roosevelt (October 1912). Involved the use of a Colt .38 calibre Police Special. This is likely to have been the 1896 pattern, firing six rounds and with a 4.5in barrel, but a smaller, more practical model was made in 1905.

Fanny Kaplan's attempt on Vladimir Lenin (August 1918). An FN Browning M1900; not a revolver (as in some translations of Kaplan's own statement in court). It was a Belgian-made 'blowback' relying on inertia and a spring to delay the opening of the breach. The British Army tried the gun in the early 1900s but decided against it.

Giuseppe (Joe) Zangara's attempt on Franklin D. Roosevelt (February 1933). Unknown, except that this was a second-hand revolver.

Griselio Torresola and Oscar Collazo's attempt on Harry S. Truman (November 1950). Collazo carried a German-made Walther P.38, a gun widely used during the Second World War. In fact, it was so popular that the Mauser company making it could not keep up with demand. It fired eight rounds from a detachable box in the butt. Torresola's weapon was the eight-shot Luger, after the Colt 'Peacemaker' probably the most famous handgun in the world. It was a 9mm Parabellum.

Jean-Marie Bastien-Thiry's attempt on Charles de Gaulle (August 1962). Unknown sub-machine gun.

Samuel Joseph Byck's attempt on Richard Nixon (February 1974). This resulted in the shooting of a police officer. A .22 calibre rifle, make unknown.

Lynette Alice Fromme's attempt on Gerald Ford (September 1975). This was a M1911 pistol, almost certainly a Colt-Browning. 'Squeaky' Fromme did not know how to load the chamber from the box magazine, which she claimed was because she did not intend to shoot the president, merely make a point.

Sara Jane Moore's attempt on Gerald Ford (September 1975). Unknown pistol.

Raymond Lee Harvey's attempt on Jimmy Carter (1974). A .22 calibre handgun, make unknown.

John Hinckley's attempt on Ronald Reagan (March 1981). The gun used here, which can be seen online and is in a museum, was a Rohm RG14 22LR revolver. With its 2.5in barrel, it looks like a toy. Having fired all six bullets, Hinckley would have had no time to reload.

Mehmet Agca's attempt on Pope John Paul II (May 1981). The gun was a Browning Hi-Power semi-automatic pistol. Unlike most of the assassins in this book, Agca was a professional. Even so, although firing from close range, he managed to hit two innocent bystanders and did not succeed in his mission.

Marcus Sarjeant and Christopher Lewis's attempts on Queen Elizabeth II (June 1981). Sarjeant fired a starting pistol of the type used for athletics competitions. Unless modified by an expert, such guns cause no harm. Lewis used a .22 rifle, type unknown.

Francisco Duran's attempt on Bill Clinton (October 1994). Involved the largest gun in this book, a SKS semi-automatic rifle of the type used widely by military forces all over the world. It is similar in range, weight and efficiency to the better-known Kalashnikov.

Robert W. Pickett's attempt on George W. Bush (February 2001). The gun was a Taurus .38 calibre special revolver, firing six shots from a conventional cylinder.

Oscar Ortega-Hernandez's attempt on Barack Obama (November 2011). Another large weapon, like the SKS, the Cugir semi-automatic rifle was made by the Cugir Arms Company of Romania which had been making firearms since 1799 when Romania was still Wallachia and part of the Austro-Hungarian empire.

Michael Sandford's attempt on Donald Trump (June 2016). It was possibly because he was British that Sandford carried no weapon of his own. Instead, he grabbed the pistol of a policeman on duty that day. Most US law enforcement officers carry a 9mm Glock 17. Thomas Crooks' attempt on Trump in 2024 involved an AR-15 semi-automatic rifle.

Bibliography

Aaronovitch, David, *Voodoo Histories*, Jonathan Cape, 2009
Ayton, Mel, *Plotting to Kill the President*, University of Nebraska Press, 2017
Belfield, Richard, *The Secret History of Assassination*, Magpie Books, 2008
Bruce Lockhart, R.H., *Memoirs of a British Agent*, Macmillan, 1932
Bullock, Alan, *Hitler: A Study in Tyranny*, Pelican, 1962
Clarke, John, *The Life and Times of George III*, BCA, 1972
Dale, Iain, *The Presidents*, Hodder, 2021
Durschmied, Erik, *The Hinge Factor*, Coronet Books, 1999
Fido, Martin and Skinner, Keith, *The Official Encyclopedia of Scotland Yard*, Virgin, 1999
Fleming, John, *The Assassination of Fidel Castro*, Absolute Crime Books, 2013
Gash, Norman, *Sir Robert Peel*, Longman, 1986
Kunhardt, Dorothy and Kunhardt, Philip, *Twenty Days*, Newcastle Publishing, 1965
Lewis, Bernard, *The Assassins*, Phoenix, 2003
Marshall, Dorothy, *The Life and Times of Victoria*, BCA, 1972
Moore, Jonathan J., *Shot, Stabbed and Poisoned*, New Burlington, 2018
Murphy, Paul Thomas, *Shooting Victoria*, Head of Zeus, 2012
Peterson, Harold L., *The Book of the Gun*, Paul Hamlyn, 1962
Rees, Laurence, *The Dark Charisma of Adolf Hitler*, Ebury, 2013

Roberts, Andrew, *George III*, Allen Lane, 2021
Sanders, Ed, *The Family*, Panther, 1972
Shirer, William L., *The Rise and Fall of the Third Reich*, BCA, 1960
Sifakis, Carl, *Encyclopedia of Assassinations*, Headline, 1993
Speer, Albert, *Inside the Third Reich*, Phoenix, 1970
Stern, Jessica and Berger, J.M., *ISIS*, Harper Collins, 2015
Thomas, Hugh, *The Murder of Adolf Hitler*, St Martin's Press, 1995
Trow, M.J., *Enemies of the State*, Pen & Sword Books, 2010
Trow, M.J., *The JFK Assassination*, Pen & Sword Books, 2024
Vassiltchikov, Marie, *The Berlin Diaries 1940–1945*, Pimlico, 1985
Walter, John, *Handguns*, Quercus, 2013
Williams, Nigel, *Elizabeth*, BCA, 1972

Index

Arthur, Chester 40, 85, 123, 208
Assassins
  Agca, Mehmet Ali 183-8, 211
  al-Zaidi, Muntadhar 146
  Arutyunian, Vladimir 146
  Bastien-Thiry, Jean-Marie 178-81, 210
  Bean, John 73-6, 80, 91-2, 193, 208
  Bellingham, John 38-9, 92
  Bonzon, Claudio 125
  Booth, John Wilkes 21, 97, 99, 190
  Britain, Jonathan 58-9, 207
  Byck, Samuel 132-4, 210
  Celik, Oral 183-4
  Chail, Jaswant 88, 193
  Collazo, Oscar 131-2, 210
  Crites, Austyn 154
  Crooks, Thomas 204
  Cubela, Rolando 162
  Czolgosz, Leon 41-3
  de la Tocnaye, Alain 178, 180
  Despard, Colonel Edward 12-13, 15-16, 64-6
  Duran, Francisco 143-4, 211
  Elser, Georg 104-106
  Fawkes, Guido 3-4, 6-7, 9, 26, 32, 190, 199
  Ferrier, Pascale 155
  Fieschi, Guiseppe 75
  Francis, John 71-5, 80, 92, 208
  Fromme, Lynette 134-7, 191, 210
  Gerard, Balthasar 56
  Gonalez, Omar 148
  Guin, Ramon 162
  Guiteau, Charles 39-41
  Hadfield, James 12, 63-4, 71, 89, 192, 194, 207
  Hamilton, William 76-8, 82, 208
  Harvey, Raymond 137-8, 210
  Hinckley, John 138-42, 210
  Kaplan, Fanny 169, 174-6, 191-2, 209
  Laurence, Richard 95-6, 208
  Levingay, Gregory 154
  Lewis, Christopher 88, 211

M'Naghten, Daniel 88-94, 96, 208
Maclean, Roderick 84-6, 193, 209
Magee, Patrick 27-8, 30-1, 33
Meyers, William 123, 208
Moore, Sara Jane 136, 210
Nekrasov, Nikolai 172
Nicholson, Margaret 60, 62, 64, 192
Noetling, Dr John 123, 208
O'Connor, Arthur 80-4, 193, 208
Orta, Juan 160-1
Ortega-Hernandez, Oscar 152, 211
Ortiz, Oswaldo 137-8
Oswald, Lee Harvey 4, 38, 137
Oxford, Edward 68-75, 91-2, 192, 208
Pate, Robert 78-80, 92, 193
Pickett, Robert 145-6, 211
Pietro, Pierre 124-5
Prevost, Jacque 178, 180
Princip, Gavrilo 37, 194
Ravaillac, Francois 57
Rogofsky, John 124
Sandford, Michael 154, 211
Sarjeant, Marcus 87, 211
Scarfo, Alejandro 127
Schrank, John 101-103, 194, 209

Thistlewood, Arthur 10-11, 15-21, 25, 38, 191
Torresola, Griselio 131-2, 210
von dem Bussche, Axel 111
von Stauffenberg, Claus 113, 115-20, 194
Wright, Arthur 100, 209
Yaleb, Noske 125
Zangara, Guiseppe 128-30, 194, 209

Albert, Prince 67-8, 71-3, 76, 78, 80, 90
Al-qaeda 44, 51, 133, 145
Arthur, Chester 40, 85, 123

Berghof 107-108, 111-14
Bethlehem Hospital (Bedlam) 62, 64, 71, 75, 92
Biden, Joseph 201-202, 205
Brighton Bombing 26-32
Broadmoor 71, 85-6, 94
Brown, John 80-2, 84-6
Bush, George H. 142-3, 166
Bush, George W. 145-6, 150, 196, 211

Caesar, Julius 34-6, 38, 43, 98
Carter, Jimmy 50, 132, 137-9, 166, 210
Castro, Fidel 48, 50, 167-68, 178, 196, 198

Catesby, Robert 3-4, 6-7
Cato Street Conspiracy 3, 11-12, 14-21, 23, 25, 27, 32-3, 37, 64-5, 191
Central Intelligence Agency (CIA) 47-51, 159-68, 186-7
Cleveland, Grover 124, 141, 194, 209
Clinton Body Count 144-5
Clinton, William 134-5, 166, 211
Coolidge, Calvin 125

De Gaulle, Charles 176-81, 210
Drummond, Edward 90-4

Elizabeth I 2, 5-6, 54-6, 206
Elizabeth II 87-8, 144, 193, 211
Executive Action 48, 158

Ford, Gerald 50, 134-7, 150, 166, 192, 195, 210

Guns
   .38 Police Special 101, 137, 194, 209
   7.62 FAL rifle 162
   9mm Browning semi-automatic 184, 211
   AR-15 semi-automatic rifle 204, 211
   Bulldog revolver 39
   Colt-Browning M1911 134, 136, 210
   FN Browning M1900 174, 176, 209
   Luger 112, 131, 210
   Magnum 357 134
   Rohm RG14 139, 210
   Smith and Wesson 134
   Taurus .38 145, 211
   Walther P38 131, 210
Garfield, James 36, 39-42, 85, 100, 102, 123, 142
George III 12, 15, 58-60, 62, 64, 66, 71, 191, 194-5, 207
Gunpowder Plot 1-10

Harrison, Benjamin 123, 142
Hashashin 43-4, 51, 190
Hayes, Rutherford 123, 208
Henri III 57, 60
Henri IV 1, 56-7, 60
Hitler, Adolf 34, 104-21, 128-9, 157, 159, 163, 178, 182, 196-8
Hoover, Herbert 122, 126-8

ISIS 44, 150-1

Jackson, Andrew 95-7, 122, 208
James I 1-2, 13, 22, 32, 34, 56-7, 90, 191
John Paul II 26, 87, 181-5, 187-8, 199, 211

Kennedy, John F. 33, 38, 48, 50, 69, 107, 122, 134, 137, 140, 142, 155, 159-62, 195, 199, 202, 204

Lenin, Vladimir 125, 169-76, 192, 209
Lincoln, Abraham 21, 36, 97-100, 102, 123, 125, 128, 142, 190, 199

M'Naghten Rule 40, 89-94, 142
McKinley, William 36, 41-3, 100, 102

Newgate Prison 19-20, 69-70, 72
Nixon, Richard 132-4, 165, 210

Obama, Barack 146-54, 196, 211

Peel, Robert 76, 88, 90-1, 94, 208
Perceval, Spencer 38-9, 65, 92
Peterloo 14-15, 19
Pitt, William 12-13, 22, 62
Putin, Vladimir 46-7

Reagan, Ronald 45, 50, 87, 138-41, 143, 166, 185, 210
Roosevelt, Franklin D. 128-30, 194, 209

Roosevelt, Theodore 42, 100-103, 122, 194-5, 209
Secret Service (US) 100, 122, 129, 131-4, 136-7, 140-2, 144-5, 147, 149-50, 154-5, 194-5
Sicarii 43-4, 190
Stalin, Josef 34, 45-6, 113, 157, 162, 171, 182, 197

Taft, William 99-101, 124, 209
Thatcher, Margaret 21, 26-32, 34, 138, 191
Trotsky, Leon 46, 48, 157, 170, 174
Truman, Harry S. 130-2, 210
Trump, Donald 101, 145, 148, 153-5, 169, 201-205, 211

Valkyrie 113-15, 117, 194
Victoria 58-9, 70-3, 76, 78-82, 84, 86-7, 90, 92, 94, 192-3, 208-209

White House 95, 97, 100, 122-5, 130-4, 141-5, 147-53, 158
William of Nassau (the Silent) 56-8, 63, 67, 206
Wilson, Woodrow 124-5
Wolf's Lair 108, 110-11, 113-5, 117, 119, 194